SOCIAL WORK ON TRIAL

The Colwell Inquiry and the state of welfare

Ian Butler and Mark Drakeford

THE COLLEGE OF SOCIAL WORK

First published in Great Britain in 2011 by

The Policy Press
University of Bristol
Fourth Floor
Beacon House
Queen's Road
Bristol BS8 1QU
UK

t: +44 (0)117 331 4054
f: +44 (0)117 331 4093
tpp-info@bristol.ac.uk
www.policypress.co.uk

North American office:
The Policy Press
c/o International Specialized Books Services
920 NE 58th Avenue, Suite 300
Portland, OR 97213-3786, USA
t: +1 503 287 3093
f: +1 503 280 8832
info@isbs.com

British Library Cataloguing in Publication Data
A catalogue record for this book is available from the British Library.

Library of Congress Cataloging-in-Publication Data
A catalog record for this book has been requested.

ISBN 978 1 84742 868 4 hardcover

Cover design by The Policy Press.
Front cover: image kindly supplied by Getty Images.
Printed and bound in Great Britain by Berforts Group.

Contents

Sources   iv

Acknowledgements   v

Preface   vii

one   The second week of January 1973 ...   1

two   November and December 1972 ...   19

three   The state of social work   59

four   The public inquiry   91

five   Social work on trial   129

six   Afterwards ...   161

seven   The trial continues ...   193

Appendix 1: Maria Colwell – synopsis   215

Appendix 2: Maria Colwell – a chronology   219

References   221

Index   233

Sources

All material in this book is derived from sources that are publicly available.

Acknowledgements

We would like to thank in particular the following for their invaluable help in writing this book:

Adam Trimingham, the 'sage of Sussex', for his generosity in sharing his memories of the Colwell Inquiry and of Brighton in the 1970s and for access to his unpublished manuscript on the subject.

Olive Stevenson, for providing us access to the daily transcripts of the Colwell Inquiry and for providing us with her perspective on events from the point of view of someone who was central to the Inquiry.

Mel Nowocin, for helping us to navigate the archive of the *Argus* and for her time and expertise.

Dan Butler, researcher, for the days he spent in the National Archive in Kew and for his scrupulous note taking and keen sense of what we needed to know.

Preface

In producing this account, we have been sensitive to those who knew Maria personally and who might read this book. We have received correspondence from family members, who, although they have made themselves known through the press, have asked us to respect their privacy. Accordingly, we have not made reference to the names of any of Maria's brothers and sisters, many of whom now have children of their own.

It is easy to forget, given the iconic status of the Maria Colwell 'case', that woven into it is a network of individuals whose lives continued long after more public attention turned away from them. In Brighton, the media invokes her name almost every time there is a case of child abuse reported. Commenting on one such case, one of Maria Colwell's brothers is reported as follows:

> "I think more could have been done to save those other children going through what they have been through. It's terrible."
>
> His sister was fostered by the Coopers from 1966 to 1971, while he was looked after by his grandparents.
>
> Their mother went to court to get Maria back, despite having had another family with Kepple.
>
> Mr Colwell said: "Maria should never have gone back.
>
> "Every week I go down and put flowers on her grave. I always say 'you shouldn't be here.'
>
> "She would have been 34 this week and would probably be married with children of her own. If Doris and Bob Cooper had kept her, she would be here today.
>
> "Not only did social services fail Maria, even the law did as well because he only got four years."
>
> Kepple was sentenced to eight years for manslaughter, but had it reduced to four years on appeal.
>
> Mr Colwell said: "He only did four years and he kicked her to death. How can you get four years for kicking and tormenting a child to death?
>
> "The anger I felt towards him was unbelievable. I just wanted to put him through what he put my sister through."

We are mindful that for some, this will never be a former 'case' of child abuse but will be a continuous reminder of a part of their own experiences. Throughout this book, we have tried to respect that. For the same reason that we do not make reference to any of Maria Colwell's brothers or sisters by name, we have not given the reference for the newspaper report from which the preceding extract is taken.

The justification, if there is any, for risking evoking painful memories and trespassing on the privacy of individuals, is recognised by those whose lives were touched by this tragedy and those whose lives are touched by other, similar ones. As Maria's brother's partner said in the same newspaper article:

> ... her children were coping well with this latest case and were following the *Argus*[1] stories.
>
> She thought the publicity that they have tried to avoid was worth it this time.
>
> She said: "If it's helping other children and stopping them from being neglected, then I think people should stand up and say 'no more'."

We are unsure how much has been learned from child abuse scandals, in terms of effective policy making or professional practice, but we think that it is vitally important that we should continue to try and learn all that we can from them. We are both qualified social workers who have spent many years in the field and who have considerable firsthand experience of child protection work. We have an idea of the devastating effects that child abuse has on individual children and young people and on those around them. We understand that the death of Maria Colwell is not a remote experience that can be analysed and understood dispassionately. In a way, that is a further justification for the kind of close examination of her life and death that this book includes.

Behind each 'case' of a child's death through abuse is a real child who must be remembered; not memorialised or mythologised as has happened in some instances recently but simply and respectfully remembered. This book is one way in which, we hope, the memory of Maria Colwell will be preserved.

Ian Butler
Mark Drakeford
October 2010

---

[1] The *Argus*, Brighton's own evening newspaper, is variously identified in documents used in this research as the *Brighton Evening Argus*, the *Evening Argus* and, most often, as simply the *Argus*. For the sake of simplicity we have used the final form throughout this book.

ONE

The second week of January 1973 ...

The news headlines on the morning of Saturday 6 January 1973, were little brighter than the prospect of the short, misty and chilly day that lay ahead.

In Belfast on the previous evening, two 15-year-old boys shot dead an 18-year-old as he was putting air into the tyres of his car at a service station on the Shore Road. Another 18-year-old was shot in the abdomen and thigh outside his house in Hannahstown, South Antrim. In Portadown, a grenade was thrown at a Roman Catholic priest and 10 shots were fired at a passing bus on the edge of Belfast. The UDA (Ulster Defence Association) issued a statement calling for the killings to end.

President Nixon informed Congressional leaders that his national security adviser would be leaving for Paris on Monday to resume peace talks over Vietnam. This 'goodwill gesture' came after the 11-day aerial bombardment 'above the 20th parallel' had ended on 29 December. Operation Linebacker II (or more commonly, 'the Christmas Bombings') had involved 273 missions by B52 bombers, the largest heavy bomber strikes launched by the US Air Force since the end of the Second World War.

On mainland Britain, with possibly the same degree of optimism that would accompany Henry Kissinger to Paris, Anthony Barber, Prime Minister Edward Heath's Chancellor of the Exchequer, was in talks with the Trades Union Congress (TUC) on 'Phase Two' of the government's anti-inflation strategy and as far as that other armed conflict was concerned, the 'cod wars' (a dispute between Britain and Iceland over fishing rights) had reached the International Court of Justice at the Hague. Much further afield, the end of the Empire took a step nearer as General Idi Amin ordered 88 British companies to prepare for takeover by Ugandans.

There was some good news, of a sort. Most of the papers on that Saturday morning reported that the Distillers company had offered nearly £22 million by way of compensation to the 410 children affected by thalidomide, and the film version of 'Oh Calcutta' ('a nude romp') was passed for viewing in London. There was too, for those who could afford it, the prospect of a summer holiday to look forward to: £33 could buy seven days in Rome and £37 would secure 'guaranteed Sicilian sunshine'.

In the meantime, exceptionally loyal supporters would have to have left very early to watch Brighton and Hove Albion playing at Sunderland. Many more would have to be content with the results on *Final Score* on BBC 1 at 4.40 pm, followed by *Basil Brush* and *Dr Who*, after the news. Later, Cilla Black would be on, ahead of *Match of the Day* and *Parkinson*. Alternatively, there was the prospect of a 'Carry On' film on ITV, with the *Val Doonican Show* to follow.

The television was on for much of Saturday at 119 Maresfield Road, Brighton, as it was every day. For more than two years this had been the home of the Kepple family.

Maresfield Road is east of Brighton's famous pier, on the rising ground that leads up to the racecourse. It is the Whitehawk Estate that, in the 1970s, was to be described by a former journalist, Adam Trimingham, in the local newspaper, the *Argus*, as 'bleak, hilly, unsavoury and unattractive' and as a place to which 'many of the town's problem families had been sent to live' (Trimingham, unpublished[1]). On the outside, no. 119 is identical to the other houses on the hill, built in the mid-1930s, a redbrick semi, set back from the road, reached by a flight of a dozen concrete steps. The small gardens to the rear are set into the slope and back onto allotments and open ground. No. 119 is uphill of no. 117 and is separated from the neighbours at no. 121 by a gated alley. It is a modest three-bedroom house, the living room on the left of the front door and the kitchen at the rear, with the bathroom and toilet also downstairs, either side of the kitchen.

According to Acting Inspector Jack Wright of the Sussex Constabulary who had cause to visit the house in the early afternoon of Sunday 7 January:

> The living room was poorly furnished and untidy, with clothes and other things piled up in heaps. The kitchen was dirty and the larder did not appear to have been used.

[1] Adam Trimingham worked for the *Argus* in Brighton at the time of the Colwell case and reported daily on the progress of the public inquiry into Maria's death. Subsequently, he began to write a book on the case but never completed his account. Adam very kindly spoke to us at length about his experiences at the time and allowed us to draw on his uncompleted manuscript for the purposes of this and other chapters.

There was a dog locked in the toilet and what seemed to be human excreta and urine in a bowl in the kitchen. There was some food in the kitchen cabinet and everything was dirty and untidy. The front bedroom contained a double bed, one single bed and a cot. The double bed was made, the others were unmade and the bedding was dirty. The larger rear bedroom appeared unused and it was possible for the door handle to be removed. The small rear bedroom was better furnished than the other two rooms and contained two beds, one with bedding, and a sideboard. There was an electric fire in the room and it was possible to remove the door handle from the outside. [NA: Director of Public Prosecutions 2/5197/2]

One of Inspector Wright's colleagues, WPS Gillian Fry, noted how 'exceedingly cold' the front room of the house was although she would say in a statement prepared for court later 'that the conditions in the house were not exceptional for a family on low income.... I have certainly seen houses in far worse condition. The impression I got was more of untidiness than of filthiness' [NA: DPP 2/5197/1: S25].

Inspector Wright and WPS Fry were at 119 Maresfield Road to investigate the circumstances surrounding the death of Maria Colwell, aged seven, who had lived there and who, sometime between 11.30 pm on Saturday 6 January and the early hours of Sunday morning of the 7th had died there.

The police had been called by staff at the Royal Sussex County Hospital (approximately 15 minutes walk down the hill from no. 119). Here, at around 10.30 am, Maria had been seen by Patricia Weller, the staff nurse on duty in the children's area of the hospital. The staff nurse had been unable to find a pulse in Maria who showed no signs of life on first examination. Dr Adey, who was called to attend Maria, observed that the body was very cold, and concluded that Maria 'had been dead for some time'.

Beginning at just after 8 pm on Thursday 11 January at Brighton Public Mortuary, then, as now, on Lewes Road, Brighton, Dr James Cameron, forensic pathologist, Honorary Consultant in Pathology at the London Hospital and Professor of Forensic Medicine at the University of London at the London Hospital Medical College, began a post-mortem examination of Maria. Professor Cameron described himself, in evidence used in later criminal proceedings, as having 'been involved in research on "battered babies" since 1965' and the 'author of several papers on the subject' (with a textbook shortly to be published).

'The number of cases of child abuse ... both living and dead' that he had examined, he submitted in evidence, 'must number several hundreds'.

Professor Cameron found Maria to have been underweight by about 30 per cent. Such weight loss, he concluded must have taken place over 'several months' and 'could not have occurred during the space of a few days'. Her thinness 'should have been apparent to a reasonably observant person on looking at the child, either unclothed or clothed'. Professor Cameron recorded 'excessive bruising' on Maria's body, not all of it new. He noted bruising to the left side of Maria's head, her eyes, her neck, her thorax, 'finger-tip type' bruising of varying age over the whole of her right leg and bruising to her limbs. He wrote that, 'It was the worst bruising I have seen in the whole of my experience with battered children.'

Her internal injuries included evidence of a 'healing, relatively recent fracture of the tenth rib' as well as extensive and fatal damage to her intestines and stomach. The post-mortem report concluded that the 'injuries were inconsistent with self-infliction and were inconsistent with a fall'. Cause of death was recorded as 'multiple injuries'.

Maria had been wheeled in a pram to the hospital by her stepfather, William ('Bill') Kepple. Bill Kepple was 42 and described in the formal 'Police report on the character of a prisoner' as a 'native of Cork City, Eire'. He had come to the UK as a 'Bevin Boy', aged 18.[2] Kepple had worked in the coalfields of South Wales, Yorkshire and Staffordshire and as a steel erector with a Middlesbrough company. He was married while working in the North East and had two children, a boy aged 21 (in 1973) and a girl aged 19. After his wife divorced him 'for cruelty', he had come to Brighton in 1965 and had worked in 'numerous jobs as a labourer with road construction and cable laying companies in the Sussex area'. He had been unemployed through illness for about two months by the second week in January and was drawing about £18 a week in sickness and supplementary benefits.

Maria's mother, Pauline Kepple (née Tester), had accompanied her husband to the hospital. Pauline had married Bill Kepple on 20 May 1972, at Brighton Registry Office. She had previously been married to Raymond Colwell who had died, aged 28, on 22 July 1965. It was not long after Raymond Colwell died that she had begun 'to keep

---

[2] The Bevin Boys scheme was introduced in 1943 in response to a shortage of labour in the coal mining industry. The scheme involved recruiting men aged between 18 and 25 to work in coalmines rather than serving in the armed forces.

company' with Bill Kepple and they had lived together for over six years by the start of 1973.

Maria was Raymond Colwell's daughter.[3] She was the fifth and youngest of the marriage and Mrs Colwell's sixth child. Raymond died when Maria was barely four months old. Faced with looking after five young children, Pauline Colwell had gone 'completely to pieces' (DHSS, 1974a, p 13). Within a short time, her care of the children was the subject of warnings by the NSPCC and Hove Children's Department.

In August 1965, Pauline had taken Maria to the home of Raymond Colwell's sister, Doris Cooper, who agreed to take her in and look after her. Pauline, with help from her mother, Lillian Tester, continued to look after the four older children. However, on 15 December 1965 they were placed in the care of East Sussex County Council following 'a considerable deterioration in the situation' (Report for Hove Juvenile Court, 11 January 1971). Maria continued to live with the Coopers until June 1966, with 'occasional and spasmodic' contact with her mother (DHSS, 1974a, p 15).

In June 1966, Pauline Kepple removed Maria from the Coopers; the removal coincided with her intention to set up house with her future husband Mr Kepple (DHSS, 1974a, p 15). However, within a matter of days, Maria had come to the attention of the NSPCC. On 17 August 1966, Maria too was placed in the care of East Sussex County Council and she returned to live with the Coopers, where she stayed for the next five years.

For all bar a few months of her infancy and childhood, Maria had lived with her paternal aunt. However, for reasons to be explored in later chapters, in October 1971, aged just over six-and-a-half, Maria was 'returned home on trial' to live with her mother, Bill Kepple and her half-brother and sisters at no. 119. On 17 November 1971, Hove Juvenile Court revoked the Care Order in respect of Maria and made a Supervision Order in favour of the County Borough of Brighton, in whose area Maria would live for the remainder of her life. It was agreed, however, for the sake of continuity, that the 'duties of supervision' would be undertaken by East Sussex, who retained the care of the four other Colwell children.

Bill and Pauline Kepple had had children of their own too – a girl aged five, a boy aged four and another girl, aged two-and-a-half, all with good saints' names. Pauline Kepple was seven months pregnant with her tenth child.

---

[3] A detailed synopsis of Maria Colwell's life and an index of key dates are provided in Appendices 1 and 2. See p 213.

The three young children had been left at home by the Kepples while they wheeled Maria to the hospital. When the police arrived at the house, the two older children were already dressed. According to WPS Fry:

> The younger girl ... was barefoot and dressed only in a dirty vest and a nightdress. She appeared to be very cold and had a nasty cough. [One of the children] told me that [the youngest child's] clothes were in the sideboard. On opening the sideboard door, I found it crammed with screwed-up clothes, all of which felt slightly damp to the touch.... The children told me that they had not had anything at all to eat or drink that day. They were therefore brought to the Police Station, where they were given lunch and looked after until 6.30 pm when they were taken to a local authority home, as both of their parents were at that time still detained in custody on suspicion of having murdered the children's seven-year-old sister, Maria. [NA: DPP 2/5197/2]

These are almost all the known facts concerning the events of Saturday and Sunday 6 and 7 January 1973. From this point on, it becomes a matter of interpretation. Now the struggle to account for what happened to Maria and to provide an explanation for her death began. It was from here onwards that Maria's life and death began their transformation from an individual tragedy into a public scandal.

The scandal of Maria Colwell

First, the Kepples were to tell their conflicting stories. These would be interpreted by the police, the prosecuting authorities and several courts. Accounts would appear in local newspapers and then the national press. There would be a public inquiry. Maria's name would become familiar to the leading politicians and opinion formers of the day and it would be recorded in *Hansard* as a new law was passed in her name. Future generations of social workers will be taught how to practise their profession by reference to what happened to Maria. In short, the very particular, painful and distressing death of this unique seven-year-old girl will be transformed into something of extraordinary significance.

We have described elsewhere what we mean by the 'scandalising process':

... whereby events that are local and personal become
national and public; the process whereby the specific comes
to stand for the general and where meanings and historical
significance become attached to acts and events that at
other times might have passed almost unobserved. (Butler
and Drakeford, 2005, p 1)

We do not mean to diminish the fact of Maria's death but we have no
reason to think that child abuse was any more or less common then
than it is now. We know nothing of the 'several hundreds' of cases
known to Professor Cameron, who carried out the post-mortem
on Maria, mentioned by him in his statement, for example. Tragedy
does not necessarily produce scandal. Indeed, as we believe we have
already demonstrated, 'neither the chronic administrative failings, small
carelessnesses and institutional brutality of the long-stay hospital, nor
even the abuse of children or the violent deaths of innocent bystanders
are sufficient cause for scandal' (Butler and Drakeford, 2005, p 1).

Scandals need to be 'discovered'; they need to be pursued, often with
press support. In the case of public policy scandals, they frequently need
to be mediated by a public inquiry, where the 'facts' are connected
with the operations and interests of the state and with the broader
political and social currents that flow in and around the underlying
events out of which a scandal is 'constructed'. It is the inquiry that
frequently provides the orthodox 'text' that fixes the meaning of these
events. In fact, the final report of a public inquiry is just one artefact
to be set alongside newspaper accounts, police and court records and
the personal reminiscences of those involved.

We have previously argued that scandals occur at points of unbearable
tension within the tectonics of public policy. They occur along major
social fault lines, at points of critical transition. Scandals are 'the policy
equivalent of the earthquake; they are a powerful signal that change is
occurring, or that the pressure for change has reached unsustainable
levels' (Butler and Drakeford, 2005, p 5). In the scandal of Maria Colwell,
the deeper currents are concerned with ideas of what the welfare state
is meant to do about certain, 'problem' families or indeed whether such
families exist. This case also carries the fate of social work as a form of
welfare practice into public debate. In the eddies, there are concerns
about what it means to be 'British' in deeply troubled times.

In our previous accounts, we described these processes through the
lens of a telescope, taking a broad but necessarily distant view. In this
book, we intend to use a microscope to examine the very fine grain
of this major public policy scandal. We will examine in close detail

the events and processes that took place between that second week of January 1973 and the passing of the Children Act, which received Royal Assent in November 1975. In doing so, we aim to produce a 'book of record' that draws on material from a wide range of sources and to set this alongside the canonical text of the public inquiry. In so doing, our intention is to provide a detailed and thorough account of a critical moment in the history of social work in the UK.

However, if the second week of January 1973 was to prove a pivotal point in the story of social work in the UK, it probably did not seem so at the time.

'Frustration, anxiety and stress'

On 11 January 1973, the day of Maria Colwell's post-mortem examination, the UK social work's leading trade magazine, *Social Work Today* (*SWT*), announced itself in the following terms (11 January 1973, p 2):

> The first edition of *Social Work Today* for 1973 is all about frustration, anxiety and stress; about the goals of social work, the shortage of resources and other constraints placed on social workers and the effect on them of these frustrations.

Before they had read the editorial content, however, social workers then, as now, had probably browsed the jobs pages. Although seasonably thin, the structure of the jobs section, on the surface at least, mapped the contemporary organisation of social work and hints at some of the causes of this 'frustration, anxiety and stress'.

Vacancies for social workers are organised into a number of discrete sections: hospital and medical; local authority; residential; social work services; locum; probation; child guidance; and educational. The typeface and the tone of the 41 advertisements under the heading 'hospital and medical' suggest something of a previous age. Undemonstrative and entirely text-based, the advertisements are almost always for single posts in long-stay mental health or mental handicap [sic] hospitals. The work offered is typically of a sort that would interest those with a 'strong interest in group methods of treatment and be prepared to participate in therapeutic programmes with doctors'. The rather traditional appearance of these advertisements is deceptive, however. In among the small print are clear signs that fundamental change in the structure of social work services is taking place. Numerous advertisements refer explicitly to this being a time of change or of 'modern, extensive redevelopment work', or of a 'unique opportunity to develop real continuity of care between hospital and community'. Other advertisements report 'units' being 'newly opened and rapidly developing' or of establishing 'new patterns of care within the hospital service and establishing links with local authorities in the area'.

The scale and pace of the changes taking place in the organisation of social work is much more explicit in the advertisements for local authority social workers. Here the 'block' advertisements, offering a frequently unspecified number of employment opportunities, speak breathlessly of the promise of services aiming 'to provide an easily accessible point of contact for persons of all age groups with a wide range of personal needs and problems' (Birmingham) and of social services departments offering 'a considerable number of posts at main grade level, which, if filled quickly, would enable the Department to move faster towards the provision of a first class service to areas in which the need is greatest' (Glasgow).

There is a healthy range of opportunities for 'housemothers' and married couples in the residential section of the jobs pages too. There are however, only six advertisements for posts in 'social work services', an unfamiliar term these days. Then, it referred to the voluntary, independent and private sector. Only one of these posts could be described as with a 'national' organisation; the remainder were with very small, usually faith-related and geographically specific projects. There were almost as many posts available in the child guidance setting as there were in the voluntary sector.

For successful applicants, the rewards of a job in social work were perhaps to be found elsewhere than in the pay packet. At a time when the average earnings for a non-manual worker, working a 38.6-hour week, were £2,256.80, basic salaries for a social worker in the health service and in the local authority were £1,932 and £2,025 respectively. As an article in this first edition of *Social Work Today* of 1973 pointed out, 'In the health service even senior social workers at their maximum of £2,199 were then £257.80 pa below Mr Average Whitecollar' (*SWT*, 11 January 1973, p 1). The early career 'housemother' could look forward to a starting salary of between £933 and £1,437, less £258 deduction for board and lodging, scarcely more than the Kepple family's income from state benefits. That week in the 'Sicilian Sunshine' would cost almost three weeks' wages for many residential staff.

Nonetheless, accepting the relatively poor pay, what might await the local authority social worker taking up one of these advertised posts? According to one senior social worker, writing about conditions in Brent Social Services Department (*SWT*, 11 January 1973, p 9):

> In many cases their work environment is deplorable. A high
> proportion [of social workers in London] I spoke with sit
> in one large room, telephones ringing all over the place,
> with no quiet area for supervision and with inadequate
> interviewing space.... Most of them do not have the time
> to deliberate on their cases, especially the more difficult
> ones, nor do they have time to write up as they would
> like in order to clarify what it is they are doing and to see
> where they are going.

Such conditions were not just limited to London. Reported in the same
issue of *Social Work Today*, a survey by the Leeds and Mid-Yorkshire
Branch of the British Association of Social Workers (BASW) found
similarly poor physical conditions in which social workers had to
practise:

> In one room there were as many as 20 staff. Also on the
> debit side the survey revealed that there were no facilities for
> children in 13 of the 16 waiting rooms and that in seven of
> the offices there were no toilet facilities for clients. (*SWT*,
> 11 January 1973, p 3)

While they might avoid the overcrowding and inadequate
accommodation of the social services department, hospital social
workers could not safely assume the provision of even basic secretarial
support, to judge by the number of times reference to the availability
of 'part-time secretarial assistance' was made in advertisements,
presumably by way of an incentive to recruitment. Even in the more
hectic environment of the social services department, the replacement
of the shorthand typist by 'the erratic and inflexible Dictaphone' (*SWT*,
11 January 1973, p 10) was not meeting expectations.

The week's *Social Work Today* also provides a tangential commentary
on the leadership, or at least the management, of social work at this
point in its development. Writing about the first ever training course
for directors of social services, run by the London School of Economics
and Political Science (LSE) and the National Institute for Social
Work (NISW) in July 1971, Muriel Brown, a tutor on the course
and a lecturer at LSE, noted in relation to the advertisements that had
appeared for these posts, that:

> The range of qualities and qualifications demanded of
> applicants included both a knowledge of social work and

suitability for the larger managerial role such key positions implied. But few people existed with all the requisite qualifications and none with knowledge in any depth of the whole range of the previously separate fields of social care. (*SWT*, 11 January 1973, p 13)

The process of recruitment must have been slow, to judge by the fact that the course in which Muriel Brown had been involved had been due to take place in the autumn of 1970 but there had been too few directors available to take up places. Indeed, nine further dates were set for the commencement of the course prior to July 1971 but none proved viable. The profile of the 23 directors who did enrol for the three-week course (with a four-day follow-up six months later) provides a glimpse into the experience and professional backgrounds of those on whom the leadership of social work in the 1970s seemed to have fallen:

> The group was divided evenly between those with previous experience in child care and those from welfare, with one former deputy chief clerk. All but three had previously held chief officer status ... age range from 40 to 58 years, mostly being in their late 40s and 5 of the 23 were women.... Educational qualifications varied considerably. Four directors had degrees and four Diplomas in Social Science. Three had Diplomas in Municipal Administration and two in Public Administration. Eleven directors had some formal training in social work and others had some short course experience. Training in management was largely limited to short courses in recent years. (*SWT*, 11 January 1973, p 13)

Then there was the volume of work to consider. Nationally, there were approximately 87,000 children in care, almost 60 per cent in residential homes. This did not include:

> ... the 8,500 children in long-stay hospitals [who] were subjected to a regime devised for the short-stay patient. They had little need for nursing care and were primarily there for social reasons, having been too great a physical, emotional and financial strain on their parents. 7,000 of these children are mentally handicapped and 1,500 physically handicapped. A third are never visited and a third have no links with the

social services departments from their place of origin. (*SWT*, 11 January 1973, p 18)

In these long-stay hospitals, one might have seen:

> ... wards of tidy cots but no toys and where children were put to bed at 4 pm on a summer evening so that the nursing staff could get ahead with their routine work. (*SWT*, 11 January 1973, p 18)

These conditions were reported at the 10th Annual Conference held by the Association for the Welfare of Children in Hospital. Delegates to the conference also heard that that for every 18 children in hospital there were 30 living at home. The article notes that there were only three directors of social services among the delegates and, rather pointedly, that:

> No mention was made of the support given by local social services departments to mothers caring for the larger number of children at home. (*SWT*, 11 January 1973, p 18)

Any modern-day social worker will recognise the perennial challenges of poor pay, less than perfect working conditions, apparently high vacancy rates, debatable quality of management, the sheer volume of work and considerable administrative restructuring and reorganisation that ran through the pages of *Social Work Today* for the week in which Maria Colwell died. In that sense, the 'frustration, anxiety and stress' of the period may be familiar enough.

But there are two important differences to note. First, this was 1973 and, as such, nearer in time to the Children Act 1948 than the Children and Young Person's Act 2008. It seems highly likely that Myra Curtis, as she travelled the country collecting the information from which she would construct the report (Curtis Committee, 1946) that would form the basis of the Children Act 1948, would have recognised the conditions in the long-stay children's hospitals reported in *Social Work Today* during this fateful week. In many ways, 1973 was much closer to the start of social work as a recognised profession than may be immediately obvious.

Second, the 'frustration, anxiety and stress' that runs through the pages of *Social Work Today* was explicitly associated with the 'goals' of social work. This is another reminder that this is now and that was then. The goals of social work do not seem to excite the same degree of emotion, even among the profession, these days.

In the next two chapters we explore just how different and how contested they were. In Chapter Two, we report how complex, uncertain, 'messy' and difficult the social work with the Kepple family really was. Then, in Chapter Three, we consider the policy context in which this work was undertaken and relate this to some of the larger themes that drove both policy and practice.

Whatever we seek to make of Maria Colwell's death and whatever others were to make of it in the months that followed, it is important that we do not conceal the brutal reality of it. The *Report of the Committee of Inquiry into the Care and Supervision Provided in Relation to Maria Colwell* (DHSS, 1974a) that was to follow the public inquiry established in July 1973, refers only to 'the events which formed the basis of the indictment against Mr Kepple' (para 146). To understand the fundamental events from which the scandal of her death was constructed is to understand the unsettling mixture of the banal and the extraordinary that can surround a violent death; it is to glimpse the complexities of the private life of a family suddenly exposed to public view; it is to gain an impression of who and what those who knew Maria and her family in a professional capacity were working with; and it is to ground any assumptions that might be made by others after the event (including ourselves) in the lived experiences of real people.

Life and death at 119 Maresfield Road

The only witnesses to Maria Colwell's last few days alive to have left a permanent record were Bill and Pauline Kepple. By their own admission, they both lied repeatedly in the statements that they made to the police after their arrests at the hospital. Pauline Kepple was interviewed four times on Sunday 7 January and a further four times on Thursday the 11th. She made four separate written statements that contradicted each other in key particulars (including 'the manner in which [Maria] received any injuries'; 'the extent of the injuries'; and 'the way in which [Maria] was treated − or neglected − in the days immediately preceding her death').

In reviewing her statements as part of preparing the case for the Director of Public Prosecutions, the view of the detective chief inspector responsible for the investigation was unambiguous:

> At the time of interview she was seven months pregnant, her daughter had been murdered by a vicious beating or

beatings, and yet she was not upset in any way. Only a couple of times did she cry, and these were merely crocodile tears which she was able to stop immediately. Even when she was caught out in her lies she continued to tell further lies in order to cover up the truth of what happened … it was not until she had been arrested on suspicion herself, and the position clearly explained to her, that her position at that stage might have been regarded as criminal, did she decide to reverse her previous accounts on [sic] what happened.

I consider that she is a hard woman, unmoved by the events and I am doubtful as to what story she would tell should she be called to give evidence. [NA: DPP 2/5197/2]

This latter point is important as it explains, in part, why Pauline Kepple was not prosecuted herself. In the event, Pauline did give evidence (by deposition and orally) at her husband's committal hearing but not at his final trial.

Bill Kepple made fewer and much shorter statements to the police than his wife. At first, he maintained, as did Pauline Kepple, that Maria's injuries had been caused by a fall down the stairs on the Saturday morning. The implication was that Maria had suffered an epileptic fit. Both Kepples maintained that Maria had had such a fit on the previous Wednesday. It was on the Wednesday (or possibly the Tuesday) that Maria had suffered a serious injury to her face, causing severe bruising around her eyes. When he was interviewed at the John Street Police Station early on Sunday evening, Bill Kepple was shown an album of photographs of the bruises to Maria's body:

The accused put his head between his hands and muttered, "What a terrible thing." DCI HAWKINS said to him, "Now are you still saying that you had not seen any of those bruises?" He replied, "I never laid a finger on her, never – and she always had plenty to eat." [NA: DPP 2/5197/2]

Later that evening, just after 11.00 pm, after Bill Kepple was told that Pauline had changed her story and had said that he had indeed hit Maria, Bill Kepple admitted that he had:

DI DRISCOLL said, "How many times did you hit her?" and he replied, "Just the once." DI DRISCOLL said, "Where? On the body?" He replied, "In the chest and stomach." DI DRISCOLL said, "She's very small. How hard

did you hit her?" He replied, "Well, a good backhander."
[NA: DPP 2/5197/2]

Bill Kepple never levelled any accusations against his wife, several times saying that she was 'too soft' to ever have harmed Maria.

Bill Kepple appeared at Brighton Magistrates' Court on Monday morning (the 8th). There he was allowed to see his wife:

> When KEPPLE was in the interview room speaking with his wife, Mrs KEPPLE said to the accused, "See, Bill, I had to tell them the truth and that you hit Maria", and he said, "That's all right, Pauline. I see. How are the other children?" He then said to me, "Are you going to see that my children go back to Pauline?" [NA: DPP 2/5197/2]

Bill Kepple alone was charged with Maria's murder.

Given that both Bill and Pauline Kepple had denied much of what had happened to Maria over the previous few days, it is difficult, especially at this remove, to make any kind of independent judgement of the facts surrounding Maria's death. However, the version of events given by Pauline Kepple in her fourth statement to the police very late in the evening of Thursday and in the early hours of Friday were, in all essentials, those on which Bill Kepple was subsequently convicted. They make painful reading but they are the foundation on which the scandal of Maria Colwell was made. Somewhere in Pauline Kepple's account is the truth out of which so many other 'truths' were to be made.

In reading the extracts from Pauline Kepple's statement, it should be remembered that it was taken in an age before the routine tape-recording of interviews by the police. The statement would have been written, with the omission of questions or prompts by the interviewing officer, by hand and at dictation speed. As such, it would have taken longer to produce than to read and would probably have been more halting and less fluent than it might appear in its written form. It is also important to remember that it was taken in the early hours of the morning and at a point in the proceedings where Pauline Kepple's own possible criminal liability had been made clear to her and when the police would have been mindful that the evidence of Pauline Kepple would have been crucial in securing the conviction of her husband.

In her statement, Pauline Kepple describes how she and Maria watched the television for most of Saturday. The injuries around Maria's eyes, which had been caused on the previous Tuesday or Wednesday in a manner that was to remain uncertain, were such that her mother asked if Maria was able to see what was on the screen. She claimed that she was waiting for her husband to come home from the pub to take Maria to the hospital for treatment to her swollen face. Maria had had only a 'bit of bread' to eat all day.

From the evidence given at his trial by Margaret White, the barmaid of the Royal Standard public house in Queens Road, Brighton, Bill Kepple had arrived in the pub early that evening 'and he left at closing time and when he left he was not drunk in any way'. Margaret White also said that 'he was a non-violent man, he seemed to get on well with the other customers and there was nothing to suggest any violence of any kind in his behaviour either on that night or on any other occasion.'

On his return to no. 119 at 11.30 pm Pauline Kepple asked her husband where he had been.

> With that he said to Maria, and this was the start of it –
> "How are you Maria?" Of course, she didn't answer him.
> With that he seemed to go haywire. In a temper. That's
> when he got hold of her. Because the kids [...] were still up I
> went to the kitchen. That's when I saw him hit Maria twice
> with the hand. I said, "Oh, you shouldn't have done that."
> He never answered. I said, "You shouldn't have touched
> her." I didn't say too much to him because I was afraid I
> would have got a clout. When I say he got hold of her I
> mean he got hold of the top of her arm and pulled her. I
> said to him, "Don't you hit her." He was shouting, "Don't
> fucking shout – people will hear you." I said, "I don't mind
> people hearing – don't lay your hands on her. I am going
> to take her upstairs." When I was out in the kitchen I said,
> "Don't you ever touch her again." He said, "What do you
> mean?" I said to [Maria's sister], "If he touches Maria again
> Mummy's got this." I got hold of a knife from the drawer.
> He heard what I said. I said to [Maria's sister], "Don't worry
> darlings – in a minute I'll call out for Graham." [That's Mr
> RUSKIN [sic] at the house next door.] My husband didn't
> say anything. I lost my temper and I was shouting. From the
> kitchen I saw him punch her in the stomach twice like I
> said and kick Maria. He kicked her on the legs. I saw him
> put his foot on her neck. That's when I screamed. I tried to
> stop him from doing it further. Eventually because of me
> screaming he stopped. When he pulled her up by the arm
> he had pulled her from the chair onto the floor – then he
> pulled her up and she was standing when he hit her in the

stomach and she went down on the floor. That's when I said to [Maria's sister] about me having the knife. I could see that she was on the floor at the back of the sofa when I came out of the kitchen. [NA: DPP 2/5197/2]

Pauline Kepple then describes how she lifted Maria's head up 'like a baby and cradled her head in my arm. She wasn't knocked out or anything.' Leaving her on the floor, Pauline Kepple says that she put a quilt and blanket over Maria; 'While I was doing this my husband went out with the dog.'

There was another 'quarrel' when Bill Kepple returned from walking 'Pootchie', Pauline claiming that she wanted to take Maria to the hospital. Instead, Bill Kepple bathed her and put clean clothes on her as Maria had soiled herself, presumably as a result of the blows to her abdomen.

Maria I think was alive but she didn't speak while he was doing this and her eyes were closed. I think she was still alive. He didn't seem to have a job putting the things on. I got down to hear and put my ear to her tummy once or twice to see if I could hear her heart. I thought there was some movement but I never heard her breathing. [NA: DPP 2/5197/2]

Bill Kepple persuaded his wife that it 'was a bit late' to be taking her to the hospital and that she could go tomorrow.

I said, "Is she alright?" I kept bending down to have a listen. He said, "Of course she's alright – there's nothing wrong with her." I said, "I'll stay down with Maria." He said, "Don't be silly, she's alright." He carried her up to bed. I went up and tucked her in. She wasn't moving then. She wasn't speaking but I think she was still breathing. We both came downstairs. He went back up with the clock. [NA: DPP 2/5197/2]

Pauline Kepple started to tidy up:

There was a bit of mess on the carpet where she had been laying. There was some small lumps and some was runny.... I cleaned up Maria's mess with some paper and put some disinfectant on a floorcloth and wiped over where it had been. I didn't see any blood on the floor but I did see some on the side of the door. I hadn't seen it before he hit Maria. It wasn't running down and I didn't know if it was fresh. I picked up her clothes and put them on the table in the kitchen near the washing bag and made a jelly, put the food away and went to bed. [NA: DPP 2/5197/2]

According to Pauline Kepple, it was the next morning, after Maria had not answered her call to get up and Bill Kepple had carried her downstairs, that:

> It entered my mind she might be dead and I was very worried. [NA: DPP 2/5197/2]

Maria was put in the pram and Bill Kepple set off for the hospital. He was back within the hour, with Maria still in the pram. Kepple had gone 'near to the hospital and took [his] time'. His wife asked him why he didn't go in. What was he frightened of? She put her jacket on and they both pushed the pram the half-mile to the hospital.

How much of this account is reliable or self-serving, accurate or purposefully misleading is impossible to say. Why Bill Kepple lost his temper in the way that he appears to have done that night will never be known. This was a subject that the police pursued with both of the Kepples. A number of reasons were advanced by Pauline Kepple, especially in her third interview, late on Sunday evening. She suggested that Maria 'never really took to' Bill; lots of things that Maria did 'annoyed him' 'like when she went to the toilet she never used the paper'; 'she messed herself up'; 'she wet her bed and she called me Pauline'. Pauline Kepple told Maria that Bill was her father 'but she never looked at him like that'.

For Bill Kepple's part, in his interview with the police late on Sunday evening, after he had admitted hitting Maria, he said:

> I suppose Maria shouldn't have come back to us. I had to sign a paper that I was willing to have her with us but looking back on it, it was a mistake. There is always plenty of food in the house.... I didn't mean to hurt Maria that bad. [NA: DPP 2/5197/2]

It is not our purpose to re-investigate the reasons for Maria's death or to explain it in any way that implies a commentary on the personal pathologies of either Bill or Pauline Kepple. We tell her story only to remind ourselves and to remind you, our readers, that although it has come to have the power of myth, it is not a work of fiction.

In the next chapter we describe more of Maria's life at no. 119 and of the activity of those who were trying to help her and her family.

TWO

November and December 1972 ...

Maria's death now had to be accounted for and not just by the police and the prosecuting authorities. On the Whitehawk Estate there was anger; at first directed towards Pauline Kepple who, on release from police custody, had returned to 119 Maresfield Road. At Maria's funeral, she had to run the 'gauntlet of taunts' and cries of 'bloody murderess' (*Argus*, 25 and 26 January 1973). This anger had not abated by the time of the verdict at Bill Kepple's trial and Pauline had, briefly, to move out of the family home:

> The word "murderer" has been scrawled on her front wall and as she edged open the door today, a crowd of neighbours shouted: "Come out here and we will kill you. Let's get hold of you." They stood by a car on which had been stuck a poster that read "Bring back hanging – especially for child murderers." (*Argus*, 17 April 1973)

A number of the Kepples' neighbours, the 'ordinary, respectable people' of Brighton (*Sunday Times*, 22 April 1973), had observed Maria's life with the Kepples over the last 15 months or so since she had come to live in Maresfield Road. Some had begun to report their concerns about her treatment, beginning with a telephone call to the NSPCC by Mrs Rutson of no. 121 on 3 April 1972. Mrs Rutson was, in the words of the *Report of the Committee of Inquiry into the Care and Supervision Provided in Relation to Maria Colwell* (DHSS, 1974a, p 82), 'an honest and concerned person with the welfare of Maria very much at heart'.

On Easter Monday, 3 April, from her back garden, separated only by a wire fence from the Kepples', she had heard Pauline:

> ... shouting at Maria and calling her a "dirty little bitch" because she had dirtied herself, and this was followed by the repeated sounds of slapping; the noise came from the top back bedroom window of the Kepple's house.... (DHSS, 1974a, p 82)

Mrs Rutson did not see Maria again until 12 April:

> While in her garden on that Wednesday Mrs Rutson looked
> up at the bedroom of number 119 with the drawn curtain
> and saw Maria looking out of the side of the curtain. Her
> face was, she told [the Committee], "terribly blackened and
> she had a terribly blood shot eye – one eye was just a pool
> of blood". (DHSS, 1974a, p 84)

In later chapters we will look in more detail at the commentary
provided by the Maresfield Road neighbours, not only on the standard
of care provided for Maria but also indirectly on the way in which
others had responded, or failed to respond, to their concerns. At this
point, we seek to establish only that some of the neighbours, at least, had
a legitimate interest in wanting to know what had happened to Maria.

As we have indicated, Maria had been known to the NSPCC and to
East Sussex County Council's Social Services Department almost all
her life. The express purpose of the public inquiry that, by twists and
turns, followed her death in the summer of 1973, was 'to inquire into
and report upon the care and supervision provided by local authorities
and other agencies in relation to Maria Colwell and the co-ordination
between them' (DHSS, 1974a, p 9). The Inquiry was to serve many
other purposes too: emotional, political and symbolic, and there would
be other fora where Maria's death would have to be accounted for,
in the press and the criminal courts, for example. Each forum would
account for Maria's death in its own terms.

Yet common to all of these 'accounting' processes was a concern to
establish 'the facts' of what had happened, to make links and associations
between events, to 'make sense' of what had happened and to allocate
responsibility, even blame. It is to ask 'why' as well as 'how' Maria
Colwell died. Both questions require the construction of a coherent
and credible narrative in which the actions of those implicated in events
could be located, examined and judged. The greater part of the report
of the public inquiry into Maria's death is concerned with establishing
just such a narrative. It must be understood, however, that the task of
constructing a comprehensible and plausible account of the nearly
eight years of Maria's life was, then as much as now, a more subjective
and contestable process than might initially appear. Indeed, while the
chronology of events may be uncontroversial, the report of the public
inquiry actually reaches two distinctive sets of conclusions in relation
to the events of Maria's life and the part played by those whose job it
was to care for her. We return to this point in later chapters.

Moreover, the process of synthesis and summation necessary to tell
Maria's brief history is also a process of simplification. To construct

such a narrative is to reduce the endless possibilities of the moment, the complexity, confusion and untidiness of everyday life into a linear, causal or explanatory sequence that leads to a known end. It imposes a *post hoc* logic on events; it imparts significance to facts that they did not seem to carry at the time; it suggests an inter-connectedness that, in the moment, was obscured by other events; it relies on shorthand, short-cuts and rhetorical and linguistic devices. In this chapter, we want to reintroduce the messiness, confusion, misunderstanding and sheer complexity of just who knew what and when in the days and weeks before Maria Colwell's death. Understanding this is key to understanding how the 'local authority and other agencies' actually went about their business with the Kepples.

We have suggested already that, as well as the actions of particular social workers, social work itself as a form of welfare practice became accountable for Maria Colwell's death. Accordingly, if we are to achieve our purpose of making this a book of record, the social work practised with the Kepples must be represented as it was experienced at the time, with all the ambiguities, uncertainties and lacunae that were present then rather than how it has been abstracted, summarised and preserved in existing accounts. This means setting out, in considerable detail, what we have been able to recover of the variety of contacts that took place with and between neighbours, friends, various departments of the local authority, health professionals, education staff, the police and the NSPCC over the weeks immediately prior to Maria's death.

In what follows, we use transcripts of the evidence given in oral testimony and the written statements provided by witnesses at the public inquiry to resolve the 'confusion about certain aspects of events at the end of November and the first 10 days in December [1972]' (DHSS, 1974a, p 127) that is central to understanding *why* Maria Colwell died. Of course, we are reliant on our sources and we do not pretend to any greater objectivity than anyone else who has provided an account of this period. Nonetheless, we try to provide a much fuller account than we have found elsewhere.

It will be recalled that Maria had lived at no. 119 only since October 1971. For most of her life, she had been looked after by her paternal aunt, Doris Cooper and her husband. Maria was formally under the supervision of Brighton County Borough's Social Services Department but, under an agreement made between the two authorities, the actual duties of supervision were to be carried out by East Sussex County Council. Since April 1970, the social worker responsible for Maria had been Diana Lees. The NSPCC had known Maria since birth and their involvement continued in the person of Inspector Kirby. We take up our account at the start of this critical period, two months before Maria's death, on Bonfire Night, 1972.

November 1972

At 10.15 pm, on **Sunday 5 November,** PC Roger Pratt, who was on patrol car duty in the Whitehawk area of Brighton, was called to 119 Maresfield Road. Reports had been received from neighbours that the Kepple children had been left alone in the house. He found two children, aged about three or four years, leaning out of an open upstairs window, crying and screaming. Mr Brasil,[1] brother to Mrs Rutson, the Kepples' immediate neighbours at 121 Maresfield Road, had made the initial call to the police and he was waiting outside the house.

PC Pratt asked him to remain there, 'for the safety of the children' [Day Four: 2[2]] while he went to search for the Kepples at a number of public houses, which Mr Brasil had named, in the immediate area. Failing to find them, he returned to Maresfield Road, where Mr Brasil explained to him the history of bad feeling between the Kepples and their neighbours. According to his contemporary notes, PC Pratt then 'asked Mr Brasil to go home but he refused' [Day Four: 4]. They therefore remained there together until 11.15 pm when the Kepples came up Maresfield hill, smelling of alcohol, but not, in the constable's opinion, drunk.

An immediate argument began between Mr Kepple and Mr Brasil, with Mr Rutson emerging from No 121 Maresfield Road to join in. Although concerned for the welfare of the children, PC Pratt was soon more urgently engaged in sorting out trouble between Mr Kepple and Mr Brasil. In his evidence to the Inquiry, PC Pratt put it this way:

> Mr Kepple … immediately swore at Mr Brasil and lunged at him and I had to restrain him. Then, while holding Mr Kepple, I shouted to Mr Brasil to go away, which he eventually did. I went into the house with the Kepples, and after I came downstairs with Mr Kepple … he suddenly ran out of the house and went for Mr Brasil, who was now standing on the steps to the next door house. [Day Four: 6]

---

[1] The family's name is variously spelled as 'Brazil', 'Brasil' and 'Brashill', depending on the source. We have reflected the spelling used by the various sources as we cite them.

[2] Day Four of the Inquiry, page 2 of the transcript. This convention is used throughout the book.

In information not provided in oral evidence, but set out in his notes, PC Pratt now called for assistance, and was soon joined by two police patrol cars, a uniformed inspector and a sergeant, in a show of force which cannot easily have escaped the notice of those living nearby.

Inside the house, Mr Kepple showed PC Pratt upstairs where he found the two children who had been at the window and a younger child lying in a cot. He did not see, and was not told, that a fourth child, Maria, was living at the address. Mrs Kepple protested that she had only been away for about 20 minutes, to collect her husband, a claim that the police officer was able to refute from his own attendance of at least an hour.

While what had began as a child welfare incident had thus become one of public order, the officer nevertheless passed a report of what had taken place to the policewomen's department – standard practice, at the time, in any family matter.

On **Monday 6 November**, in the morning, the family's health visitor, Miss Bodger, made her monthly, unannounced call to see Mrs Kepple, whom she now knew to be pregnant with her tenth child. She found no one at home. At about the same time, Mrs Miles, Mrs Rutson's mother who also lived at 121 Maresfield Road, visited the head office of the housing department to complain about the Kepples.

Following PC Pratt's report, a follow-up call had been made by the police on Monday evening. WPC Luck, in her written report, concluded that a record of her visit had better be kept on file 'for future reference as I feel that this family may well come to the notice of the police again' [Day Seventeen: 46].

Tuesday 7 November was family allowance day. The top of Maresfield Road forms a junction with Manor Hill. A few hundred yards down Manor Hill, at the junction with Manor Road, are the local shops. Here, Mrs Kepple bumped into Mrs Cooper's daughter, Mrs Shirley. In Mrs Shirley's account, Mrs Kepple told her that Maria was unwell with 'a bit of a cold' [Day Seventeen: 46]. An offer to call round to Maresfield Road to visit was resisted by Mrs Kepple on the grounds that 'he doesn't like me having anyone in the house' [Day Seventeen: 46], an observation which Mrs Shirley took 'as a hint that she did not want me round there anyway'.

On the same day, a group of neighbours visited the housing office and called for the Kepple family to be re-housed, away from the area. Complaints focused on Mr Kepple, and the disturbance involving Mr Kepple and Mrs Rutson's brother, Mr Brazil, that had taken place on the previous Sunday evening (5 November).

At the housing office, 'deputations', said Mr George Smith, area housing officer and master of the bureaucratic dead bat, 'do arrive from time to time. I would not like to say they are rare and I would not like to say that they are frequent' [Day Eleven: 8]. The visitors, however, were, he thought, honest and orderly.

On **Wednesday 8 November**, in response to concerns from Maria's class teacher, Mrs Turner, concerning Maria's lateness and erratic attendance at school, the education welfare officer, Mrs Dickenson, made one of her regular and increasingly frequent visits to the Kepple household. She recorded having seen Mr Kepple who told her that Maria had been taken to Hove, to see her brother and sister.

Also on Wednesday, in response to the deputation of the previous day, Mr Topley, a housing assistant, called at 121 Maresfield Road in an attempt, in the words of the area manager, Mr Smith, 'to try and conciliate their complaints' [Day Eleven: 11]. In the event, he was handed a petition, which, while containing no allegations of violence against, or ill-treatment of, Maria, set out a series of other concerns. The burden of the petition was summarised for the Inquiry as [Day Eleven: 15]:

> ... obscene language; bad behaviour; a question of fouling pavements and other property by excreta by the children; noise due to drunkenness and leaving three [sic] small children alone in the house while out drinking.

The petition pointed out that, as far as the latter charge was concerned, 'this matter has been reported to the Brighton Police, NSPCC and Welfare Organisations'. It also concluded that, 'Other than the above mentioned Mr and Mrs Kepple being moved, we honestly feel that there is no solution to the problem.'

On **Thursday 9 November** three further contacts were made with the Kepples, by three different public authorities, with widely contrasting fortunes. Early in the day, Mrs Dickenson, the education welfare officer, was again at 119 Maresfield Road, and again she was met by Mr Kepple, standing by the front room window. He asked her in and suggested that Maria had flu. Challenged about Maria's lateness – which Mrs Dickenson believed to be caused by Maria having to go shopping before being sent to school – Mr Kepple blamed her Cooper relations. Specifically, he suggested that Mrs Shirley had been enticing her away and that a summons had been taken out against her. Neither suggestion had any basis in truth, but both were an indication of the extent to which even chance meetings with the Coopers could produce a strong allergic reaction in the Kepples, bringing back to the surface the tensions which lay buried never very far beneath.

During the same morning Mr Topley from the housing department, still in the cause of conciliation, called and saw Mrs Kepple. He described her attitude as 'apathetic and rather aggressive'. He left feeling that he had made little progress and was pessimistic about the prospects of being able to bring about a return to good neighbourly relations [Day Eleven: 18]. This impression was heavily reinforced later in the same day, when Mr Kepple paid a visit to the housing office. Mr Topley's oral evidence to the Inquiry and a written report he made at the time both convey the character of that visit. An extract from the report was read to the Inquiry during Day Eleven of the hearing. It read:

> Mr Kepple made his presence felt in due course and it became only too clear that he also felt very strongly about the matter. He hurled vicious threats and accusations in my direction and it took some 10 minutes or so to abate his belligerent behaviour. Finally, however, he began to offer some constructive information but continued to interject heatedly during most of my comments which I confined to the task at hand, that is, gaining objective information. Although denying the specific complaints Mr Kepple told me that he regularly comes home drunk from the pub. He added that his children were "free range" with regard to their toilet habits and this he considers to be quite normal bearing in mind their numbers.

In his oral evidence, Mr Topley added some further details. On arrival at the Whitehawk housing office, Mr Kepple had 'demanded to see him' [Day Eleven: 18/19]:

> He was very aggressive. He was practically violent at the time.... Extremely belligerent. I felt it was quite likely that possibly violence would ensue if I was not careful to choose my words carefully ... it took me about 10 or 15 minutes to cool him down a bit and establish the peace....
>
> The information I got from him largely agreed with the accusations in the petition. He not only agreed that they were, in fact, valid, but he suggested that it was none of his neighbours' business or mine whether or not his children were considered to be unruly. He used the term "free range" with regard to their toilet habits which I thought

was significant.... His attitude was that that was the way he had chosen to bring up his children and he felt it was quite a valid way of looking after them....

He took the attitude that it was none of my business that he frequently got drunk – daily I think he said, at least he drank a fair amount. I had the impression at the time of the interview that possibly he had been drinking before, but I could not be certain.

Both Mr Smith and Mr Topley of the housing department came under close questioning about their assessment of the Kepples, and the difficulties they posed. Here it is important only to note that Mr Smith and Mr Topley were at pains to point out that both the complaints they received, and the contact that they had with Mr Kepple was not unusual in the context of the time and place in which they worked. Asked about his interview with Mr Kepple, Mr Topley replied, 'I would not go so far as to say it was common, but I have had nastier moments – let us put it that way' [Day Eleven: 25]. Mr Smith repeated his assessment that, despite the issues raised by neighbours, the Kepples were never regarded by the housing department as a 'problem' family. They were not so regarded when they had taken on the tenancy and they paid their rent regularly and were without arrears [Day Eleven: 13].

Also on 9 November, Miss Lees, Maria's social worker, made a visit to Mrs Kepple's mother, Mrs Tester, in response to a request which she, Mrs Tester, had made. Diana Lees, who was to play such a major part in the subsequent scandal of Maria Colwell and whose role we analyse in more depth in later chapters, had been Maria's social worker since April 1970. It was her name at the end of the report that advised Hove Juvenile Court, in November 1971, to revoke the Care Order and permit Maria's return to the custody of her mother. Diana Lees had not seen Maria since early June, almost six months previously.

In her oral evidence, Miss Lees was asked about information that was said to have been passed to her during that meeting with Mrs Tester. It was put to her that Mrs Tester had told her, 'Miss Lees, there's definitely something wrong with Maria. She's so thin, and her little legs are like matchsticks: that little girl is pining for Doris Cooper – she should be taken away' [Day Twenty-Five: 5]. Diana Lees seems to have regarded these views as part of a long-established pattern in which family members used Maria as grist to the mill of dispute and animosity that had so long characterised their relationships. The potential significance of the source, coming as it did from the Tester, rather than the Colwell, side of the family, did not seem to have struck

Miss Lees as noteworthy. As Miss Sandra Tester was to say of her mother in her written statement to the Committee of Inquiry, 'she usually told her [ie, Miss Lees] everything she knew', so the observations of 9 November would, no doubt, have to be set in the context of a long history of sometimes antagonistic observations.

Later on the same Thursday, WPC Luck was again on patrol in the area, and decided to make a further follow-up call. This time she encountered Mr Kepple. 'I could see the children and obviously they were not on their own', she told the Inquiry. 'I asked could we come in, and he said, "No", and the door was closed. He made it quite clear he did not want to have anything to do with us' [Day Four: 10]. She was sufficiently concerned at her reception to look the family up in the local police records, but, searching only under the name of 'Kepple', WPC Luck found nothing.

On the following **Monday 13 November**, Mrs Dickenson called at no. 119 again. Mrs Turner, Maria's class teacher, had complained to the school secretary that Maria had been late getting to school, arriving at 9.20 am for a day which began at 8.55 am. That message had been passed to Mrs Dickenson who was, by now, in possession of specific complaints that Maria was being used to carry bread, potatoes and large bags of coal back to the house, early in the morning, pushing them up Manor Hill in an old pram. A note from Mrs Turner was passed to Mrs Dickenson informing her that, on arrival in school, Maria had told Mrs Turner, 'My mummy has told me to come and tell you I don't go shopping for coal and potatoes, but I do' [Day Five: 37].

Invited in to the house by Mrs Kepple and, without apparent irony, 'asked to sit down in front of a big fire', Mrs Dickenson trod a narrow path between putting accusations about Maria having to do the shopping directly and not making matters worse for Maria, by betraying any suggestion that the accusations had been corroborated by her. Mrs Kepple's response was to dismiss the idea, saying that Maria had 'a vivid imagination and I wish people would not take notice of her romancing, because she is always doing that' [Day Four: 21]. Asked why she did not take the matter up more directly, Mrs Dickenson was clear: 'I did not want Maria to get into trouble. What would have been the consequence if I had gone to Mrs Kepple and said, "You told me a lie – the child did go out and get coal"?' Instead, she decided 'to go around to the shop early in the morning to look for the little girl carrying it' [Day Five: 61].

Although making no progress in improving Maria's continued lateness for school, Mrs Dickenson's intervention, as noted, did help produce some temporary improvement in attendance. Maria returned

to school for the rest of the week, making what was to be her final visit
to Whitehawk Junior School on **Friday 17 November**. On the same
day, Miss Lees, not having seen the family since 16 June, wrote to Mrs
Kepple, suggesting a home visit for the following Monday, at 5.30 pm.

Somewhere about this point, possibly on **Saturday 18 November**,
the written evidence of Mrs Kepple's daughter and regular babysitter,
Miss Tester, set out an incident which the Inquiry was unable to
corroborate, but which it accepted was 'on the whole … consistent
with the general picture' (DHSS, 1974a, p 50):

> At about 9.00 pm, before Mr and Mrs Kepple went out,
> Maria, Mr Kepple and I were alone in the living room.
> Mr Kepple told Maria to go to bed – she looked towards
> me as I had already said she could stay up. Mr Kepple then
> gave Maria a double slap across the face, very hard. I told
> Mr Kepple to stop and threw a vase at him. He went for
> her again, and I pushed her out of the way. We then had
> an argument about his hitting Maria, and I told him that if
> he wanted to hit anybody he should hit somebody bigger
> than a little child. He said he had lost his temper. Maria had
> a graze on her right cheek.
>
> When I returned home later that evening I told my
> mother, Mrs Tester, what had happened. My mother was
> very angry and said she would phone Miss Lees the next
> day. The following day, when I got home in the evening,
> my mother told me she had phoned Miss Lees. Miss Lees
> came the next day to ask me what had happened, and I
> repeated to her what I had told my mother.

The evidence of Maria being slapped, and of being kept locked in
her bedroom, was also put to Miss Lees, but she denied having been
told it at the time – 'I do not remember being told about that at that
time. I do remember Mrs Tester saying something after Maria had
died' [Day Twenty-Five: 6]. Indeed, given the nature of what was said
to have been disclosed, Miss Lees agreed with the counsel for the
Inquiry that it would have been 'absolutely inconceivable' that such
a conversation, had it taken place, 'would not have found its way into
your notes' [Day Twenty-Five: 7]. In the Inquiry's account, the bruising
which would have followed such an assault could have contributed to
the difficulties which Miss Lees was to experience in getting to see
Maria, and connected to an anonymous call which the NSPCC was
to receive on 27 November, alleging bruising.

The robustness of this inference is called into question, however, by the fact that, on the next day, **Sunday 19 November**, Maria was very clearly seen by Mrs Kirby of the NSPCC, playing on the corner of Maresfield Road with other Kepple children. Mrs Kirby saw no signs of harm. Mrs Kirby recorded the sighting in her case notes, because she stopped in her car, en route to visiting her own mother who lived nearby, and spoke to the Kepple children. To her, they appeared 'the same as they always had' [Day Eleven: 51].

On **Monday 20 November** Whitehawk School was closed in celebration of the Queen's Silver Wedding anniversary. Mrs Kepple had received Miss Lees' letter. She telephoned the social services department office to explain that it was a school holiday, and that she would not be at home. She suggested, instead, that the visit should go ahead at the same time on either the Tuesday or Thursday of the same week. A reply was sent, explaining that neither of those dates was possible, but suggesting Friday instead.

On the following day, Maria was absent from school again. Mrs Kirby of the NSPCC, who had been away at the High Court on 13 November, was now absent for a further three days, a further full day at the High Court on the 20th, and two days away sick on 21 and 22 November. On **Wednesday 22 November**, the persistent Mrs Dickenson, the education welfare officer, called at no. 119 again, two or three times during the day, but without receiving any reply. On the same day, other welfare officials were following up the 'domestic incident' of 5 November. Mr Smith of the Whitehawk housing office telephoned Brighton Social Services Department to explain the situation to them. He spoke to Mr McBurney[3] whose case note suggested that this was a relatively routine call. The events were two weeks old and Mr Smith's main concern was dealing with neighbour complaints.

On the following day, **Thursday 23 November**, Mrs Dickenson, who had had no luck on 22 November, called at no. 119 again. This time, she was told that Mrs Kepple had taken the children to relatives for the day. Mrs Kepple had telephoned the social services department office, in response to Miss Lees' latest letter, cancelling the arranged visit by Miss Lees. Instead of Friday, Mrs Kepple proposed bringing Maria directly from school on the following Monday, with an appointment at the social services department office at 4.30 pm. The note taken of

---

[3] Mr McBurney was the social worker with formal case accountability for Maria's Supervision Order, the order having been made in Brighton County Borough's favour although with the duties falling to Diana Lees of East Sussex County Council, for reasons explained earlier.

the call for Miss Lees said that if convenient, 'we would confirm by letter' [Day Twenty-Five: 18]. Instead, Miss Lees replied, on the same day, to say, 'I am sorry that I shall not be able to call on you on Monday next [although this was not what Mrs Kepple had proposed], but could manage the following day, Tuesday, at 4 pm.'

In the last week of November, the sequence of events which was to end with Maria's death gathered pace and direction. On **Monday 27 November**, Mrs Kepple had received Miss Lees' latest letter proposing a visit on the following day. She again telephoned the social services department office – 'Could you make it Friday at 4 pm? Maria OK except for dysentery, easing off a bit' [Day Twenty-Five: 18]. Over a 10-day period, seven different arrangements had been proposed and found to be inconvenient to one side or the other. To the counsel for the Inquiry this 'rather looks, does it not, as if Mrs Kepple was trying to avoid you for as long as possible?' [Day Twenty-Five: 19]. Miss Lees did not agree. She pointed out that potential appointments had been turned down on both sides, not just by Mrs Kepple, and that on each occasion, Mrs Kepple had taken the trouble to contact the Office to propose alternative arrangements.

On the same day, at 3.45 pm, the NSPCC received the first of what were to be three anonymous telephone calls, each from a woman and each complaining about Maria's condition and each saying that she ought to be removed from her family. In response to an appeal from the Inquiry to come forward, this first call was traced to Mrs Betty Brazil, the aunt of Mrs Rutson, and wife of the Mr Brazil caught up in the events of 5 November. Her own account was offered to the Inquiry on the 17th day of its hearings [Day Seventeen: 28]:

> I said I was ringing in connection with little Maria Colwell of 119 Maresfield Road, Brighton. I said she had not been seen for several days again, and on the last occasion she was not seen, when she was eventually seen she had bruising around her face, and I was afraid this could be the reason again. I said, "If you do not soon take her away from that house something terrible will happen to her, and when you do go there take a medical officer with you." And the lady thanked me very much.

At the NSPCC, the call was taken by Mrs Goodman, the secretary at the Group Office who passed it to the duty officer, Mr Baker – '3.45 Keppell [sic], 119 Maresfield Road. Maria bruises, and lost a lot of weight – a stone in weight – not at school? Last seen Wednesday last week.' He in turn telephoned Mrs Kirby that evening to pass on the details of the call.

At the same time, the school authorities were again alerted by a call to the school secretary, Mrs Chapman, from Mrs Rutson (of no. 121), asking for inquiries to be made into Maria's absence. This call, and other developments, led to a new level of concern for Maria's well-being at Whitehawk Junior School. The main instigator in what took place was Mrs Turner, Maria's class teacher and a probationer, in her first year in the profession. A combination of mounting absenteeism, and growing rumours of Maria's ill-treatment among the pupils, combined to give Mrs Turner's concerns greater credence.

On or just before **Tuesday 28 November** a meeting took place at the school, attended by Mrs Turner, Mr Masters, the long-standing deputy headmaster, and Mr Cornwall, the newly arrived headmaster. According to Mr Cornwall, the meeting began with the other two staff members recounting 'rumours of ill-treatment' [Day Eight: 9] circulating among pupils. They decided to contact Mrs Dickenson (the education welfare officer), the social services department and Mrs Kirby of the NSPCC. Mr Masters made the telephone calls, in the presence of Mr Cornwall. The date is fixed, in a note which appears in Miss Lees' case notes of that date, in which she records that 'the headmaster also feels that Maria has deteriorated' [Day Nine: 37]. In his evidence, Mr Cornwall rather glosses the outcome in telling the Inquiry that assurances were received that 'these three agencies had the matter under control', and that there was 'no need to pursue the case any further' [Day Eight: 11]. In fact, what had taken place was a set of initial contacts, and consolidated concerns, which were to reverberate well into the following month. As far as Mrs Turner, Maria's class teacher, was concerned, for example, Mr Masters had reported back to her in alarming terms, saying to her [Day Three: 45]:

> Don't worry, Mrs Dickenson and the NSPCC are involved.
> It looks like being a battered baby case.

Mrs Dickenson also spoke to Mr Masters directly. He told her that, 'he had to get concerned because of the rumours – one child said that they thought she was locked in a cupboard – and he wanted to see them through. So I said, "By all means ring everybody and I will deal with it from the attendance point of view"' [Day Five: 23].

On the same day, Diana Lees was also attending to Maria's case. Her notes contain a reference to her having a telephone conversation with the NSPCC's Mrs Kirby in which, for the first time, she learned that:

'Maria had been late for school, absent and had been seen carrying coal' [Day Twenty-Five: 2]. The note, of that conversation, quoted in full to the Inquiry, reads as follows:

> Phone call from Mrs Kirby. She has been seeing Maria very frequently during the summer, passing up Maresfield Road almost every day and seeing Maria playing outside on most occasions. She has also called at the house with clothing and other goodies. Today, she said that Maria had not been at school for the last week. A neighbour reported that Maria had deteriorated and had lost weight. Mrs Kepple has told Mrs Kirby that Maria tells lies which appear to be mostly about the Colwell/Coopers and Mrs Kirby wonders whether CGC [child guidance clinic] might be of benefit. I think this is a possibility since this should not be too threatening to the Kepples. Mrs Kirby will agree to transporting Maria and her mother. She thinks she has quite a good relationship with Mrs Kepple.

During the Inquiry, the content of this note became a subject of dispute between the two parties. Miss Lees was sure that, had bruising been mentioned – as in the anonymous telephone call – she would have recorded that fact. Mrs Kirby was equally clear that a call would not have been made (and she had no record of any such call), without discussing the bruising. Yet a close reading of Mrs Brashill's own evidence shows that her own only reference to bruising was to what had happened in April 1972, rather than in November. In fact, the only call which Mrs Kirby's records do show for 28 November is one *to* Mrs Dickenson, a call which Mrs Dickenson herself was sure could only have taken place on 4 December. During that day, however, Mrs Kirby did receive a message as a result of a call from Mrs Kepple, asking her to rearrange a planned visit: 'Could you make it Friday at 4 pm?' the message read. 'Maria okay except for dysentery, easing off a bit' [Day Thirteen: 15].

It was against this background that, on **Wednesday 29 November**, Mrs Dickenson made a further home visit. Mr Kepple was at home. He told her that Maria was not in school because of a bad attack of diarrhoea and vomiting, but when she asked to see Maria, Mr Kepple replied that Maria had gone out with her mother. Asked if she believed what she was told, Mrs Dickenson replied, 'Oh no, they were such a plausible couple; they were always lying.' While she did not believe that Maria was ill, however, she was equally clear that it had not occurred to her at all, at this stage, that Maria might have been at home, having been

ill-treated [Day Five: 24]. As a witness, her credibility is strengthened
by her refusal to allow her distrust of the Kepples which, by the end
of November 1972 was self-evident, to be extended retrospectively
into recalling warning signs which were not apparent to her at the
time. She never rewrote history to make herself seem either wiser or
more active in pursuit of Maria's welfare than she had been at the time.
Nevertheless, the strongly unsatisfactory nature of her latest interview
with Mr Kepple now set Mrs Dickenson into action on a series of
fronts. She informed him, at the conclusion of the interview, that she
would now require a medical certificate to explain Maria's absence
from school, and began, immediately, to find ways of securing such a
certificate herself.

On the same day, Wednesday 29 November, education welfare officer,
Mrs Dickenson also telephoned the NSPCC Group Office, leaving a
message asking Mrs Kirby of the NSPCC to telephone her about Maria.
She followed this up with a further call on **Thursday 30 November**
and it was during this call that she learned, for the first time, of the
involvement of Miss Lees, the local authority social worker.

December 1972

Miss Lees, of all of those who were 'involved' with the Kepples, was
the only official not to have seen any members of the family during
November. Now, on **Friday 1 December**, armed with the contents
of her visit to Mrs Tester on 9 November, and following the telephone
conversation with Mrs Kirby three days earlier, she made her first direct
contact with the Kepples since June. Miss Lees' record of the hour-long
visit was a full one. She found [Day Twenty-Five: 19]:

> Maria sitting on the sofa, rest of the family present. Maria
> has certainly lost a tremendous amount of weight. I think
> she has grown a little taller but seems very thin. Mrs Kepple
> said that Maria has persistent diarrhoea and Maria herself
> confirmed this. If this is the case it could account for loss
> of weight. She looked rather pale and listless. She also has a
> recurrence of her local head infection which Mrs Kepple
> pointed out to me. I advised her to seek medical help, both
> for the dysentery and for the head infection. She says that it
> is because of Maria's ill health she has not attended school.
> I suggested it would allay people's worries if she would
> send a note down to the school or somehow notify them
> of Maria's ill health.

It was a visit which left her concerned at what she found, but not excessively so. Maria was thin, but 'certainly not' providing any impression of malnutrition [Day Twenty-Five: 21]. She was absent from school but, given her condition, 'I would not have expected her to be at school' [Day Twenty-Five: 21]. With advice to visit the doctor, and to contact the school, Miss Lees felt that matters were able to rest.

On the same day Mrs Dickenson, whose recent engagement with the case had been of a very different order, but whose involvement remained, at this stage, wholly unknown to Miss Lees [Day Twenty-Five: 20], was also in action. Although she had agreed with Mr Masters to pursue matters from 'the attendance point of view', this turned out to be a role that allowed her a fairly free rein. On Friday 1 December she made a visit to Brighton Social Services Department Office, at the end of the afternoon, to discuss a number of other cases. While there, she took the opportunity to pass on her concerns, to the duty officer, Mrs Hodgson [Day Five: 26]:

> I told her about the rumours that the children were saying. I told her everything that I knew, that we had not had any definite proof to support these rumours as being right, that it needed looking into because the children were saying these things and it seemed that it might be true.

Mrs Hodgson's own note of the conversation, left for Mr McBurney (who held formal case responsibility for Maria's supervision) to pick up after the weekend, set out Mrs Dickenson's concerns, in some detail [Day Eighteen: 9]:

> Mrs Dickenson, EWO [education welfare officer] to office, to inform of present situation in Kepple household. Maria has not been at school for a week. The implication is that she may have been beaten. Mrs Kirby has a good relationship with the family, and is aware that Maria has been beaten before. She was supposed to be visiting today. I stressed that it was definitely Mrs Kirby's territory if there was a suspicion of ill-treatment. An added dimension is that EWO feels that the physical care of the child is unsatisfactory. The appearance of her stomach suggests malnutrition or a tapeworm! The health visitor, Miss Bodger, is refused entry, but Mrs Kepple claims to have taken Maria to her GP recently, as she herself is concerned about Maria's physical position.

This information was to become another matter of dispute at the Inquiry. Mrs Dickenson believed that, on 1 December, she was yet to learn of Mrs Kirby's views. Yet it was difficult to identify any other source from which Mrs Hodgson might have learned this alarming information.

There matters rested over the first weekend of December 1972. The morning of the following **Monday 4 December** saw Mr McBurney of Brighton's social services department attending a training course at the University of Sussex. He was not to see the note of Friday's visit until at least that afternoon. Mrs Dickenson, however, was again to the fore. In her view, this day marked her first direct contact with Mrs Kirby, calling in response to her messages of the previous week. Mrs Kirby 'gave me details of the case; she told me about the previous report of the child being battered and about the fostering; she gave me a lot of information about the family'. In complete contradistinction to the view recorded by duty officer Mrs Hodgson on the previous Friday, Mrs Kirby's conclusion, relayed to Mrs Dickenson, was that 'she could not do anything because the child was on a Supervision Order' [Day Five: 27].

What is clear to us is that for almost the whole time in which Maria had lived at Maresfield Road, the connections between different social welfare services and officials who knew her had been tenuous at best, and often non-existent. It was only from this point that this began to change. On the day when Mrs Dickenson was speaking, perhaps for the first time, to Mrs Kirby, she also received a message from Miss Bodger, the health visitor, after which Mrs Dickenson made another home visit. In her evidence to the Inquiry, Mrs Dickenson pinpointed her discussion with Mrs Kirby as a turning point in her attitude towards Maria's welfare. Until that point she had felt a general disquiet and a specific concern about school attendance. As far as physical danger, however [Day Five: 57]:

> I was never concerned until the beginning of December, until I heard that a similar incident had happened before in April, and then I did all I could.

Mrs Dickenson's own record for that Monday read 'Child in bed. Mother would not bring her down' [Day Five: 47]. Despite all her many efforts, Mrs Dickenson had not actually seen Maria since her single meeting with her in July. Faced with Mrs Kepple's assertion that Maria was sleeping, and not to be disturbed, there was nothing she could do 'apart from forcing my way in, which I could not do at that stage' [Day Fifteen: 27]. Instead, she reinforced her insistence that a medical examination be carried out and, in response to Mrs Kepple's assertion that Maria would be returning to school on the following day, said that she would make an appointment for her to be seen at the school clinic. Mrs Kepple's reaction – 'She thanked me and said that she would appreciate it' [Day Fifteen: 27] – illustrates the ambivalence that characterised the family's relationships with officialdom. Mrs Dickenson's frustration at the mendacity of both partners was plain, but diffused, at least temporarily, by the apparent appreciation that was now forthcoming. In response, she rang the school clinic immediately, telling them 'about the rumours' – 'Neglect has been reported in this case and some battery – child has appeared bruised' [Day Fifteen: 15]. In response to her call, Mrs Dickenson obtained agreement that 'the child would be pushed in the next afternoon' [Day Fifteen: 28].

The following day, **Tuesday 5 December**, was potentially a pivotal moment in the history of the Colwell case and was possibly the last point at which concerns about Maria's welfare were sufficiently exposed for decisive action to have been taken. The catalyst, once again, was Mrs Dickenson. Early in the morning she telephoned Whitehawk Junior School:

> ... to find out if Maria had gone into school. She had not turned up at school, so went round to the house. I knocked on the door and there was no reply, and I kept on knocking. Eventually Mr Kepple came to the door, threw it wide open, and started swearing. He had a strap in his hand; his trousers seemed to be well supported, and the strap was held above his shoulder in this way – I think he thought he could scare me.

Mrs Dickenson, however, stood her ground, reminding Mr Kepple that a promise had been made that Maria would be returned to school that morning, that a medical certificate was now a requirement, and that 'if he did not produce a medical certificate then I would bring him before the Committee'.

A series of familiar sounding responses now followed: Maria was in bed, asleep; it was not right to send an unwell child out in the bleak and rainy weather of that day; she was already out with her mother at the doctor's, or at the shops, or visiting relations. At each point, Mrs Dickenson countered. If Maria was still at home then she told Mr Kepple that, 'I will not go away until you show me her.' If she was at the doctor's then, 'I will phone down to the doctor's because, as you say, if she were really ill, she should not be out in weather like this.' If she was at the shops, then 'I will go and look for her.'

Mr Kepple's original bluster – 'if he wanted to get a medical certificate for his wife or child he would do so, and if he did not then it was no concern of mine' – was giving way a little under Mrs Dickenson's directness. 'I said "You have told me so many lies that it is very difficult to believe you now."' He was, she thought, still 'quite worked up', but 'panicky'. The interview, all of which had taken place on the front doorstep, ended with her insistence that Maria be produced at the school clinic that afternoon – 'your wife has consented. The appointment has been made', and his counter that he would make an appointment at the family's own doctor, and take the child himself.

> "And was that the end of the conversation?", asked the Inquiry. Mrs Dickenson replied, "He said 'You will get your medical certificate', only he phrased it up a little bit more than that, and he just slammed the door."

Events of the day, however, were very far from over. Anxiety about what had taken place led Mrs Dickenson to seek an immediate interview with her own senior in the education department, Mrs Tattam. In her evidence to the Inquiry, Mrs Tattam confirmed that it was unusual to have held such a discussion about a child who had been absent from school for a bare two weeks. This was, she said, evidence of the wider concerns to which the case was now giving rise. As a result of what she heard, Mrs Tattam made two calls. Mrs Dickenson by now knew of the existence of Miss Lees and the first call was made to East Sussex Social Services Department; the duty officer made this note [Day Four: 58]:

> Telephone call from Mrs Tattam. Worried regarding Maria's welfare. Not attending school. Visit made this am. Mr Kepple holding leather belt and refused admission. URGENT visit requested for today.

Hove Office now contacted Brighton Social Services Department. Mr Rutherford, duty officer in the Brighton Office, consulted his senior, Margaret Egan, and Miss Lees consulted her senior, Miss Coulthard. She, in turn, contacted area director, Miss Wall, who agreed that 'the situation be investigated immediately' and that a Place of Safety Order should be obtained 'if it were necessary when they got there and visited' [Day Twenty-Five: 46]. Following some negotiations, it was agreed that Miss Lees would visit, accompanied by the Brighton duty officer, Mr

Rutherford. Two reasons were given for a joint visit: 'the first was the threatening attitude reported to have been shown by Mr Kepple, and the second was the possibility that a Place of Safety Order might have to be applied for' [Day Seventeen: 5].

In advance of the visit it was agreed that Miss Lees would go into the house and that Mr Rutherford would wait in the car unless or until his assistance was needed. At around 2.30 pm the visit took place. Miss Lees tried the front door, the side door and went round to the back, but to no avail. She and Mr Rutherford agreed to return to the Brighton Office and to take advice from their seniors. About two minutes into the journey, they met Mr McBurney (the case officer from Brighton Social Services Department) on Donegal Road. He was on his way to meet them at Maresfield Road. They all returned together at which point, according to Mr McBurney's case notes, Miss Lees phoned the NSPCC [Day Seventeen: 3/4]. The content of that call, and a further one, was recorded in Miss Lees' notes of the day [Day Thirteen: 25]:

> During the course of today between visits to the Kepples I spoke to Mrs Kirby on the 'phone. She was worried because she had been away and had not seen Maria for a fortnight, but was reassured when I explained I had seen the child last Friday. I phoned her again later, having seen Maria, to reassure her as to Maria's well-being.

Having returned to the office and considered matters further, a second attempt was made to visit the home. Miss Lees and Mr McBurney now travelled out in separate cars. Mr McBurney told the Inquiry [Day Eighteen: 11]:

> I went with Diana Lees to the door and went up the steps. At the door I asked her if she wished me to accompany her in ... she said she would prefer to go in alone and that she knew she could call me if she needed me. I returned to the car.

Miss Lees' own account of what took place was set out, as usual, in some detail in her case notes [Day Twenty-Five: 22/23]:

> I found Mrs Kepple and the children at home, Mrs Kepple on the point of putting some potatoes in the oven to roast. A warm cheery fire was burning in the grate and all the children were playing quite happily. Mrs Kepple showed

me a bottle of medicine which she had obtained for Maria from the doctor and also some ointment for the child's head. She said that Maria appeared to have a spot on her shoulder which she had picked which might have been related to the head infection (I had seen this previously), but assured me that the infection had not spread to the rest of her body. I asked if I could have a look to see and was able to see the whole of her body and her legs and the lower part of her arms. There was no evidence of other infection and no sign of any bruising or other ill treatment.... Maria looked quite unharmed and, in fact, had more life in her than when I saw her last.

Miss Lees thus left Maresfield Road on 5 December, believing that, far from finding a family in crisis, she had found matters improving. Mr McBurney's case notes of that day confirm this impression [Day Eighteen: 12]:

Miss Lees returned after half an hour, said she had seen Maria; situation as before and Miss Lees considered not appropriate for any other action. Material deficiencies in home, blankets would be helpful. Promised Miss L to see if anything could be provided.

Despite this rather bathetic note, the real sense among the social workers was one of 'great relief' that matters were not as serious as they had been reported.

Meanwhile, a number of different strands were coming together on the same day at the NSPCC. Mrs Kirby had already spoken to Mrs Dickenson. She now received a call from Mrs Tattam (Mrs Dickenson's senior) who recounted the earlier visit by the education welfare officer. According to Mrs Tattam, 'she [Mrs Kirby] was a little hesitant about visiting in this particular case because of the Supervision Order and the child being the responsibility of a social worker, but I pressed her and told her we were anxious and she did agree to visit' [Day Seven: 16]. Mrs Tattam's call was reinforced by a reminder of the urgency with which Mr Masters (deputy headteacher at Maria's school) had wanted to contact Mrs Kirby – 'I don't know if I emphasised that the deputy headmaster wanted to speak to you when I gave you the message' [Day Four: 61]. Mrs Kirby made a call, but spoke only to the school secretary who 'advised me that he [Mr Masters] wanted to let me know Maria's teacher was worried because Maria came to school late in the morning and was very thin, and sometimes ate more than one dinner' [Day Four: 55].

If visits were over, the activity of the day was not. Maria was not produced for examination at the school clinic. Following Mr Kepple's insistence that an appointment would be made at the family's own GP, Mrs Dickenson found out who that might be. She telephoned the surgery and [Day Five: 30]:

> I spoke to the receptionist. I asked her if an appointment had been made, and she said, it had not. I put her into the picture as to why I was eager for the doctor to see the child.

As noted earlier, however, the pressure on Mr Kepple had mounted during the day. Before the end of afternoon surgery Dr Barley, the family's GP, already briefed about Mrs Dickenson's concerns, had taken a call from Mr Kepple which he recalled for the Inquiry [Day Fourteen: 54]:

> ...he wanted me to go to see Maria on account of abdominal pain, which, on further questioning, she turned out to have had over a considerable period of time, also diarrhoea. My usual reaction to that sort of request, especially if it comes during an afternoon surgery, is to think, why did they not phone earlier? Why did they not phone in the morning or anything like that? I therefore offered to stick in an appointment to see her as soon as possible the next day, and he readily agreed to this.

Mrs Dickenson now telephoned the surgery for a final time. She was told that an appointment had been made for 4.20 pm on the following day. And there, for a brief period, matters rested.

Despite the reassurance that she had already received from Miss Lees, Mrs Kirby decided to visit no. 119 on **Wednesday 6 December**, arriving after 3 pm. She took with her some baby clothing and bedding for the child that Mrs Kepple was expecting in March. Alerted to the considerable concerns of others, the visit itself – made unannounced – had the opposite effect than she might have anticipated [Day Eleven: 53]:

> I was warmly received.... I thought there was a great improvement in Mr Kepple's attitude towards Maria.... He spoke to her kindly. He told her to go and get the dog

so that that I could see the tricks that the dog and the cat
could do. It was a very, very happy visit. It was the first
time I had really seen Maria laughing and all the children
were laughing at the antics of the puppy and the kitten....
I always felt that she was a serious little girl. But her attitude
was most spontaneous on this occasion when I called, and I
felt that there was a marked improvement in the happiness
in the home generally.

These general impressions were reinforced by physical examination of
the property and of Maria:

Mr Kepple told his wife to show me the bedroom he had
just redecorated. So I did go upstairs and have a look round.

As to medical examination, the Kepples told Mrs Kirby that Maria
had been suffering from gastro-enteritis and 'spots'. They 'willingly'
let Mrs Kirby undress Maria and examine her. Apart from continuing
thinness, and a dermatitis-like scab on her head, there was nothing to
observe – and 'certainly no bruising' [Day Thirteen: 22]. Mr Kepple
confirmed that an appointment had been made for Maria to see the
family GP. Mrs Kirby offered to call back at the house and give them a
lift to the surgery. Although the offer was declined, she was convinced
that the appointment had been made, and would be kept, because it
was apparent that Mr Kepple 'had been under pressure to produce
a medical certificate'. The pressure, of course, had come from Mrs
Dickenson – 'that education woman', as he referred to her. Mrs Kirby's
recollection of the visit was that Mr Kepple was determined never to
let Mrs Dickenson in the house again [Day Eleven: 55]:

He was very anti Mrs Dickenson at this stage. He said she
had demanded to go upstairs and he was not going to
allow people to enter his house and go over it without his
invitation.

Mrs Kirby left the home that day 'satisfied that there was nothing to
worry about'. Her assessment differed from that of others because
'they had not seen the child, but I had', and 'in close proximity' [Day
Twelve: 39]. She now left a general message at the NSPCC office, to
be passed to all enquirers [Day Thirteen: 31]:

... anyone rings, Maria Kepple is well. Spent long time with her yesterday. Dermatitissy spots on head. Mrs K perfectly satisfied.

For both Miss Lees and Mrs Kirby, therefore, Wednesday 6 December was a day of passing reassuring messages. They spoke to one another, and contacted the school. Mrs Tattam, at the Education Department, received calls from both, and both confirmed their impression that 'nothing much was wrong' [Day Seven: 16]. Mrs Tattam's records show that Mrs Kirby had told her that 'In her opinion nothing was wrong with Maria. The child was thin, but she thought that was because the child had grown rather quickly' [Day Twelve: 17] – although this was not, in fact, the case. At some stage in her contact with Miss Lees, and most probably during this call, Mrs Tattam exchanged rather heated words, in response to what was said to be an assertion by Miss Lees that the social services department 'wanted [Maria's placement] to be successful', to which Mrs Tattam replied 'successful at whose expense – the child's?' [Day Seven: 16].

Mrs Dickenson also learned of the two visits and their outcome. She was not reassured by what she heard [Day Five: 33]. In her contemporary notes, she recorded that, 'I learned that Miss Lees the social worker had seen Maria twice during the last few days: she hadn't found any reason to be concerned' [Day Six: 11]. The ambiguity of this note is striking. It could be taken at face value – no cause for concern had been found. It also, however, could be taken as an implied suggestion that Miss Lees had, in a self-serving, or self-fulfilling way, failed to find any reasons to be concerned. Mrs Dickenson shared her own concerns, again, with Miss Bodger, the health visitor, who had also telephoned the surgery that morning to check on whether an appointment for Maria had been made.

Mr Kepple, in the meantime, had made his way to the Education Department and demanded to see Mrs Tattam, Mrs Dickenson's senior. As she told the Inquiry, 'I heard him shouting at one of the juniors in our small reception office', and decided that the best course of action was to ask him in. The burden of Mr Kepple's message was 'that I was to keep Mrs Dickenson away from his house. I think he referred to her as "that woman". I asked him why. He said that Mrs Dickenson had called him a liar.... Then Mr Kepple said I had no right to send Mrs Kirby and Miss Lees to his home' [Day Seven: 17].

Mrs Tattam's conclusion was that, while Mr Kepple was demanding, his presence was not disturbing – 'he did not swear' – and that he had made his case forcefully but not aggressively. He made the point to her that 'Miss Lees visited once a month ... that she had, in any case, been to the house quite recently and she was satisfied about the child' [Day Fifteen: 2]. As a result of the visit, Mrs Tattam discussed the situation with Mrs Dickenson, giving her the chance to withdraw from the case because of Mr Kepple's hostility. She declined.

Having made his views known to Mrs Tattam, Bill Kepple now took Maria to see the family doctor, Dr Barley. The GP's conclusions were that Maria was 'just a small, rather thin girl', who showed no evidence of ill-treatment or violence [Day Fourteen: 57], whose condition gave him no cause for concern. He dismissed any suggestion that what he found gave any reason to consider referring her to the Brighton Children's Hospital and agreed that, from a medical perspective, any thought that she might need to be removed from home 'would have been totally unjustifiable' [Day Fourteen: 63].

Dr Barley's examination ended with two conclusions – first, that Maria was fit to be returned to school – 'and I told the parent that that was where she ought to be' [Day Fourteen: 58] – and that a follow-up appointment should be made for the following week. This was duly done, and Maria returned home.

At the time when Dr Barley carried out his examination he was aware, from the telephone calls received at his surgery, that Maria was the cause of anxiety to a number of social welfare workers interested in her well-being. It was not until the following day, however, **Thursday 7 December**, that he received a call directly from Mrs Dickenson. He confirmed to her that, other than on the previous afternoon, he had not seen Maria for many months – 'and certainly not in the last few weeks, when Mrs Kepple told me the doctor was visiting the house' [Day Five: 31]. He confirmed that a follow-up appointment had been made for the Wednesday of the following week. Mrs Dickenson recalled Dr Barley as having said that he would 'be delighted' to provide a report, should matters ever get to court – an ambiguous conclusion, in which he was sure he had referred only to matters of non-school attendance, but which might be understood as referring to wider welfare concerns. On the same day, and in response to a note from Mrs Dickenson, Miss Bodger, the health visitor, called at Maresfield Road but, once again, without obtaining a reply.

On **Friday 8 December** Mrs Dickenson went to see Mr McBurney, at his office in Brighton's Social Services Department in order to discuss other cases. At that point, she was unaware of his responsibility for Maria, but soon learned of it. They were later to disagree about the nature of their discussion. To Mrs Dickenson, Mr McBurney appeared to suggest that the social services department was actively looking for evidence that would back up a court application to have Maria removed from the home – with Mr Kepple as the focus of their concerns. Mr McBurney disagreed. When Mrs Dickenson's account was read to him by the Inquiry he said: 'The paragraph suggests that we were waiting to pounce upon Mr and Mrs Kepple. This is just not so' [Day Eighteen: 13]. Rather to the contrary, in his recollection, he had 'talked at some length with Mrs Dickenson about reasons for not taking a Care Order and the difficulties in taking it' [Day Eighteen: 13]. Nevertheless, he attempted to contact Miss Lees by telephone during the discussion, but finding her not available, 'I did not pursue the matter'.

Friday ended with Mrs Dickenson putting the events of the week in a report that she presented to Mrs Tattam, and which set out her intention to continue her efforts to engage with the Kepple family after the weekend.

Saturday 9 December saw Maria out and about. A neighbour, Mrs Brashill, had already made an anonymous call to the NSPCC, complaining of Maria's declining condition. Now on Saturday 9 December [Day Seventeen: 35]:

> I saw her playing about four or five doors away from where she lived on the bottom of some steps with [her sister] and another couple of children.

Mrs Brashill saw the children from a car which was being driven by Mrs Rutson of no. 121. The car was going slowly 'because of the children there, and also we were near the end of the road'. She told the Inquiry that she got Mrs Rutson to stop the car so that she could get out to take a closer look at Maria, because, from the car, she thought she could see a mark on her cheek. As she approached Maria, however, she ran away towards her home [Day Seventeen: 35]:

> My intention was to get out of the car and if I could have got hold of Maria I was going to take her, her face being like I said it was, to the hospital or doctor to have her examined.…
> I thought she had had another smack on the face.

When **Monday 11 December** came around, Maria was still not in school. As Miss Lees had suggested to them during the previous week, Mr or Mrs Kepple contacted the school to say that she had a 'bad stomach' [Day Five: 35]. Mrs Dickenson, despite the events of the 5th, went around again to the home, but without obtaining any reply. In all, she called on three separate occasions during the day, all without success. At the Inquiry she was asked how long she persisted in attempting to get an answer, replying that she did so:'Until I realised that possibly if there were anybody in they would not open the door to me' [Day Five: 34]. The resolute refusal to admit Mrs Dickenson – who was never to have direct contact with the family again, despite further attempts – can be seen as providing some support to the general social services department strategy of patient engagement with the Kepples. Mrs Dickenson had been able to get access to the home until she quarrelled with Mr Kepple. Once that had happened she was unable to obtain access of any sort and a potentially vital source of support and surveillance was cut off.

At the end of the school day, Mrs Dickenson reported her lack of success to the school secretary, Mrs Chapman, who told her that concerns within the school about Maria had not abated. Knowing that Maria had another appointment with Dr Barley, Maria's GP, Mrs Dickenson again telephoned him and 'Dr Barley himself told me that he had made an appointment I think it was for Wednesday of that week.'

Wherever Maria had in fact spent the day, she was seen in the local area. Mrs Muriel Smith was another sister of the late Raymond Colwell. She worked at Vines sweet shop, at 34 Manor Hill, the group of local shops that served Maresfield Road. On 11 December she recalled seeing Maria, in one of those encounters which formed a substantial thread in the evidence of family and neighbours and which suggested that Maria was regularly treated less well than the other children [Day Seventeen: 20]:

> Maria came into the shop with the other children, the Kepple children. The Kepple children all had money for sweets. I was serving on the sweet counter. I said to Maria, "What are you going to have?" She said, "I haven't got any money.". I said, "You can choose what you like and I will pay for it." All she chose was a small bar of Cadbury's chocolate, I think they are about 2p.

Mrs Dickenson, by contrast, despite her real reservations about the family, and her own conflicts with them, still reminded the Inquiry that, as far as treatment of Maria by her family was concerned, 'I never had a definite complaint about Maria, nor had I anything to complain about myself' [Day Five: 26].

On **Tuesday 12 December** Mrs Rutson, of no. 121 Maresfield Road, made her final attempt to intervene on Maria's behalf. She had 'seen Maria at the back garden and I thought she would only weigh about three stone. She looked terribly unkempt and she was dirty and had dirty clothes on her … she looked more or less than a skeleton. Her socks would not even stand up on her legs' [Day Two: 6]. Mrs Rutson telephoned Miss Lees directly to report what she had seen. Miss Lees was not at the office, but a message was left. Mrs Rutson telephoned again during the afternoon and, according to Miss Lees, she too attempted to return the call, both on the 12th and on the following day. No call was successfully made on either side.

Wednesday 13 December, at about 11 o'clock in the morning, Miss Bodger, the health visitor, made a further visit to no. 119. Since her last failed attempt to make contact on 7 December she had been in contact with Mrs Dickenson again, and knew that the education welfare officer was 'very concerned about the child, in the first place, and was doing her best to get this child to Dr Barley'. At the time of her visit, however, Miss Bodger did not know that Maria had been taken to the doctor on the 6th.

Miss Bodger found a comfortable and improving domestic scene. Presided over by Mr Kepple – 'I know he had been away from work; he was supposed to have hurt his back. I did know that' [Day Fourteen: 12] – whom she was meeting for the first time, Miss Bodger saw that:

> "P" and her sister [sic], Maria, were there … sitting on quite a nice, comfortable easy chair by the nice fire….They both looked nice and clean to me, but I noticed Maria was pale…. I had only seen Maria once before, and this was just a paleness.

As far as Maria was concerned, Miss Bodger saw no evidence of malnutrition, or marks or bruises and, as she told the Inquiry 'I looked well'. Asked specifically if she had seen 'signs of dislike or hatred on the part of Mr Kepple towards Maria', Miss Bodger replied that she had not. During the visit, Mrs Kepple returned from shopping. She went upstairs and returned with a prescription written by Dr Barley that had yet to be dispensed. Asked by Mr Kepple to tell Maria not to scratch her face and bite her nails, she advised them to take this up with Dr Barley at a visit which, she was told was due to take place later that day. More generally, standards of comfort within the home were 'much improved…. The room had recently been decorated the furniture was improved; the whole cleanliness of the room was improved' [Day Fourteen: 10]. As she left, she commented on how much brighter the room seemed since she had last been inside it and, 'Mr Kepple said, "I am trying to make a better home for the children", or a "nicer home for the children", some such phrase as that'.

Nevertheless, Miss Bodger told the Inquiry, she left the visit anxious at Maria's welfare. She had checked directly with Mr Kepple whether she was happy in the home, being told, 'Yes and she loves her brother and sisters' [Day Fourteen: 12]. Something in the 'merry and bright and carefree' attitudes of her brother and sisters was missing in 'quiet Maria', and Miss Bodger's conclusion was that Maria remained insecure and unhappy.

Also on 13 December, Mrs Dickenson again called at the house, but with no reply. She concluded that the door may deliberately have not been answered because of her quarrel with Mr Kepple. With the holiday fast approaching, this was her last attempt to make contact during school term time [Day Five: 35].

Visits to Maresfield Road on 13 December were not yet over. Unknown to each other, Miss Lees, as well as Miss Bodger and Mrs Dickenson, paid a home visit. Since 5 December, when she believed matters to be improving, she had been involved in further telephone calls with Mrs Kirby and knew that Mrs Rutson had tried to contact her. Now she visited again in order, in the words of the Inquiry's counsel, 'to keep an eye on the situation' [Day Twenty-Five: 26]. Her conclusion was that circumstances had improved further:

> The whole family, including Mr Kepple, present. Mrs Kepple again on the point of cooking. The children all looking lively and well. Maria seemed much improved – still very thin but playing well with the other children. She was swinging them around in turn and [Maria's sister] was also swinging Maria (although having more of a job as Maria is much taller than she is). The jealousy between [Maria's sister] and Maria seems diminished and Mrs Kepple herself commented on this.

The case record then sets out a different element in the conversation, and one which struck a rather more cautionary note. Mrs Kirby had previously raised the possibility that a referral to the local child guidance clinic might have been a way of helping the family to understand better the feelings and fantasies which Maria experienced. Miss Lees was more sceptical, both about the likely efficacy of any referral and of the family's likely participation. Nevertheless, she raised it at the visit on 13 December. She found that Mrs Kepple was 'not very anxious for me to speak to Maria on her own and I would not push this point as I think it might result in Maria being coached as to what to say to me. Anything which I might later say to the Kepples which could be construed as criticism might be blamed on the child.' Even if things were improving, generally, negotiating a path through the different tensions in the Kepple household remained one of considerable difficulty.

Two further contradictory elements are recorded as part of that day's visit. On the one hand, and very positively, Miss Lees recorded that:

> On this visit, for the first time, I heard Maria spontaneously speak to Mr Kepple, initiating the conversation, and calling him "Dad".

On the other, hand, her continuing concerns for Maria's medical condition were such that she concluded that, 'if her condition does not improve, I think it might be helpful to seek referral to the children's hospital for her' [Day Twenty-Five: 27]. Miss Lees had been clearly led to believe that Maria had attended the doctor by 5 December, which she had not. Again, on the 13th she was told by Mrs Kepple that Maria was 'taking her medicine' [Day Twenty-Five: 26], when it was clear that the prescription provided by Dr Barley on 6 December was yet to be dispensed. Nor was there any suggestion to Miss Lees of the follow-up appointment, due to be kept on the day of this, her final visit, and which was about to be broken.

Miss Lees concluded that 'following this visit, I felt very much happier about the family and it seems as though the situation might be improving a little again'.

The business of the missed appointment was taken up directly with Dr Barley during his evidence to the Inquiry. He agreed that he had concluded that the appointment had been missed because the condition had improved. While she may not have been to the doctor, Maria had been seen for the second time in a week, by her aunt, Mrs Smith, at Vines sweet shop, calling at about 4.30 pm [Day Seventeen: 21]:

> She did not come in, she stood on the step of the shop, and my son came in and said, "Maria is outside on the step." He said, "She has not got any money for sweets." The other children were in the shop. I said, "Take her out this iced lolly."

On **Thursday 14 December**, Miss Bodger, the health visitor, tried to telephone Mrs Kirby of the NSPCC to discuss the outcome of her visit of the previous day, but without success in speaking to her – 'message left' [Day Fourteen: 13].

Miss Bodger was busy again on the following day, **Friday 15 December**, when she called at the home 'to deliver a carry-cot which I had collected on the previous day' [Day Fourteen: 13]. No one was at home when she called, and, despite her view that material conditions at Maresfield Road were improving, she was obliged to leave the cot 'through an open space, broken glass in the door'. During the same afternoon, however, Mrs Kepple 'came to my child health clinic in the Lewes Road on Friday afternoon, the 15th December ... to thank me for delivering the cot'. Mrs Kepple had [Maria's brother and sister]. with her, but not Maria. 'Did you ask about Maria?', Miss Bodger was asked. Her reply was clear:

> I was very, very busy, but I did still ask about Maria and Mrs Kepple sort of said all right, as far as I recall.

Maria, in the meantime, was seen for the third and final time at Vines [Day Seventeen: 21]:

> She came down again, It was on a Friday. It was a fortnight before Christmas. it was half past four because all the papers were coming in. [Maria's sister] came in she was getting an *Evening Argus*, and my son came in and said Maria was outside. I called her in ... but she did not answer, she did not turn around, she ran away from the shop.

As Mrs Kepple called at the clinic, she may have been on her way to or from her mother's. Despite the deteriorating relations between them, at the end of November, Mrs Tester had invited Maria to spend Christmas at her home, in order to be with her brother and sister, who remained in her care. Now Mrs Tester repeated the invitation, to be told by [Maria's sister], 'No, she isn't, because my dad said so' [Day Seventeen: 56].

Miss Lees also visited on the 14th. She found Maria 'playing quite happily with the others', and 'certainly better than she had been on the 1st December' [Day Twenty-One: 47]. She looked closely at Maria and saw that 'the ointment that was being used for Maria's face was a yellowy colour and perhaps that this had been mistaken for bruising; but certainly she did not see any bruises on her at all' [Day Eleven: 57].

Saturday 16 December was the date of the annual Brighton NSPCC Christmas Party, to which Mrs Kirby had invited Maria, and to which both Mr and Mrs Kepple had agreed to her attending, during her visit of 5 December. In the event, on the previous morning, they telephoned the NSPCC where Mrs Goodman, the office secretary, noted in her telephone message book that, 'Maria Kepple will not be going on Saturday; still has head infection' [Day Twenty: 15]. Nothing further was seen of Maria over the weekend. On **Monday 18 December** the NSPCC received their second anonymous telephone call, noted at 2.45 pm by Mrs Goodman. That note reads [Day Thirteen: 24]:

> A phone call from a woman who said that although she did not live in Maresfield Road, she did not want to give her name or address, but she talked about Maria and said that she had seen her with her face bruised. I asked her when this was and she said last week. I established that it was bruising (as I knew the child had a head infection). She went on to say that not only was the child treated like this, she was left out of the things that the others did etc etc and that she should be taken away from her parents. I rang Mr Baker about this and he said that I should put this in the post to you and also leave a message for Mr Baker to get in touch with you with it, if you did not ring in until later tonight, after I had left.

It was the evening of that day before the call was relayed to Mrs Kirby. Her notes read, 'Face all marked again. Maria Kepple face is bruised. Seen last week – anonymous phone call' [Day Thirteen: 24]. It was the following day before she was able to discuss it with Miss Lees [Day Eleven: 57]. Miss Lees gave her view that any reported bruising was the result of the skin ointment.

Tuesday 19 December: as the end of the term drew near, Mrs Turner, Maria's class teacher, became more and more concerned about her absence. She had become, she told the Inquiry, 'desperately worried at not having seen her'. She asked a local youth worker, Ms Ruby Barrow, to try to 'get into the house and tell me how that child is' [Day Three: 46]. Ms Barrow planned to run activities for young people on the estate during the Christmas holiday, and agreed to try to include Maria in them, although nothing was to come of her attempt.

On the same day, Miss Bodger, the health visitor, finally made direct contact with Mrs Kirby, recording in her notes that she had: 'Discussed case of Maria with Mrs Kirby, NSPCC Mrs Lees, Hove Children's Dept, has Supervision Order here. Maria? to be seen by [Child Guidance

Staff]' [Day Fourteen: 15]. Mrs Kirby's note of the conversation was put to Miss Bodger during cross-examination:

> She says this: she rang you by request and she says: "She" – that is, referring to you – "has only recently known the Kepple family and wanted to know how involved I" – that is Mrs Kirby – "was. She" – that is again referring to you – "too is warmly welcomed when she visits. The beds the children have were given by her, also a carry-cot. Advised Miss Bodger" – that is Mrs Kirby advised you – "I have a cot which I will deliver one evening when it is dark." I feel the Kepples are under some pressure from the neighbours.

Miss Bodger agreed that practical help was the focus of their discussion and her own intervention.

The latest anonymous telephone call gave rise to a rather different call between Mrs Kirby and Miss Lees. Mrs Kirby recorded in her case notes the reassuring news that Miss Lees 'is to visit today [19 December] as she is making arrangements for Mrs Kepple's two sons to visit' [Day Eleven: 77]. In fact, no such visit took place. Miss Lees was indeed involved in making arrangements for a visit from Maria's two brothers, which was to take place two days later. These arrangements, however, were all made by telephone, rather than by visit, including a telephone conversation with Mrs Kepple [Day Twenty-Five: 19]. On the same day, however, Miss Lees again telephoned Mrs Kirby. The NSPCC records for that day show: 'A message from Miss Lees confirmed no bruising on Maria', a reassurance presumably based on Miss Lees' observations of almost a week earlier.

Wednesday 20 December saw a further meeting between Mrs Kepple and Mrs Kirby [Day Eleven: 59]:

> This was at St Anne's Church Hall.... Mrs Kepple had written to the *Argus* to ask for a Christmas parcel or for toys to help with Christmas. She did not realise that when people write to the *Argus* ... the letters come to me. So she had been invited to call to collect her Christmas *Argus* parcel.

As in the visit which Mrs Kepple had made to Miss Bodger's clinic at the end of the previous week, she had two of Maria's older half-siblings with her, but not Maria. Nevertheless Maria's welfare was discussed. Mrs Kepple told Mrs Kirby that Maria was happy, 'but she still tells lies sometimes. I said I hoped that there was help on the way in this respect' [Day Eleven: 60].

At St Anne's, Mrs Kirby had picked out the best dolls she could find, and 'put them aside for the Kepple children'. Indeed, so large was the final parcel – it included clothing as well as toys – that it was both too heavy for Mrs Kepple to carry, and too big for Mrs Kirby to get into her car – "It was an enormous parcel." Instead, arrangements were made for it to be delivered along with grocery vouchers and 'gifts for her other children who were with her mother and the two who were in care' [Day Eleven: 60]. If Maria did not go to the Church Hall, Mrs Kirby still saw her 'on the very same day'. Mrs Kirby had left St Anne's and was walking in Maresfield Road delivering parcels when she saw Maria at the living room window. 'She looked happy', she told the Inquiry, 'and she waved to me'. It was the last time she saw her.

During the evening of the same day, Miss Tester, Mrs Kepple's daughter, came to babysit. She arrived at about 8.30 pm and found Maria already in bed [Day Eighteen: 35]:

> I asked Pauline if I could go up and see her and she said yes.... She was in bed and she was just laying looking up at the ceiling ... she seemed quite happy.

Asked how long she supposed the conversation went on, she replied:

> At least half an hour or so because I was asking her if she would like me to buy her something and giving her money and that.

Thursday 21 December was the end of the school term. It also saw a visit to the Kepple household by two other members of the social services department who, otherwise, had no connection with Maria, as such. Miss Pauline Edwards was responsible for the supervision of Maria's brothers, aged ten and nine. They were fostered at some distance from Brighton, and 21 December was to be their Christmas visit to their mother. Miss Edwards arrived at around 10.15 am, and stayed about 10 minutes. She could neither recollect seeing Maria, nor having heard her name mentioned. Her recollection was that any discussion centred entirely on Mrs Kepple's desire to see the boys have more regular visits home [Day Ten: 8]. In days well before anti-discriminatory practice, Miss Edwards was asked to sum up her experience of the conditions in which she found the family. She took a line which was very different

from almost all the social welfare professionals in regular contact with
the Kepples. She told the Inquiry [Day Ten: 8]:

> I would say it was a very poor house. It sounds rather trite,
> but it was what we would call a family with problems, and
> there was a family-with-problems-type smell, the look of
> the furniture and the general décor.

In preparation for giving evidence to the Inquiry, however, she had
visited the two boys again and taken notes of their recollections of the
visit. In their account, Mr Kepple was present on their arrival, reading
a newspaper – Miss Edwards could not remember seeing him at all.
He left almost immediately to go to work. Thereafter, in the boys'
account, the day had an entirely positive character. All five children
played in the garden during the morning. They went together to get
chips and potatoes for lunch, Maria carrying the money and [Maria's
sister]. carrying the goods. The only notes to resonate directly with
other accounts of the time was that, after tea, the other children watched
television, while Maria washed up. While that was happening, [Maria's
sister] went into the kitchen and came out crying. 'Mrs Kepple got
cross with Maria, but no crosser than any ordinary Mum would be'
[Day Ten: 10].

At the end of the afternoon, ancillary social worker Mr Paddy Mees
came to collect the boys to return them to their foster parents. The
door was answered by Mrs Kepple who had the boys ready. On the
journey, they talked happily about the day, and the enjoyment they
had from it, but without, as far as Mr Mees could recall, mentioning
Maria specifically in any way.

On or around the following day, **Friday 22 December**, Miss
Tester was again at Maresfield Road during the evening. Mr Kepple
was working away and due to telephone Mrs Kepple at a telephone
box on Manor Road. Mrs Kepple decided that she had 'better take
the children with her'. All but Maria were dressed. Miss Tester went
upstairs to get Maria, only to find that:

> ... the door to her bedroom was locked and the handle
> had been removed. I asked Pauline if I might see Maria,
> to which Pauline agreed, and put the handle back in the
> door and opened it. The room was in darkness. I spoke to
> Maria and asked her if she was alright; she seemed very
> unhappy and frightened. She did not say anything but
> merely looked at me as if she wanted to tell me something

but was too frightened to tell me (normally Maria did not say much unless asked about a particular subject). I kissed her good night and left the room. Pauline again removed the handle, and I asked her why Maria was in bed and why she needed to take the door handle out. Pauline said it was because Maria had run away once to a relative of Mr and Mrs Cooper nearby, and if she did not take the handle away she would do it again. I did not think that Maria should be left alone so I stayed downstairs while Pauline went to the phone box with the other children. I stayed the night at Pauline's, but a few days later I told my mother. I do not know for certain whether my mother reported this to Miss Lees, but she usually told her everything she knew, and I would expect that she passed on this information to her. [NA: DPP 2/5197/2: Statement 61a]

On the same day, Mrs Dickenson, too, seems likely to have called again at Maresfield Road.[4] As she told the Inquiry, she had deliberately been waiting until the school holidays had begun [Day Five: 36]:

I wanted to get back to a fairish relationship with Mr and Mrs Kepple after the incident of the 5th, and usually if I visit during holiday time I get a better reception because the child is legally out of school on holiday and I am received better then.

She received no reply when she knocked.

On **Saturday 23 December** Mrs Brashill (ie, Mrs Brazil) saw Maria for the final time. Mrs Brashill was sitting in a car, parked at the side of the road waiting to be taken home at 2.30 pm. She saw Maria in the front downstairs window and she waved 'feebly' twice [Day Seventeen: 31].

On the same day, Miss Lees went to see the Coopers to collect Maria's Christmas presents. According to Mrs Cooper's written evidence, 'we were always told that she was getting on fine and coming out of her shell after the change-over. Even on the 23rd December, 1972, we were told she was growing and attending school regularly' [NA: DPP 2/5197/2, Statement 17A].

---

[4] The evidence was ambiguous. She remembered that she had made such a visit, but it was not recorded in her notes. It is likely that she did so, but not conclusively provable that she did.

On **Sunday 24 December**, Christmas Eve, Mrs Rickworth, a neighbour from 99 Maresfield Road, told the Inquiry that she had seen Maria at the living room window apparently alone [Day Five: 64/65]:

> She must have been alone in the house because she was sitting on a table or a high chair by the window sill. She was looking out of the window and she looked very thin in the face. She called out, "Hello, Aunty Rita" and I looked up and saw her. I was going to take her shopping with me, but I changed my mind because it was too cold and she didn't look very well.

On Christmas Day, **Monday 25 December**, Mrs Rutson, her mother and sister visited her father's grave at the cemetery. It was a cold Christmas, and the windows at no. 119 had been covered in ice. Mrs Rutson's mother had suggested that they ought to call and let them have some coal. On their return they saw Mr Kepple, walking up over Race Hill, with [Maria's brother and sister]. on either side of him. They seemed 'happy and normal and looked very nice. They were very well dressed' [Day Two: 7/8]. Maria was not with them; Mrs Rutson never saw her again.

From this time onwards, the contact between Maria and the outside world grew much less. On **Wednesday 27 December** Miss Sandra Tester went to visit 119 Maresfield Road. On the 18th day of the Inquiry she was questioned closely about the visit. She went round, she said, 'just to see "K"', whose birthday was coming up. Mrs Kepple was at home but not Mr Kepple. 'I do not know whether he was working or not' [Day Eighteen: 40]. According to her written evidence, 'Mr Kepple was away that week working in London' [NA: DPP 2/5197/2, Statement 61]. On her return, later that evening she found Maria up, but ready for bed. Maria seemed, according to Miss Tester's statement, 'quite normal'. In cross-examination, Miss Tester told the Inquiry that 'She was quieter, that is all.... I asked her what was wrong. She just sort of looked at me as if I was not there. I asked, "Are you tired?", and she just nodded her head that was all' [Day Eighteen: 40].

Once the holiday period was over, normal civic activities began to resume. On **Wednesday 3 January** Brighton Social Services Department had reopened, and was dealing with a request to the WRVS to supply single blankets and sheets to Mrs Kepple. A letter to that effect was issued by the receptionist – presumably to Mrs Kepple herself [Day Eighteen: 3].

On **Friday 5 January** Mrs Dickenson called at the house again. In her written evidence she recorded that [NA: DPP 2/5197/2, Statement 14]:

> I went round to the house again with the intention of encouraging Mr and Mrs Kepple to ensure that Maria should go back to school when the Spring Term began again in a few days time. This was part of my routine. There was no reply; nobody was in.

We have already narrated the events of 6 and 7 January.

On **Monday 8 January** before any of what had taken place was known to anyone, Mrs Dickenson received a report that Maria was not at school [NA: DPP 2/5197/2, Statement 14]: '... I went immediately to her home, but there was nobody there. At 3.00 pm I heard on my car radio the news of Maria's death.'

On the same day, Miss Lees attended Brighton Police Station and made a brief statement. While at the station she met Mrs Tester, in a state of extreme shock and distress [Day Twenty-Five: 36]. Either at that encounter, or in a subsequent telephone conversation, Miss Lees recalled Mrs Tester telling her that 'Sandra was in a state of considerable distress. She had seen Mr Kepple hit Maria, and now she wished she had said something about it at the time' [Day Twenty-Five: 36].

On **Tuesday 9 January**, there was a third anonymous telephone call made to the NSPCC.

Who knew ...

The report of the Committee of Inquiry makes its judgements on what could and should have been known by everyone concerned with the Kepple family and the care of Maria. In a period of eight weeks before Maria Colwell's death, we have counted at least 28 different visits or attempted visits by the social worker, the NSPCC inspector, the education welfare officer and the health visitor to 119 Maresfield Road. There had been involvement with the family GP, the police and the housing authority, as well as the WRVS and the social workers looking after Maria's older brothers. There had been several anonymous telephone calls to the NSPCC. There had been numerous sightings of Maria, in the street, at the shops and at the window of no. 119. There were case notes and telephone calls. There were other children to be watched out for and visited. There were apparently clear signs of improvement and equally clear reasons for concern; there was optimism and counter-balancing anxiety. There was cooperation and 'disguised compliance'. There was a great deal to 'know' but, and this is the critical point, very little of what was known to one person was known to another and no one outside of no. 119 actually knew very much at all.

Throughout November, Mrs Dickenson, the most active caller to no. 119 (at least eight visits) was concerned primarily with Maria's attendance at and her lateness to school, allegedly because she was having to go to the shops before school began. What other concerns she could have had would have been based on playground rumours and the (infrequent) observations of her class teacher. Mrs Dickenson may have been guided by her instincts but she did not have 'any definite proof to support these rumours'. Diana Lees, Maria's social worker, knew nothing of her involvement during this period. She had heard, from the housing authorities and two weeks after the event, of a neighbour dispute. She did have concerns expressed by Mrs Tester but these did not allege any violence towards Maria, although this point is disputed, but not convincingly, by Miss Sandra Tester. Mrs Kirby had seen Maria on the 19th and had no reason to be concerned. Even the first anonymous call to the NSPCC referred to bruising arising from a much earlier alleged incident and this may well not have been communicated to Diana Lees effectively by Mrs Kirby. Before the meeting at the school on the 28th, it would have been impossible for Diana Lees and very difficult indeed for Mrs Kirby to have identified the causes for concern that become apparent only with the omniscience afforded to the Inquiry by hindsight. Even the recollection of the meeting of the 28th varies. When Diana Lees did visit the family on 30 November, she was not unduly concerned by the evidence in front of her.

At the beginning of December, armed with information from her first contact with Mrs Kirby of the NSPCC, Mrs Dickenson, who had still not seen Maria since July and who had not contacted Diana Lees directly, made her last productive visit to no. 119. After Mr Kepple's complaints about her intrusions, she was no longer a welcome caller but Mr Kepple's threatening manner precipitated an urgent visit from Diana Lees, the effect of which was, ironically, to reassure her that matters were improving. On her next visit, Mrs Kirby too was considerably reassured. Having examined Maria physically, Mrs Kirby left the house 'satisfied that there was nothing to worry about'. The health visitor too, who had finally gained access to the family on the 19th, was not exactly reassured but nor were anxiety levels unduly raised. In response to Mrs Rutson of no. 121's concerns, Diana Lees visited twice more and on both occasions saw evidence of an improving situation. The concerns of family members and neighbours which grew more intense at this time were only partially communicated to anyone else.

There may be an argument for any one or all of the principals concerned having been more active in their pursuit of understanding what was happening to Maria but our conclusion is that outside of no. 119, no one actually did know very much and very little of what was known pointed to the events of the first weekend of January.

But the need for others to know what had happened was being strongly expressed, not least by the Kepples' neighbours, as we noted at the beginning of this chapter. Little of this initial anger was deflected by the promise of a 'very full and careful investigation' of the Colwell case made by the director of social services for East Sussex County Council, immediately on the conviction of William Kepple (*Argus*, 17 April [a] 1973) (see Chapter Four, this volume, for a detailed account).

This 'need to know' is not only a concern with finding out the 'facts' about how Maria Colwell died but it also reflects a fundamental distrust of those who might know, or should have known or who indeed might know a great deal but who were reluctant to explain. It would be this drive to 'know' that would expose the relatively new profession of social work, as well as the practice of particular social workers, to the forensic gaze of wider constituencies of interest and which would put social work on trial.

As already noted, the bare facts are never enough to make a scandal, as they are all too common. Nor is it enough for those bare facts to be exposed in response to a passionate and insistent demand for an explanation. We look in detail in the next chapter at how the everyday tragedy of one child's death was transformed into the iconic event it has become. The most telling question to ask in relation to this or any other welfare scandal is 'Why?', or more particularly, 'Why now?' Along what social, political, administrative and policy fault lines did these events lie such that they could be transformed 'into something extraordinary ... whereby the specific comes to stand for the general and where meanings and historical significance become attached to acts and events that at other times might have passed almost unobserved' (Butler and Drakeford, 2005, p 1)? What was it about social work as a form of welfare practice that needed to be accounted for alongside the actions of the individual social workers implicated in the sad and violent events at 119 Maresfield Road, Brighton?

THREE

The state of social work

This 'right to know' was listed by Frederic Seebohm as a persistent example of a series of what he considered to be the social ills of his time. In a speech he made at the London branch of BASW in 1977, commenting on the fate of the report he had written in 1968, *The report of the Committee on Local Authority and Allied Personal Social Services*, he said:

> I am still fascinated by the complex nature of society and regret that we have not got further than we have in understanding the basic causes of distress, nor found any simple answers to the problem of developing a happy and contented community, nor of stemming the increase in violence and other demonstrations of a basic frustration shown by so many, even though they may be a small but very audible minority. In industry and commerce there is an ever growing demand to participate at all levels and an evident "passion to know" or at least to obtain an assurance that there is "nothing to know". (Seebohm, 1977)

Seebohm's remarks are of interest not simply because they follow the popular emotional currents that flowed around the death of Maria Colwell, but because Seebohm could claim to have designed the structure of social services that was judged to have failed her and it is to that which we now turn.

Before Seebohm

At least some of the 'frustration, anxiety and stress' facing social workers in the early part of 1973 (see Chapter One, this volume) arose out of the major structural changes that had been introduced by the Local Authority Social Services Act 1970. To a degree that remains contested, this Act gave legislative substance to *The report of the Committee on Local Authority and Allied Personal Social Services* that had been presented to Parliament in July 1968 (the 'Seebohm Report').

In short, Seebohm recommended that out of the plethora of existing arrangements to deliver welfare services at municipal level, there should be created (Seebohm, 1968, para 2):

> ... a new local authority department, providing a community based and family orientated service, which will be available to all.

It was to these new local authority 'social services departments' that the 'block advertisements' in *Social Work Today* were recruiting, as described in Chapter One, and it was the working conditions in these departments that were being described in that first issue of January 1973.

The immediate origins of the Seebohm Committee have been identified by Hall as lying in the rapid expansion that had taken place in local authority welfare services since the 1950s:

> ... the consequent growth in expenditure brought the welfare services into the spotlight as never before.... In the UK, total expenditure on child care and local welfare services increased by almost 180% (at constant prices) between 1952 and 1968 ... this growth was particularly rapid in the local welfare services, for the elderly and handicapped [sic], but both child care and welfare expenditure far out-stripped the general rise in total public expenditure. (Hall, 1976, p 7)

Since the early 1950s, welfare services for children had largely been delivered through the children's departments of local authorities that had been established by the Children Act 1948. This Act had placed on local authorities a duty to provide 'a comprehensive service for the care of children who have not the benefit of a normal home life' (Section 1). Other local authority departments also provided welfare services to children and their families, including the health, education and housing departments. However, 'patterns of organisation and administration [were] immensely varied' within 10 years of the Act, according to the report of the Younghusband Committee in 1959 (Younghusband, 1959, para 412). This Committee had been established in June 1955 to inquire into 'the proper field of work and the recruitment and training of social workers' (Younghusband, 1959, para 1). Matters did not seem to improve into the 1960s, and Hall (1976, p 6) notes that, by 1968, the organisation of services at municipal level was 'chaotic', with responsibilities and functions divided between various committees of the local authority according to little more than local preference and historical accident.

As well as causing or exacerbating problems of organisation between local authority departments, rapid expansion had not been 'without pain' in other respects too (Watson, 1973, p 47). In the children's departments, the growth in the number of staff had been inexorable: from 1,549 full-time childcare officers on 31 March 1963 to 3,591 by the same date in 1969, an increase of 130 per cent in six years. These rapidly developing departments also required internal adjustments to be made:

> Departments had to work out new patterns of working and new ways of communicating. Decentralisation became essential, and through decentralisation area teams built up new loyalties. These individual cells of worker-bees had to be woven together into a total organisation which maintained common aims and common standards while allowing the maximum flexibility possible for each team. (Watson, 1973, p 47)

The situation at local authority level was mirrored at national level where the Ministry of Health was responsible for services delivered by 'health and welfare' local authority departments (such as health visiting, psychiatric services and disability services), the Home Office was responsible for children's departments and the juvenile courts with the Ministries of Housing and Education also having responsibilities for some welfare services. A variety of administrative devices to improve planning across central government departments, including joint ministerial committees, had been attempted but with little success (see Hall, 1976 pp 9 ff).

The degree to which the resolution would be found in improved coordination or wholesale reorganisation remained finely balanced for some time, however. For example, in 1960, *The Royal Commission on local government in Greater London* (The Herbert Commission) had heard strong arguments both for and against the need for structural change despite observing, in relation to social services:

> ... in many places the services were working reasonably well at ground level because the field workers were making personal contacts with one another but in some counties this was in spite of the scheme of organisation rather than

because of it. (Herbert Commission, 1960, pp 150-2; see also Hebbert, 2008)

A year earlier, in February 1959, the Younghusband Committee had found that 'much talk of multiplicity of visiting and overlapping of effort' that they had heard in evidence was 'overstated and unsubstantiated' (Younghusband, 1959, para 1098). For the Younghusband Committee, the resolution to any duplication or waste of resource lay in improved teamwork 'and integration of effort' (para 1103) rather than reorganisation of services. In other words, coordination was as much a matter of professional practice as it was a matter of administration, relying on 'communication and good working relations ... common understanding, and in professional matters, a common code of ethics' (para 1103).

Even the highly influential Ingleby Committee, which reported in 1960, had approached the issue of reorganisation very cautiously. The Ingleby Committee had been established by the Conservative government in 1956 in response to increasing concern over the rise in juvenile crime since the Second World War. Importantly, its conclusions hastened a political and intellectual consensus, which had been developing since the early years of the 20th century, that delinquency could be best understood in the context of deprivation and the family rather than in terms of moral deficiency on the part of the offender (see, for example, Blacker, 1952; Timms, 1964).

Consistent with this view, the Ingleby Committee had recommended an extension to the powers of local authorities to engage in preventative work with children and their families. In considering this, the Committee acknowledged the potential that a 'unified family service' might possess, and it urged 'the importance of further study by the government and by the local interests concerned' of such a service (Ingleby Committee, 1960, p 19). The Committee also noted, however, 'the obvious and formidable difficulties' that would arise 'in a reorganisation of the various services concerned with the family' (Ingleby Committee, 1960, p 19). In the event, the Children and Young Persons Act 1963, which rested heavily on Ingleby, conferred the duty on local authorities to 'make available such advice, guidance and assistance as may promote the welfare of children by diminishing the need to receive children into care ... or to bring them before a juvenile court' (Section 1), but said little about how that duty should be exercised, requiring only periodic reports to the Secretary of State on such matters as he [sic] might specify (Section 4).

It was this new 'preventive' duty that had accelerated the expansion of children's departments, described by Watson, earlier. The sheer scale of the growth was not the only issue, however:

> The child care service was 15 years old before it was given legal sanction to work to help children receiving unsatisfactory care in their own homes. Before that the official policy was that of "the fresh start" ... the doctrine was that of rescue from an unsatisfactory environment and compensation by the provision of a substitute home....
> (Watson, 1973, pp 45 ff)

It is hard to recreate, even at this relatively short distance, the degree to which the Poor Law ideology of 'less eligibility' and the associated 'technologies' of the long-stay institution operated in the shadows of welfare practice in the period prior to the Act of 1963 and for some years afterwards. Certainly, Seebohm was aware of it (see Seebohm, 1968, para 484, and later).

Sylvia Watson, Director of Social Services for Cambridgeshire and the Isle of Ely, captures something of a passing age as much as the dawning of a new one when she continued her reflections (1973, p 49):

> For some workers it has not been easy to find as great a satisfaction in their new role of giving indirect help to children through supporting parents as in their old quasi-parental role of working directly with children as provider, protector, home finder. Supporting adults whose immature behaviour resembles that of overgrown children and helping them to be good parents demands of the worker great resources of maturity and tolerance, and the satisfactions derived from such work may be neither immediate nor obvious.

Perhaps she too was one of those 'older' children's officers who felt that through this period of rapid growth and rapid change:

> ... something precious had been lost, and that from being a close-knit band of workers united in a common aim, departments had become large, amorphous conglomerations with diffuse aims, where size and rapid turnover made individual workers feel more like cogs in a machine.
> (Watson, 1973, p 47)

Nonetheless, the legislative momentum was decisively in favour of 'community based and family orientated' services (Seebohm, 1968, para 2), and the 'revolutionary step' of the Act of 1963 (Heywood, 1973, p 11) had to find an effective form of administrative expression that could accommodate the growing number of social workers employed by local authorities and the new philosophy of care that they were developing, not always apparently with enthusiasm, as an alternative to the 'fresh start' of a previous age (see Pinchbeck and Hewitt, 1973; Hendrick, 1994).

Alongside accommodating the growing pains of an expanding workforce, new ways of working and thinking, a further factor influential in building a case for changes in the structure of welfare services was, what Hall (1976, p 11) has called, the development of a 'common identity amongst social workers'. Organisations representative of social workers had pressed for a common form of training throughout the 1940s and 1950s and the first generic social work training programme had begun at LSE in 1954. Younghusband, in a chapter of her report entitled 'The "general purpose social worker": patterns of future development', approached the idea of the generic worker from the point of view of the client served (Younghusband, 1959, para 640):

> Appreciation of the common social and personal factors in the needs of those using the [welfare] services is a first and vital consideration. There is always a risk in any type of specialisation of concentrating on a particular aspect at the expense of the whole. We ourselves have seen how this can lead to a focussing of effort on a particular need or handicap, rather than on the effect of these on the individual in his family and social setting. Our inclination is thus away from specialisation as far as social work is concerned and towards some form of combination of functions....

While Younghusband argued against specialism and in favour of a more integrated approach, she clearly recognised the distinctive contribution that social work could make. Her Committee noted a tendency, in the absence of trained social workers, for emphasis to be placed on the 'health aspects [of a problem] without recognition of the corresponding social factors' (para 714). She also noted, disapprovingly, that 'local government, like nature, abhors a vacuum and if there is a job to be done someone will do it whether or not it is part of their particular function or appropriate to his training' (para 959). Younghusband's conclusions are unequivocal (para 867):

> In our view, the essential case for training is that a body of
> knowledge now exists which individual workers cannot
> acquire by experience alone, and that social work practice
> now rests upon a systematic method and principles of work
> for which individuals need training.

Thus, not only did Younghusband recognise the distinctive contribution
that social workers could and should play in the emergent 'psycho-
social' welfare paradigm (Younghusband, 1959, para 866), she did so in
such a way that would explicitly professionalise the practice of social
work through claims to a distinctive knowledge base and the necessity
of formal training. On the basis of Younghusband's recommendations,
a Council for Training in Social Work was established in 1962; the
qualifying award for social workers became the two-year, generic
Certificate in Social Work, and, in 1963, the National Institute for
Social Work Training was formed. Each of these developments added
impetus to the emergence of a distinctive, new class of local authority
professional, the social worker.

Once common training, skills and tasks had been identified, the
bewildering administrative distinctions operating at local authority
level appeared increasingly unsustainable, especially where they seemed
simply wilful. Ingleby identified 'inter-service rivalries' (Ingleby
Committee, 1960, p 16) as a barrier to the efficient delivery of services
and even Younghusband (1959, para 1093)

> ... came across instances in which it was a matter of pride
> to keep information from another department rather than
> work in co-operation with it.

Through a rapid but *ad hoc* expansion of health and welfare services,
paradigm shifts in philosophies of care and the forging of the 'new'
profession of social work that was still far from at ease with itself, the
case for the reorganisation of services at local level continued to build
steadily through the early years of the 1960s.

A family service?

As well as at administrative and practitioner levels, political pressure for
change in the structure and organisation of welfare services also grew
through the early years of the 1960s.

The Ingleby Committee's interest in a 'family service' had been
substantially informed by the evidence the Committee heard from

leading members of the Fabian Society, including Mary Stewart, Peggy Jay, David Donnison and Peter Townsend (see Donnison and Stewart, 1958; Donnison et al, 1962). The 'family service' that they envisaged recognised the achievements of the Beveridge welfare state in ameliorating the 'chaos, cruelty and social wastage of the Poor Law' (Donnison et al, 1962, p 7), but recognised that there were still families whose needs did not fit easily into services as they were currently constituted or who had complex, multiple needs preventing them from accessing services in the first place. The 'Fabian' family service therefore was one that:

> ... must set out by concentrating on the few families that get into serious difficulties, but would be available from the beginning to all those who wish to make use of it (it would be a "family casework service", not a "problem families service"). It must be manned by workers with a sensitive understanding of family relationships, and special skills in mobilising the will and energy of the bewildered, anxious and aggressive people (thus it would be based primarily on the skilled use of personal relationships, rather than on the provision of material help and expert advice). (Donnison and Stewart, 1958, p 7)

Given that the focus of Ingleby was on delinquency, Clarke (1980, p 77) sums up the Fabian position:

> Thus delinquents merely form one segment of a much more significant group, those in need of care through the breakdown of family arrangements, not through illness, death and destitution – thanks to Beveridge – but because of the inability of parents to cope with human relationships. It is here that the work of the proposed family service is situated.

Clarke goes on to locate this approach squarely in the 'revisionist position of the Labour Party in the late fifties' (1980, p 80). This implies an acceptance of the postwar welfare state (with some reservations) and a strategy that amounts to little more than 'administrative rationalisation', a response which he sees as firmly within the 'tradition of the Webb's administrative socialism' (Clarke, 1980, p 80).

Within four years of Ingleby, considerable momentum was added to the pressure for a reorganisation of welfare services into some still to be operationally defined 'family service' from another left-wing source, namely, by the work of the Longford Study Group. This Group, for similar reasons to those that had prompted the establishment of the Ingleby Committee, was intended 'to advise the Labour Party on the recent increase in recorded crime and the present treatment of offenders' (Longford Study Group, 1964, p 1).

Based less on an analysis of juvenile crime than on a critique of the current state of the nation, where 'men and women are brought up from childhood to regard personal advancement and ruthless self interests as the main considerations' (Longford Study Group, 1964, p 5), the final report of the Study Group argued, as had Donnison et al, for an understanding of delinquency as a marker (one among many) of difficulties located within the family:

> Chronic or serious delinquency in a child is in the main, we believe, evidence of the lack of care, the guidance and the opportunities to which every child is entitled. There are very few children who do not behave badly at times; but the children of parents with ample means rarely appear before the courts. The machinery of the law is reserved mainly for working class children, who more often than not, are also handicapped by being taught in too big classes in unsatisfactory school buildings with few amenities and opportunities for out of school activities. (Longford Study Group, 1964, p 21)

It is important to re-capture the strong ideological positioning of Longford's (and the Fabian Society's) conception of what it was a family service should be. According to Clarke (1980, pp 90 ff), Longford was interested not so much in crime as in the personal deficiencies and structural inequalities (especially before the law) that had arisen or at least that had been maintained, through the postwar reconstruction and the establishment of the 1948 welfare state. Accepting that the remaining challenges were in the operation of the state rather than in the structures of society, Longford's aim was to express a socialist, humanised and civilising alternative vision for society which would disavow the 'get rich quick' culture and 'substitute the ideal of mutual service and work towards a society in which everyone has a chance to play a full and responsible part' (Longford Study Group, 1964, p 21).

Whereas for the Fabians this might be achieved purely administratively, Longford extended the argument in favour of the 'family service' to emphasise its critical role in the socialising process. The family service was not simply an argument in favour of changes in the apparatus of the state; it argued for a change in the relationship between the state and the family. According to Clarke (1980, p 92):

> Welfare capitalism is understood to have largely accomplished the "incorporation" of the mass of the working class into some form of stable involvement in English [sic] society.... The family service is the agency through which the new working class "residuum" – those who have not adjusted to this new stability – can be helped to an adjustment, and taught to catch up....

Or, in Longford's own words, a family service would be one:

> ... with the aim of helping every family to provide for its children and the careful nurture and attention to individual and social needs that the fortunate majority already enjoy. (Longford Study Group, 1964, p 16)

While in the modern context, this radical critique of Longford seems almost quaint, it was a consistently expressed theme of those who would challenge the recommendations of the Seebohm Committee and it is a powerful reminder that just below the administrative surface, strong ideological currents run. It would not be long after Seebohm reported that a very similar analysis of the problems of the welfare state emerged, but this time from a right-wing perspective. This would lead to a very different and far less benign model of tutelage and a very different conception of the role and functions of the welfare state. At this stage, it is important merely to note that no less than seven of the Longford Study Group's members were to take up posts as ministers in the Labour government that followed the 1964 general election.

Although it may not have seemed so at the time, those who have since placed the Labour governments of the 1960s in historical context are at pains to point out that it represented 'the middle of the "golden age" of expansion of welfare state spending' (Johnson, 2004, p 223). Tomlinson (2008, p 136) quotes Joel Barnett's assertion made in 1969 that Labour's 'purpose in political life was to expand the social wage through large increases in public expenditure on education, health, housing and the social services'. Harold Wilson himself told the Labour Party Conference of 1969 (the last before the intended general election of 1970) that,

> We have put in hand a dramatic deployment of resources
> in favour of those in greatest need, in favour of the under-
> privileged, on all fronts of social action – social security,
> health and welfare, the housing of our people, the education
> of our children and our young people – the most massive
> ever carried through ... the figures I have given you [a 45
> per cent rise in social spending in four years] represents our
> social priorities. (cited in Timmins, 2001, p 213)

It was in this context that Alice Bacon, who had been a member of
the Longford Study Group and who was, in 1964, Minister of State at
the Home Office (responsible for children's departments as well as the
juvenile courts), was eager to see the Longford Study Group's vision
of a 'family service' put into effect. She began work immediately on
a draft White Paper that proposed a substantial reform of court, penal
and welfare services for young offenders, including a considerable
development of preventative work, delivered through a family service.

Contemporary with Alice Bacon's arrival in the Home Office,
Douglas Houghton, Harold Wilson's successor as chair of the House
of Commons Public Accounts Committee, a man with a reputation
for tenacity and attention to detail, had been appointed as Chancellor
of the Duchy of Lancaster, a senior Cabinet position. His duties
included chairing the Cabinet committees on home policy and social
services. His appointment was, in part, yet another administrative device
intended to improve the planning and coordination of welfare services
across Whitehall departments. He took the opportunity provided by
his position to develop his own proposals, in consultation with Alice
Bacon, for a family service, although his scope to develop these was
somewhat overtaken by events.

In April 1965, at the Royal Society of Health Conference in
Eastbourne, Richard Titmuss, Professor of Social Administration at
LSE, and an influential commentator on the development of the
postwar welfare state, declared that he was 'not happy' with the
'fashionable' argument being made at the time in favour of family
service departments (see Hall, 1976, pp 22 ff). Titmuss's objections
were, essentially, that the proposals were too narrowly drawn, both
in terms of the recipients of welfare services ('too family-centred
and child-centred') and in terms of the range of existing services to
be included in any possible reorganisation or reform. He was also
'doubtful whether [a family service department] would effectively
bring together within one administrative structure all social workers in
the employ of a single local authority' (cited in Hall, 1976, p 23). After

the Conference, a group began to gather around Titmuss to develop these ideas. The group included no less than six members of staff or governors of the National Institute for Social Work Training, including its first principal, Robin Huws Jones, a close friend of Dame Eileen Younghusband and a member of her Committee as well as, shortly, of the Seebohm Committee.

In May 1965, the group wrote a memorandum to Douglas Houghton, copied to other ministers with relevant departmental interests. The case they made effectively formed the mandate for the Seebohm Inquiry that was to follow. The memorandum made its case for comprehensive change on the basis that the 'services in which social workers are employed have developed *ad hoc* in recent years and not in response to any general policy'. The resultant

> ... overlapping is confusing for the people being helped, uneconomic for the community and frustrating for the social worker. (quoted in Hall, 1976, p 50)

This resulted in people having their needs unmet as 'everybody's business becomes nobody's business' (quoted in Hall, 1976, p 50). It was only the 'high sense of personal responsibility of most people employed in social services' that prevents 'gross breakdowns' (quoted in Hall, 1976, p 50). The memorandum called for an urgent and speedy inquiry into the 'departmental structure and organisation of social work services at the local level and their relation to other relevant services in the community' and a clear warning note was sounded:

> If separate and isolated developments are allowed to continue, the welfare of large numbers of people will be affected adversely, especially the welfare of the most socially handicapped [sic] and vulnerable members of the community. (quoted in Hall, 1976, p 50)

Titmuss had close contacts with senior members of the newly elected Labour government, as did Robin Huws Jones. In particular, Titmuss was a close friend of Richard Crossman, who was Minister of Housing and Local Government in Wilson's Cabinet, and Huws Jones was close to Kenneth Robinson, Minister for Health. Both ministers gave their support to the Titmuss view and in his diaries of the time, Crossman notes:

The moment the idea was looked at departmentally it was clear that we couldn't introduce a family service without careful consultation with the local authorities. The first time I heard it mentioned was when I got a letter signed by Titmuss and practically every other social scientist that I respect, urging me to insist on a really independent inquiry into the local authority services to sort out how responsibilities should be divided.... The package had been forced on Douglas Houghton, as chairman of the Committee, very much against his will. (Crossman, 1978, p 284)

Seebohm

Thus, in October 1965, Frederic Seebohm was asked to chair a small, independent committee, to 'review the organisation and responsibilities of the local authority personal social services and consider what changes are desirable to ensure an effective family service' (Seebohm, 1968, para 1). In an early, and telling tussle, the Home Office entered an adamant refusal to allow the probation service to be brought within its remit, while, according to Cooper, it was made clear to the chair, by ministers themselves, that 'the question of departmental responsibility in central government was precluded as essentially a machinery of government matter', and hence something for the Prime Minister of the day to decide (Cooper, 1983, p 64).[1]

Colonel Seebohm was a figure who combined an impeccable social welfare pedigree, as a member of the Seebohm Rowntree dynasty, with

---

[1] In a personal communication in 1976, the Home Secretary of the time, James Callaghan, explained that his reluctance to loosen his grip on the 'children's side' of the work of his department was not only a matter of high or even of low politics but also because he was under some pressure from his wife Audrey to maintain his interest. Audrey Callaghan had served with distinction on the Children's Committee of the London County Council, visiting children's homes and returning to County Hall with numerous recommendations. At this time, she had begun her association with what would become the National Children's Bureau, prior to her lifelong commitment to Great Ormond Street Children's Hospital. Callaghan, too, regarded the children's work as a relief from 'all the murderers on licence and difficult immigration work' that passed across his desk. He was in no particular hurry to see his department reduced to being one serving only the 'wicked and the undeserving' (quoted in Bilton, 1979, p 9).

senior experience in the field of business. He had been a director of Barclay's Bank since 1947, and had a record of involvement in social welfare which stretched back over 30 years, since becoming treasurer of the Sheffield Council of Social Service before the Second World War. He was also a founding member, chair and later president of the National Institute for Social Work Training (later the National Institute for Social Work, NISW).

Once the Committee got underway it rapidly took a maximalist view of the terms of reference that had been provided to it. Indeed, Cooper (1983, p 67), writing with the benefit of many years' experience within government, concluded that it had taken a 'cavalier' attitude towards the remit with which it had been provided that was 'rare in the history of committees'. Seebohm wished immediately to have the now contentious term 'family service' removed from his Committee's terms of reference. He was unable to persuade the Home Secretary to share his view. Undeterred, Seebohm promptly sought to ensure as much distance from the Home Office as he could by reinterpreting 'family', quite literally, as 'everybody' (1968, para 32). The Committee equally quickly reached a set of conclusions about the nature of the problems that it needed to solve: lack of resources, inadequate knowledge and divided responsibility (Hall, 1976, p 41).

Moreover, very early in its deliberations, it resolved the issue that provided its primary raison d'être – structural reform. Hall suggests that the whole issue 'consumed little of the committee's time' (1976, p 59). The need for a single, local authority department was, she concluded, a 'largely pre-existing belief amongst most of its members' and one which became a settled part of the report's final landscape 'only months after the committee began sitting' (Hall, 1976, p 61). Issues of training (fewer than 20 per cent of field social workers had any professional qualifications in 1967, the Committee found), qualifications to be regarded as essential in the chief officers of the new departments, the inclusion (or otherwise) of professional groups such as health visitors or education welfare officers – all of these were to take up substantial time in the Committee's deliberations, but all were predicated on the basic belief that, in order to compete successfully for resources, and on equal terms, to remove stigma and to improve access, then 'a door on which everyone could knock' had to be created. Indeed, Seebohm, writing 20 years after the completion of his Committee's report, suggested that he may have been convinced after hearing the evidence of the Committee's very first witness, Richard Titmuss, who:

...set the pattern of our thinking by giving us the following advice: "To succeed", he said, "your service must be acceptable, accessible and comprehensible." These three principles helped us throughout. To be acceptable, it must finally destroy the memories of the most hated Poor Law, and people must feel as free to go for social help as they do for medical help. To be accessible it must come out of the forbidding portals of the Town Hall; to be comprehensible it must greatly simplify the proliferation of departments and regulations that have taken place since the Poor Law. (Seebohm, 1989, p 31)

These new departments were to have 'responsibilities going beyond those existing local authority departments' (Seebohm, 1968, para 3), but they would include the children's departments, the welfare departments, educational welfare and child guidance services, home help services, the social work services provided by health departments and some functions carried out by housing departments too.

The universalist aspirations of Seebohm were very clear (1968, para 2):

The new department will, we believe, reach far beyond the discovery and rescue of social casualties; it will enable the greatest possible number of individuals to act reciprocally, giving and receiving service for the well-being of the community.

How far such a belief in voluntary action was heir to the tradition of Beveridge is a moot point, but Seebohm regarded the potential of community work very seriously indeed. Far from taking a 'nostalgic' or romantic view, Seebohm, like the Fabians, understood the part played by the 'community' in the maintenance of personal well-being. He also recognised the contribution it could make to social order and stability (1968, para 476, para 477):

Such ideas point to the need for the personal social services to engage in the extremely difficult and complex task of encouraging the development of community identity and mutual aid, particularly in areas characterised by rapid population turnover, high delinquency, child deprivation and mental illness rates and other indices of social pathology. Social work with individuals alone is bound to be of limited

effect in an area where the community environment itself
is a major impediment to healthy individual development.

Such a view was later to be characterised as 'a sharpening of surveillance,
and its displacement over as wide a field as possible' (Collison, 1980,
p 63) but, at the time, these sentiments reflected a developing critique
of the 'casework model' that had grown in influence in social work
practice as part of the 'therapeutic familialism' of the postwar period
(Rose, 1985, p 157).

Although strongly associated with but not confined to the family
service units (which had had an important part to play in defining the
'problem family' of the 1940s and 1950s; see Philp and Timms, 1962
and also Chapter Five, this volume), the limits of the 'psychodynamic'
casework model of intensive psychological support to families had
been questioned by the Ingleby Committee (1960). The Committee
noted a 'certain reaction against the indiscriminate application of
intensive or deep case work for family or personal difficulties', and
had recommended that attention should first be paid to 'simple
forms of social aid' (Ingleby Committee, 1960, p 17). Several leading
social scientists, including Barbara Wootton, Thomas Simey and
Richard Titmuss in particular, had also made their views clear that by
concentrating on the psychology of the individual, there was a risk of
'ignoring both wider social problems and administrative realities' (see
Starkey, 2001, p 107). By the early 1970s, pioneering research by Mayer
and Timms (1970) suggested that even the clients of social workers
preferred a more straightforward approach and particularly valued the
provision of material aid over more complex forms of intervention.

The relative explanatory potential of 'psychological' or 'sociological'
accounts of social problems is, of course, a version of a much older
debate about 'nature versus nurture'. Nonetheless, this ancient
problematic was later to be central to the Colwell Inquiry's attempts
to define and refine the social work task.

At this point in the narrative, it provided an opportunity for some
on the left, in practice and in academic social work, to imagine a more
radical model of social work developing than perhaps Seebohm himself
envisaged and one that extended well beyond simply new administrative
forms. Adrian Sinfield, an Oxford academic at the time and later chair
of the Child Poverty Action Group in the 1970s and the 2000s, at the
time of the report's publication approvingly invoked Clement Attlee's
view that, 'Every social worker is almost certain to be an agitator.' He
continued by arguing that social workers' skills:

... should be attuned to the needs of the citizens, and not, as seems to have happened so often, the citizens needs be redefined to fit the social worker's own special concerns, or departments' own convenient administrative pigeon holes. The immediate and persistent objectives of policy must be to make the knowledge and skills of a more socially-orientated social work profession more available to the community, both by increasing the accessibility of social workers and by sharing some of their work and knowledge with others in the community. (Sinfield, 1970, p 64)

Only a little later, in 1973, but possibly further to the left, Bob Holman (1973, p 30), at this point, a lecturer in Social Administration and Social Work at the University of Glasgow, was writing enthusiastically of the potential for 'community action groups and client organisations ... to create societal change, especially in the power structure controlling the social services and other resources'. While Holman's subsequent career is a testament to what can be achieved on the basis of such beliefs, in truth, community social work as a form of practice, even by the early 1970s, was a 'method of social work ... still more talked about than carried out' (Hammond, 1973, p 31). Talking in 2005, Holman (2005, p 23) was to describe as 'one of the great failings of social services departments ... that they let community social work go', having got the 'orange light' from Seebohm. But even if community work did not develop sufficient momentum from Seebohm, the radical strain in social work found other causes around which to caucus, not least the risks inherent in the greater professionalism and professional status of social workers, especially one predicated on the somewhat rarified caseworker model that many associated with NISW. Sinfield again (1970, pp 64), with an uncanny prescience of what became critical issues as far as the scandalising of Maria Colwell's death was concerned, notes the possible advantages of the professionalisation and unification of social workers but sees also the danger of 'rigor professionis':

The social work profession may unify and very largely withdraw into itself. It may continue to refine and develop its existing skills but neglect its responsibilities to adjust to the changing needs and expectations of the people and the community it exists to serve. There is a danger too that current disillusion with and opposition towards bureaucracies, and officialdom – the whole structure of establishment – may lead to an increase in the ever present tension between the community and its official caretakers.

However strong and however enduring this radical strain in social work was, its very presence testifies that social work's relationship to its clients, their communities, its own administrative forms, each other and to other professions was far from settled by the publication of the Seebohm Report. How far radical social work was ever likely to offset the 'accommodations' of the respectable left, including Donnison and Longford, that had brought Seebohm into existence is beyond the scope of this book (see Bailey and Brake, 1975, 1980; Corrigan and Leonard, 1978), but it is yet another reminder that social work was an important political as well as administrative and professional concern in the years immediately before and after Maria Colwell's death.

Seebohm was central to this. It was, as Cooper (1983, p 69) notes, the first major study of personal social welfare services since *The Royal Commission on the Poor Law* more than 60 years earlier. The whole process of shaping the content of the Report, arguing for its conclusions and lobbying for its translation into legislation meant that, for the first time, the social work profession, as Hall (1976, p 108) concludes, 'became a coherent political force'. For the personal social services themselves, the Report represented 'a great leap forward' (Timmins, 2001, p 230), in which access to services was claimed as a social right, based on citizenship, rather than client status. Social welfare, for so long 'the most marginal and residual sector of the post-war welfare state' (Gladstone, 1999, p 34), had moved closer to centre stage.

However, as Harris (2008, p 662) cautions, 'consideration of social work's history suggests that it is a contingent activity, conditioned by and dependent upon the context from which it emerges and in which it engages'. In 1969, on the surface, at least, social work seemed set to take its place as a full member of the welfare state family – a comprehensive, professional, public service, available to all on the basis of need. Yet, even at this moment of greatest triumph, other tides were also running. Within Labour circles there was unease at the notion that profound social problems were best addressed through individual adjustment. While some figures in the Labour Party, including key ministers, were convinced that the rationalisation of services into a single local authority department would provide dividends in terms of efficiency and effectiveness, others remained far more sceptical about the case for social work as the organising principle on which such departments should run. And behind all of this, there lay a concern for the nature of the state's relationship to the family and behind this a conception of the proper role and place of the state as a provider and guarantor of the welfare of its citizens. There was also the quotidian and messy world of politics and it was into this that the Seebohm Committee's report now entered.

From Seebohm to the Local Authority Social Services Act 1970

Once the Report was completed and presented to government, it faced a new series of challenges. It became the responsibility of Richard Crossman in April 1968. Crossman had been appointed Secretary of State for Social Services, as 'overlord' at a newly formed 'super-Ministry', bringing together the responsibilities for health, social security and local government. It was the first time since Bevan had resigned from the Attlee Cabinet in 1951 that some of these portfolios had been represented at the Cabinet table. The Crossman diaries record an early encounter in his new office:

> Wed 24 April: "My first job was to see Seebohm of the Seebohm Committee. He's a tall man with a reddish moustache, and I found him nervy and depressed. He was worried about the publication of his Report and I gave him an absolute assurance that directly the text was delivered I would personally look after publication and press relations and make sure we got as much coverage as possible. I think he was a little disconcerted by these assurances since he'd come to complain. I was the fourth Minister he'd had to deal with and that really was one or two too many for him. After he calmed down he told me in great secrecy what was to be the central recommendation of the Report. I didn't particularly want to know but he informed me that it was going to be a demand for the reorganisation of social services, cutting across local authority boundaries, and he was anxious to get his Report out before my Ministry of Health Green Paper which is to be published fairly soon."
> (Crossman, 1977, pp 22-3)

In the event, matters were to be far less straightforward. The new minister had inherited a set of reports into different aspects of his responsibilities that had arrived at mutually exclusive conclusions. He was faced with a report emanating from the former Ministry of Health which proposed that local government social services responsibilities should be transferred to the NHS, while a report from the local government department proposed bringing the health service under the democratic control of local authorities. Overarching both of these proposals were the emerging conclusions of the Kilbrandon Commission into the future organisation of local government as a whole. In addition to competing professional perspectives, the different proposals also gave rise to some political contests between the responsibilities of central government ministries – and therefore, between ministers.

In the immediate period prior to publication, scheduled for 24 July 1968, the Seebohm Report ran straight into the cross-fire. On Wednesday 17 July, Crossman discovered that, without his prior knowledge, the Report had been scheduled for discussion at the following day's meeting of the full Cabinet. The Crossman diaries again give some indication of what was at stake, as he dashed across Whitehall to Downing Street, in the hope of finding the Prime Minister who was presiding over a reception for the blind (Crossman, 1977, p 142):

> He was floppy, airy, pleased with himself, with perhaps a little bit of drink in him ... he said in his own Harold fashion, "Well, you ought to get what you want but we can't push it too hard and maybe I shall have to do the job for you myself. But I'm not sure whether you are in the right." "Well, if unifying the social services isn't in the right what on earth am I at the merged Ministry for?" I replied very indignantly. "Of course you're in the right in that sense," he replied, "But you don't know what pressure Callaghan is putting on me. He sees enormous Home Office prestige at stake and feels that he's fighting for his life." I got nothing out of him except a vague sloppy support and I was fairly unhappy.

Only a few months earlier, at the end of November 1967, James Callaghan had resigned as Chancellor on what he described at the time as 'a point of honour' following Wilson's devaluation of the pound. Although now Home Secretary, Callaghan's political fortunes were still at a low ebb and Wilson was not necessarily exaggerating in describing Callaghan's resistance to any apparent reduction in the scope of the Home Office's responsibilities. In the event, as Crossman recorded in his diary, the Cabinet's reaction to the Seebohm Report was uniformly hostile: 'everyone said it was a contemptible report' (quoted in Hall, 1976, p 82). In a later interview with Phoebe Hall, Crossman told her that he had found it 'both boring and unconvincing', and in particular, that the Committee had failed to justify the faith it placed in social work, 'accepting it instead as a self-evident good' (Hall, 1976, p 83). It had taken a good deal of persuasion to convince Crossman that the personal social services 'constituted an activity or set of activities which merited a local authority Department with status comparable with that of education or housing' (Hall, 1976, p 83). Cabinet discussion revolved around a choice between outright rejection of the Report's findings, or its referral to the Cabinet's Social Services Sub-Committee, with a final determination in favour of the latter.

Outside government, too, the Report, once available for public consumption, produced a set of hostile reactions from a range of organisations that regarded its proposals as inimical to their best interests. The medical profession, especially, which had been largely sidelined within the Committee itself, now mounted a vigorous attack on what it regarded as an assault on its pre-eminence in the social care field. Local authorities, too, were ambivalent, at best, and often directly hostile to the detail of the Report's proposals. District councils opposed the transfer of housing responsibilities to the new departments, because it would mean transferring this function to county councils. Within the counties, education departments opposed the notion that education welfare officers should move into social services. Only social work endorsed the Report with any degree of enthusiasm and some of this was less than wholehearted, as we have seen.

Faced with the possibility of the Report making little further progress, members of the Committee, rather than simply handing over their Report as a job well done, decided, as Hall puts it (1976, p 75), 'that it was necessary to publicise their proposals by "stomping" the country' in their support. Within social work, too, a lobby group was hastily put together, as the danger of losing the whole reform opportunity began to become more apparent. The Seebohm Implementation Action Group was effective in bringing political pressure to bear, with Crossman soon worrying about delays in implementation giving rise to 'a great outcry from social services workers in papers like *New Society* and terrible disappointment amongst the progressive forces' (Crossman, 1977, p 572). It did little to dispel accusations, however, which had long dogged the Committee itself, that the whole Seebohm enterprise had been over-dominated by interests which regarded it as an outstanding opportunity to establish social work as a fully-fledged profession in its own right, and on a par with the other great interest groups of the welfare state.

Back in Westminster, it was not until a compromise was sorted out between ministers that momentum in favour of legislating on the Seebohm proposals began to gather. Crossman agreed with James

Callaghan that, for as long as he, Callaghan, remained Home Secretary, central government responsibility for children's services would be retained at the Home Office. The result was remarkable. Hall (1976, p 96) suggests that, within the 12 months of the Report's publication, 'the Cabinet's position on the committee's major suggestions changed totally from a complete rejection of the report to a general commitment that its main conclusions would be implemented'.

A series of important, tactical, decisions now followed, in order to secure a legislative slot, against a timetable in which a general election was looming as an ever more likely possibility. While more ambitious proposals for reform of local government and the health service were both too politically contentious and technically complex to be placed in the programme, a narrower, and simplified measure, dealing only with social services, could be accommodated. Cooper (1983, p 5) concluded that 'the legislative strategy devised by the civil servants was the single-minded pursuit of the cardinal principle of the unification of the personal social services.' Even so, the translation of the Report into legislation remained on a knife edge to the end. As late as January 1970, Richard Crossman was fighting off a proposal from Local Government Minister, Tony Crosland, to leave it up to each local authority to decide whether to implement a Seebohm-style department or not (Crossman, 1977, p 780). At the final, formal Cabinet of the Wilson administration, he had to argue, again, for inclusion of the Bill in the last three days of parliamentary 'ping pong' (Crossman, 1977, p 921), when Bills move rapidly backwards and forwards between the Houses of Lords and Commons in order to complete their final stages. Even against this background, despite paring the legislation to the 'bare minimum' (Hall, 1976, p 108), and confining it to a 'machinery' more than policy measure (Cooper, 1983, p 5), it still proved necessary to curtail debate in the House of Lords in order to see its parliamentary passage completed – the very last Act of the Labour government.

For Conservative politicians, who during the passage of the Bill 'faced in all directions at once' (Bilton, 1979, p 9), the calculation of hesitation and advantage was different. Less than two weeks before the Bill was published, the Shadow Cabinet had held its pre-election conference at the Selsdon Park Hotel, near Croydon. It was widely reported as marking a new shift to the right in its political thinking, with a vigorous emphasis on selectivity, rather than universality, in welfare services, and a renewed and critical focus on those who, despite economic prosperity and the generosity of the welfare state, failed to look after themselves. Within such a paradigm the more ambitious visions of Seebohm would be in retreat, but the practical usefulness of social work, as a means of targeting the misfits and the marginal, would be on the rise. Of course, as the Local Authority Social Services Act received Royal Assent on 29 May, and the general election campaign of 1970 got underway in earnest, that was an outcome that appeared increasingly remote. It is to that campaign, and its aftermath, that this chapter now turns.

Social work, Sir Keith Joseph and the 'cycle of deprivation'

The 1970 General Election appeared to be conducted in a country largely at peace with itself. The economy, following a very difficult period, was well on the mend. Socially, the liberalising impulse of the 1960s had produced a new tolerance in many aspects of everyday life. The Prime Minister had skilfully kept the UK out of direct participation in the Vietnam War and difficulties nearer home, in Northern Ireland, appeared to have been contained with a popular mixture of firmness and fairness. Those voices which seemed to break through this surface contentment – Enoch Powell on the right who had been sacked as a Shadow Minister after his infamous 'rivers of blood' speech in April 1968 and an emerging Wedgwood-Benn on the left – were largely ignored or repudiated by their own parties. In a month of unbroken summer sunshine, Mr Wilson ran a highly Baldwinesque campaign of a 'Trust Harold' variety, in which he avoided policy controversies and reserved novelty for such 'newfangled' campaigning techniques as 'walk-abouts' in shopping centres and other public places.

While the passage of the Seebohm reforms into law had dominated the last hours of the 1966 administration, the election itself paid no attention whatsoever to its subject matter. Labour's 'safety first' message meant that there was little scope for any campaigning which appeared to smack of fresh thinking or new policy departures. Indeed, in their account of the whole election campaign, Butler and Pinto-Duschinsky (1971, p 350) identify Richard Crossman's 'efforts to involve people in new ideas about the social services' as standing out sharply against the general unwillingness, by both parties, to offend against the received wisdoms of the middle ground. Even here, Crossman's radicalism was focused on pensions and Labour's new national superannuation ideas, rather than on social services themselves.

As the election drew to a close, leading commentators queued up, one after another, to declare the result a foregone conclusion. Nora Beloff, in *The Observer* (7 June 1970), let it be known that, 'Both party leaders are now recognising that only a bolt from the blue ... can save Harold

Wilson from becoming the first Prime Minister in British history to win three general elections in a row'. The far less sympathetic Ronald Butt told *The Times* readers on 14 June that 'short of a miraculous turn-around in public opinion, Mr Wilson is headed straight back towards 10 Downing Street, probably with an increased majority' (quoted in Butler and Pinto-Duschinsky, 1971, p 165).

Yet, within an hour of polls closing at the now later time of 10 pm, it was clear to the 20 million people who stayed up to watch the results, that the Conservatives had won the election. The swing from government to opposition, at 4.7 per cent, was the largest of any postwar election. Under the surface of apparent indifference – the turnout, at 72 per cent was the lowest since 1935 – there were signs of a substantial shift in the politics of Britain.

The legislation that had created the new social services departments was thus inherited by a new Conservative government, headed by Edward Heath. Conventional accounts tend to emphasise the continuities which existed between this administration and those which had gone before it in the postwar period and, indeed, Mr Heath himself was 'a One-Nation Tory, in the line of Churchill, Eden and Macmillan, and believed in an active role for the state, not least in the provision of welfare and in promoting economic growth' (Kavanagh, 1996, p 367). Nevertheless, despite this, more recent, revisionist historians have emphasised the extent to which the 1970-74 period represented 'the main turning point in post-war British history' (Seldon, 1996, p 1).

In this sense, the period represents a bridge between the certainties of the welfare state – strong social spending, positive pursuit of equality, public services – and those of the Thatcher era, only five years distant. From the perspective of this book, and the account that it offers of social work, it is the balance between continuity and change that has to be considered and assessed.

The Conservative Party Manifesto for the 1970 General Election was unusually detailed and specific. It contained, as one of its four main pledges, 'greater selectivity in welfare', in an effort to target scarce resources at those most in need. Yet, of all in-coming administrations in the postwar period, the new Conservative ministers inherited an economy in surplus and offering the prospects of reform against a benign background of stability and growth. The dividend of that growth could be seen, substantially, in the level of additional investment that was applied to the new social services departments during their term of office. Lowe (1996, pp 196/7) characterises these years as ones of 'administrative extravagance in the reorganisation of the personal social services where between 1972 and 1974 alone the number of senior supervisory staff and social workers employed by local authorities increased by over 40%', with expansion redoubled still further during the reorganisation of local government in 1973. Hall (1976, p 122) concludes that, in the period after their inauguration, in April 1971, both the scale of activity within the new departments, and the scale of their resources, grew even faster than previously:

> ... the average annual growth rate in personal social service expenditure (at constant 1970 prices) between 1968 and 1973 was 17.4% compared with an average of 3.2% for public expenditure as a whole. Between 1969/70 and 1973/4 capital expenditure on the personal social services increased by £63 million (125% at 1974 survey prices) and current expenditure by £169.9 million (58%). In all, this accounts for a growth of 68% in five years. (Hall, 1976, p 122)

Hence, an administration that came to office offering better government, enhanced economic success and reduced public spending, ended with a record that belied all three promises. In governance terms, it stands out as a period in which the conventional machinery of administration was often suspected and neglected (virtually no use was made, for example of Royal Commissions as a means of developing long-term policy; see Ramsden, 1996, p 30), yet this government's term of office witnessed 5 of only 12 states of emergency to be declared in the UK since the passage of the Emergency Powers Act in 1920 (Seldon, 1996, p 8). Economically, a government that used its first Queen's Speech to set out 'a renewed commitment to full employment' saw unemployment go above one million for the first time in a quarter of a century. Public spending, far from reducing, 'was followed by the highest rise in social expenditure of any post-war government [while] the commitment to reduce the size of government was followed by a 10 per cent increase in public employment' (Lowe, 1996, p 191).

When Mr Heath called an early election, in March 1974, it was against the background of oil shocks, food price inflation running at 20 per cent and a monthly balance of a visible trade deficit of £383 million. In the foreground was a bitter dispute with the National Union of Mineworkers that had produced the three-day week and regular power cuts. Bogdanor (1996, p 378), in analysing what he calls the 'collapse of the Heath government', suggested that it represented a collapse, not simply in political authority and consent, but a destruction of consensus in social relationships that was to last for a further two decades and beyond. Against this background of a collapsing paradigm in the fundamentals of economic and social policy, as well as of the political settlement on which postwar Britain had been fashioned, the fate of social services in general, and social work in particular, fell to one of the Conservative Party's leading theorists, Sir Keith Joseph.

Sir Keith, in so far as he is remembered today, is mostly recalled as one of the main gurus of Thatcherism, a man who, in his own words, did not become a Conservative until 1976, by which time he had sat as a minister in three different Conservative administrations, becoming a Cabinet member for the first time as early as 1962, as Minister for Housing and Local Government under Harold Macmillan. From the point of his conversion to monetarism onwards, much of Sir Keith's career was given over to a repudiation of the record of the Heath government of 1970-74 and his own part in it. Certainly, as Secretary of State at the Department of Health and Social Security (DHSS), much of his attention had been taken up in grand plans for the (very expensive) up-scaling of major public services in health and local government. In expenditure terms, he presided over what Timmins (2001, p 292) has called 'an expansionary frenzy', overseeing annual average rates of growth in spending of 12 per cent between 1970 and 1973 – with much greater rates in some services. Timmins concludes that 'even advocates of the social services came to regard the expansion as "uncontrolled"' (2001, p 292) and quite certainly, this was a point of view of which Sir Keith was later to become a foremost advocate.

Yet, a closer examination of his record during the Heath administration reveals a far more complex picture than the later, recanted Sir Keith, allowed. As minister for both social security and social services he followed an unwavering line of selectivity in policy development. Selectivity in the way in which it was used by Conservative politicians of the period had two essential meanings. On the one hand, it referred to the means testing of social security and other benefits, so that, as its proponents put it, help could be concentrated on those who needed it the most. On the other hand, it tapped into an even older tradition in British social welfare, in that it sought to select between those who deserved, and those who did not deserve, help. In the field of social security the two elements came together most clearly in the measures taken to deal with what the Conservative 1970 Manifesto had called 'shirkers and scroungers'. In a phenomenon to be repeated even more intensely during the 1980s, as unemployment rose, so too did the pressure to deal more harshly with the unemployed. For the first time in the post-Beveridge era, the 'benefit cheat' became an object of sustained press and political attention. By the time of the Inquiry into Maria Colwell's death, Bill Kepple had already been convicted of Maria's manslaughter. Yet much energy was expended on attempting to establish the nature of his relationship with the dole office – was he working? was he ill? was he working and claiming?

In the social services, selectivity, for Sir Keith, famously meant focusing attention on those families where, he believed, problems were at their more intractable. In June 1972 he gave a speech to the Pre-School Playgroups Association (Joseph, 1972) in which he referred to the notion of a 'cycle of deprivation' (Alcock, 2002, p 177). The speech had been the subject of considerable preparation, and was used to signal the establishment of a Working Party (Such and Walker, 2002, p 185) to study the concept of 'transmitted deprivation' further. In it, he posed his central question as why, in spite of full employment, rising living standards and a huge expansion in public services since 1945, deprivation as maladjustment 'so conspicuously' persisted (Welshman, 2005, p 309). The answer, he suggested, was the existence of 'problem families', relatively few in number, but equally disproportionate in their impact, who passed their difficulties from one generation to the next. If the problem lay in a poverty of lifestyle, rather than material poverty, then the answer lay in services to address such lifestyles.

Bill Jordan, writing in 1974, when these debates were still in common currency, was at pains to point out the way in which selectivity in poverty relief and in social services came together in the cycle of deprivation: they were forms of help which, for many families, were 'best given in conjunction with one another' (Jordan, 1974, p 3), because poverty and maladjustment were conditions connected through the feckless and moral inferiority of those experiencing such conditions. The purpose of social work, more and more, would be to act as a filter through which those seeking material help of one sort or another would have to pass. Denham and Garnett (2002, p 194ff) argue that Sir Keith's motivation throughout was essentially moral, rather than political or practical. They set out a series of examples in which his speeches elide together unemployment with malingering and fraud, and where distinctions are drawn between the 'unfortunate' and 'genteel' poor on the one hand, and the able-bodied poor on the other. The latter were, essentially, the authors of their own misfortunes. They were to be found among what Welshman (2005, p 314) calls a larger set of groups, 'deprived children, deserted wives, families of alcoholics and prisoners, and those who had experienced broken marriages or broken homes'. What they had in common was that their problems were inflicted 'from within': they were 'home made casualties' (Welshman, 2002, p 202).

For social work, as Jordan (1974, p 98) makes clear, this all represented a fundamental retreat from the universalism that had been held out to it in the Seebohm reforms. Not only was social work itself to be selectively employed to concentrate on problem families, but it was, itself, to be the instrument of selectivity in relation to other services.

Of course, Sir Keith's conceptualisation of 'problem families' was not original. Macnicol (1999) has traced its antecedents to the eugenic theories which were popular in late Victorian and Edwardian Britain and which, in far more muted form, were still to be found in the post-1945 period. He points to the influential Women's Group on Public Welfare study of evacuation, *Our Towns*, which showed no hesitation in identifying a group of: 'problem families', 'always on the edge of pauperism and crime, riddled with mental and physical neglect, a menace to the community, of which the gravity is out of all proportion to their numbers' (1943, p 70). Welshman (2002, p 200) goes further into social work's history, tracing a century of different inventions and re-inventions of an 'underclass', 'each of which was manifested in apocalyptic language and purported to discover, seemingly for the first time, a significantly new and qualitatively different kind of poverty, contained within a growing intergenerational underclass, owing its condition either to heredity or to socialisation'. He quotes the American sociologist Herbert Gans, as arguing that the history of the underclass discourse points to a system of 'label formation', in which a process of 'sorting' or 'replacement' in which a new label becomes popular after an old one has lost favour (Gans, 1995, pp 18-22).

What marked out Sir Keith's discovery of persistent, intergenerational transmission of deprivation, was both his search for some scientific basis to support his theory and the commitment with which he set about putting into practice a two-fold solution to the problem he had identified. The search for science fell to the Working Group that met for the first time in the month following Sir Keith's Pre-School Playgroup speech. Its membership was drawn jointly from the DHSS itself and the Social Science Research Council (SSRC). Chaired by the chairman of the SSRC himself, Professor Robin Matthews, its heavyweight character could be seen in the remainder of its membership, which included: Professors Tony Atkinson, the economist then at Essex, Maurice Freedman, from the Institute of Social Anthropology at Oxford, Roy Parker, from the Department of Social Administration at the University of Bristol, Michael Rutter, from the Institute of Psychiatry, University of London and Peter Willmott, of the Institute of Community Studies (Welshman, 2005, p 320). The Group was, in time, to commission a large-scale, eight-year long, research programme, producing 19 research studies, 14 literature reviews and 4 feasibility projects at a cost, in 1970s prices, of an enormous £750,000. The heterogeneous nature of the material produced militated against the easy drawing of general conclusions, and a final attempt to summarise and synthesise the findings concluded that while intergenerational continuities were undoubtedly apparent, no single, simple explanation of deprivation had emerged from the research (Brown and Madge, 1982).

A decade earlier, however, the absence of evidential confirmation of these views did not prevent Sir Keith from embarking on two practical solutions to the problem, as he perceived it. First, and most famously, he advocated family planning. Welshman's (2005, p 317) researches in the Public Record Archive have identified a series of departmental instructions in which Sir Keith encouraged sterilisation 'for really bad problem families'. Sir Keith was not concerned, he said, with issues of population *per se*, but with reducing the 'casual breeding and unwanted pregnancies' among those families 'so incompetent, indifferent or overwhelmed that they are from birth virtually doomed' (Welshman, 2005, p 317). For those who shared this perspective, it is difficult to imagine an individual more likely to attract such an attribution than Pauline Colwell, nor a family more fitted to the description than the Kepples. In the month following Kepple's conviction for murder, for example, the *Argus* carried a letter which declared that: 'sterilisation – that's the only answer ... if the high grade cretins usually involved in this most repulsive type of crime are to be prevented from spreading their poison into the rest of us then compulsory sterilisation is inevitable. It is in their own interests, as much as ours, in fact more so' (*Argus*, 19 May 1973).

Six months later, in November 1973, with the Colwell Inquiry in full flow, the *Sunday Times* launched its 'Battered Babies' campaign (*Sunday Times*, 11 and 18 November 1973); it received an avalanche of readers' letters. In the second week of the campaign two full pages of these letters were printed. One, from a Mrs Pomfret of Liverpool, echoed directly the theme much rehearsed by Sir Keith: 'One way to reduce the cases of child murder, child neglect and battered babies is by sterilisation' (*Sunday Times*, 25 November 1973). The most startling evidence of the extent to which Sir Keith's ideas were more widely shared, however, came in a letter from Brighton's medical officer of health, which led the *Sunday Times* 'battered babies' letters page on 18 November. Dr William Parker did not provide oral evidence to the Inquiry, but his views were set out with remarkable clarity. His letter made it plain that, as far as he was concerned, the 'hideously mutilated body' of Maria Colwell was evidence of a much more widespread social malignancy. Throughout the country there were households without order, organisation or proper care. Their children were alive, but 'unloved, rejected and brutally mishandled'. These children were the result of 'the casual matings' of the 'socially subnormal'. While Dr Parker did not propose sterilisation directly, his propositions amounted, in practice, to the same thing. New powers should be provided to magistrates to define such families as 'socially inadequate'. They would then 'be deprived of all adult rights', their children removed from them, and being put under the care of the director of social services for up to two years, in which the 'feckless' would be taught to 'lead reasonable lives'. Failure to reach the required standard would result in the renewal of the 'socially inadequate' Court Order that Dr Parker advocated.

Dr Parker's proposals were a recognition that family planning, however desirable, was not a remedy that could be applied to those already born. Here, he endorsed Sir Keith's second solution – additional help from social services. The 'shaping forces' of poor housing, degraded environment, economic difficulty and so on, were not the answer for those who had, so evidently, failed to take advantage of the opportunities already available to them. Instead of reforming society to meet their needs further, the adjustment had to be made by individuals. Where, in sentiments that have their direct antecedents in 19th-century philanthropy and philosophies of care, such individuals could summon the moral fibre to move from state help to self-help, then assistance would be given. Where that effort could, or would, not be made, then surveillance and social control must follow. In either case, social workers and allied social welfare professionals were the instruments of such selectivity.

Something of this message appeared in a lengthy interview with Sir Keith, given to Fleet Street doyenne, Marjorie Proops, and carried in the *Daily Mirror* (29 November 1973), just as the Colwell Inquiry entered its final week. For an avowedly Labour paper, it was a remarkably sympathetic account of the Secretary of State's thinking. The first sentence read: 'No one in the country is more deeply concerned about battered babies than Sir Keith Joseph.' The article quotes Sir Keith as saying, 'we all want an effective, caring society and it'll be a long time before we get it. The present state of barbarity is appalling.' Ms Proops asked Sir Keith about Maria Colwell's 'shocking fate', 'and he said we'd got to learn lessons from her martyrdom'. Those lessons were primarily to be found in 'work he has instituted on a subject which he is passionately involved – the phenomenon of transmitted deprivation…. It means that each generation of deprived families tends to produce yet more deprived families: the problems therefore multiply at an alarming rate with each new generation.... And so the breeding of disaster goes on and on and on.' Throughout the interview he admitted that, 'I know I keep getting back to family planning, but I do think it can reduce the problem.'

In the meantime, the interview contained a defence of social work. Sir Keith said, 'social workers do a desperately difficult and often thankless task. Many of them are overworked, but most have an enormous sense of responsibility – otherwise they'd have chosen some other, less demanding career.' Ms Proops commented: 'I was glad he said this. I'd like to underline my total agreement with him. There are too many people who dismiss social workers as nosey-parker do-gooders. I often wonder how much real do-gooding their critics ever engage in. Or if they have any idea of what social work is all about.' However, in the remainder of this interview, Sir Keith did not elaborate on what he considered to be the essential social work task. One imagines that the newly trained, post-Seebohm social workers may have had a different set of ideas than that of the minister.

Accounting for 'What went wrong?' after the introduction of his reforms, Frederic Seebohm quoted a speech made by Joan Cooper in the Younghusband lecture she gave at the Social Services Conference in 1975. She said (quoted in Seebohm, 1989, pp 26 ff) that Seebohm was about 'structural reform and not social reform', and that this had been the cause of the unease that had surrounded its implementation:

> Unease because there are rival claims to ideology and panacea competing for dominance in the amalgamated services. Social problems and private sorrows are not rooted exclusively in the economic, social or political structure. Neither are they rooted in biology, character or personality. But the personal social services are a ready battle ground for the protagonists of either perception.

Neither the form nor the function of social services departments had been decided at the point at which Maria Colwell was killed, more than three years after the Act that put in place the Seebohm reforms. More importantly for our purposes, neither was social work itself clearly established as a form of welfare practice, both among its practitioners and among other welfare professionals. Hardly out from under the penumbra of the Poor Law and its mission to rescue the feckless and the indigent from themselves; unsure as to whether its new professional status and interventive techniques were too radical ('agitator') or not radical enough ('caseworker'); expanding rapidly in scale but not necessarily accompanied by a similar widening in public understanding of what social work was for and what social workers did ('nosey do-gooders'); caught in a moment when the welfare state was beginning to find itself in an economically enforced but ideologically accelerated retreat; unsure as to its role in providing a 'door on which anyone could knock' or an effective form of surveillance over those who perhaps could not be entrusted even with their own breeding; dealing with the problems families faced or merely dealing with 'problem families'; caught up in the small-scale politics of ministers and the large-scale politics of opposing political parties, both the organisation and the practice of social work were indeed a 'battle ground'. And much of that battle would be fought out in the public inquiry into the death of Maria Colwell.

FOUR

The public inquiry

We noted in Chapter Three earlier the expressed anger of the Kepples' neighbours and their concern to find out what had happened to Maria Colwell. However, just as the mere facts of a case may not be sufficient to fuel a scandal, neither are demands for an explanation, no matter how forcefully made, necessarily sufficient to secure an inquiry. As we have argued already, for this to happen, there has to be also a clear resonance with wider social and political constituencies of interest. Those interests were to meet face to face on 18 May 1973, when the Member of Parliament for Brighton Kemptown, Andrew Bowden, was ushered into the office of the Secretary of State at the DHSS, Sir Keith Joseph. This chapter describes both how that meeting came to take place and how the subsequent public inquiry came to be established. We describe also something of how the Inquiry went about its business.

This chapter is concerned also to reflect the fact that this was a *public* inquiry. It became important not just for those involved to know what had happened to Maria but also that the account of what had happened should be rendered in public and to the public. In this way, it satisfied what Frederic Seebohm recognised as 'an ever growing demand to participate at all levels and an evident "passion to know" or at least to obtain an assurance that there is "nothing to know"' (Seebohm, 1977; see Chapter Three, this volume) that seemed to be part of the general mood of the times.

As well as being present in the public gallery and in the queues outside on certain days, the 'public' were to be 'represented' at the Inquiry through the evidence provided to it by family members and by the Kepples' neighbours on the Whitehawk Estate. The neighbours, in particular, contributed to the construction of one of the most important commentaries on the events surrounding Maria Colwell's death. They can be understood to represent the voice of the proverbial 'man on the Clapham omnibus', the voice of Everyman (although, in this case, they were almost all women), the voice of 'common sense' against which the practice of social work would, in part, be judged and found wanting.

The relationship between scandal and 'common sense' is an intimate one. Much of the making of a scandal revolves around the extent to which particular incidents or pieces of individual behaviour can convincingly be explained as ordinary rather than extraordinary;

blameless rather than blameworthy; reasonable or beyond belief – with 'common sense' being invoked as the key arbiter.

Our primary focus in this chapter is on the landmark public inquiry that followed Maria's death. However, this was neither the first nor the only 'tribunal' in which the facts of the case were subjected to scrutiny. Several of the themes that would dominate later accounts of Maria Colwell's death were first established at the trial of Bill Kepple and yet, it all began very quietly. The *Argus*, which was to become so pivotally involved in recording and shaping public reaction to Maria Colwell's death, reported the successive remands in custody of Mr Kepple, in January 1973, in tiny paragraphs, placed in the most obscure pages of the paper. The news that 'New vicar is the East Sussex man' (*Argus*, 22 January 1973), for example, was reported, at considerably greater length, and with greater prominence, than the Colwell case. Even the committal proceedings (where reporting restrictions were not lifted) were recorded in the *Argus* in a strictly minimalist 34 words on 5 February.

It was not until the reporting of the trial itself, which took place in April 1973, that public attention became more prominent. Mrs Kepple, having given evidence at the committal proceedings, now resolutely refused to enter the witness box again. Her latest child was born on 5 April, the day on which Mr Kepple's trial at Lewes Crown Court was due to begin. Nevertheless, strenuous efforts were made to persuade her to appear. The case was taken out of the lists, and rescheduled for Friday 13 April. The presiding judge, Mr Justice Sir Stanley Rees, took the highly unusual step of dispatching a probation officer to her home, to make one final attempt to secure her attendance [NA: DPP 2/5197/2].[1] When that failed, it guaranteed that much of the first day of the trial was taken up in legal disputes as to the admissibility of key elements in the prosecution's case, including objections by the defence, at various points, to what they regarded as attempts to put Mrs Kepple's evidence before the jury without her being present for cross-examination. On almost all points, the judge concluded in favour of the prosecution.

---

[1] The papers concerning the trial for the murder of William Kepple are preserved in the National Archive in file DPP 2/5198. Originally scheduled to be closed until 2073, the papers were released as part of the research carried out for this book. Available documents now cover both the original trial and the appeal that followed. The 'short transcript' of the trial runs to approximately 90 pages. It contains verbatim accounts of those elements that were subject to appeal, but not of the main body of the hearing that, in any case, occupied less than a day.

Six witnesses were called by the prosecution including Maria's foster mother, Mrs Cooper, her GP Dr Barley, the forensic pathologist, Dr Cameron and the two main social workers in the case, Mrs Kirby of the NSPCC and Diana Lees of East Sussex Social Services Department. Twelve witness statements, from police officers, school teachers, neighbours and others, were read to the jury. Mr Kepple was not called to the witness box.

In his final, 66-page, summing up, Mr Justice Rees advised the jury to draw no inferences either from Mr Kepple's silence, nor Mrs Kepple's refusal to give evidence. The crucial period, he instructed the jury [NA: DPP 2/5198], was not to be found in Maria's previous history (which he proceeded to set out in some detail), nor the actions of social welfare workers (he did not once use the term 'social workers', preferring instead variations on 'social welfare worker', 'social visitor' and 'social welfare visitor'), but the disputed period between 11.30 pm on Saturday 6 January 1973, and 3 am the following morning. The jury had to be satisfied, he said, that Maria died as a result of a deliberate and unlawful blow struck by her stepfather, and that at the time he intended either to kill her or to cause grievous bodily harm. The direction to the jury was to find the accused guilty or not guilty of murder; there was no question of a manslaughter verdict. The jury retired at 3.10 pm and returned only 50 minutes later with a verdict of guilty of murder.

Almost immediately, Kepple's defence lawyers put forward, as grounds for appeal, all the points that they had previously made to the trial judge and that had been dismissed by him. They argued that the verdict was unsound, for example, because the prosecution had been allowed to adduce evidence obtained by the police after they had sufficient evidence to charge Mr Kepple while the decision to allow post-mortem photographs to be shown to the jury had been prejudicial rather than probative and 'against the weight of evidence'.

The Court of Appeal dismissed these particular points on 19 July 1973. However, the appeal was upheld on one ground, 'whether the question of manslaughter should properly have been left to the jury rather than having to consider whether the defendant was guilty or not of murder only'. The trial judge had been in error, the Court of Appeal determined, in not allowing the jury itself to resolve this matter, rather than having the possibility of a manslaughter verdict denied to them. A manslaughter verdict was substituted, and the original indeterminate, life sentence on Kepple was replaced by a fixed term sentence of seven years imprisonment.

The conclusion of the trial broke a damn of local public concern that had already been fermenting in Brighton. The terms of that concern, however, were shaped not simply by the verdict, but by the struggle for meaning that the trial had represented. By its conclusion, while any legal ambiguity over responsibility for Maria's death had been resolved, the court of public opinion had already been populated with a far wider collection of putative heroes and villains – neighbours and foster parents, social workers and Mrs Kepple. The tussle for 'authoritative sense-making' (Brown, 2003, p 95), which was to culminate in the Inquiry report itself, had already begun.

Origins of the public inquiry

William Kepple was convicted of Maria Colwell's murder on 16 April and, on the 17th, East Sussex County Council announced an emergency meeting of its Social Services Committee. The intention emerged to set up a review panel to examine the handling of the case by social workers. Interviewed by the *Argus*, Director of East Sussex Social Services Department, Denis Allen, could not say if the panel would meet in public, or if its findings would be made public (*Argus*, 17 April [a] 1973). That uncertainty immediately gave rise to a strong, negative, local reaction. Echoing views that flooded in through readers' letters, the *Argus* began to lead a campaign to have any review panel meet in public.

The paper expressed strong opposition to the idea of the investigation being held 'in secret' (*Argus*, 26 April 1973), to use their terms. The local Conservative councillor, Danny Sheldon who would shortly become the first mayor of the new borough of Brighton after local government reorganisation in 1974 and whose name was still carried on a Brighton and Hove double-decker bus as recently as 2009, was clear when he attended a meeting of local residents that he intended to campaign for a separate and wider Home Office inquiry (*Argus*, 28 April 1973).

The local MP, Andrew Bowden, was quick to lend his weight to the campaign and an approach was made to the Home Secretary, Robert Carr. A petition bearing 7,500 signatures was organised by the chair of the East Brighton Residents' Association and handed in on the steps of the Town Hall (*Argus*, 11 May [a] 1973), which added substance to Councillor Sheldon's earlier claim that, 'The public conscience has been aroused and demands that its views cannot be ignored' (*Argus*, 5 May 1973). The *Argus* made much of the 'public's right to know' (*Argus*, 24 April 1973), and correspondents expressed fears of the 'old pals act' (*Argus*, 27 April 1973), were the Inquiry to proceed in private.

Andrew Bowden insisted that justice had to be 'seen to be done' (*Argus*, 8 and 12 May 1973), and declared that, 'the people of Brighton and the nation have a right to know what went wrong'.

For a short while, however, the East Sussex County Council simply pressed on with its intention to set up a local review panel. Within 10 days it had announced the names of the five people who would sit on it. The panel would be led by the chair of the local Police Authority, Brigadier Sir Edward Caffyn. The Council reiterated, and stoutly defended, its intention to have the panel meet in private. That announcement served only to increase the temperature of local public opinion in favour of an open, wider and more official inquiry. The letters, now carried daily in the *Argus*, came mostly from local Brighton residents, but also from further afield and from prominent individuals, such as the composer and Master of the Queen's Music, Sir Arthur Bliss (*Argus*, 30 April 1973), as well as national bodies, such as the National Union of Townswomen's Guilds (*Argus*, 17 May 1973).

Councillor Sheldon again made explicit his concern that the inquiry should not only be impartial but public:

> People who have authority vested in them must always be aware that they are servants of the public. I believe that to proceed with the inquiry [in private] can only bring lack of confidence in those who administer the public's affairs. (*Argus*, 15 May 1973)

On the following day, the *Argus* published an account of events provided by Mrs Ann Turner, Maria's primary school teacher. She appeared to confirm that Maria's death had been entirely preventable. On the following day, the newspaper's editorial described the County Council's reasons for proceeding in private as 'utter nonsense':

> Nothing can possibly be considered confidential in a case of this kind. For the public need to arrive at a true picture of what really happened just as much as the inquiry panel.... In a secret inquiry only the members of the panel will hear the explanations offered by the Social Services Department and the NSPCC. If the inquiry were open, however, the public would hear what took place in the words of the people who were there at the time, rather than in the official jargon of a carefully worded report published weeks or even months later. (*Argus*, 16 May 1973)

The 'public's right to know' was now almost as much an issue as the circumstances surrounding the death of Maria.

The first meeting of the County Council's panel took place on 15 May. It proved to be the only occasion on which it met because, in Whitehall, matters now gained a new momentum. On 17 May the *Argus* reported that Mr Kepple's legal team were to mount an appeal against his murder conviction, and that Andrew Bowden's letter to the Home Office had been transferred to the DHSS for attention (*Argus*, 17 May [a] 1973). On the following day, 18 May, the meeting took place between the MP and Sir Keith Joseph. The County Council immediately announced that it was to halt its own inquiry, pending any decision that Sir Keith might make (*Argus*, 18 May 1973).

Reporting on his meeting, Mr Bowden told the *Argus* that he had been 'deeply impressed' by the minister's detailed knowledge of the case, and his own 'personal concern and deep sorrow' at what had taken place. 'It is my impression', he said, 'that Sir Keith is very anxious himself to have a ministerial inquiry', but that he needed further, detailed, legal advice and more discussion with the Home Office in order to come to a final determination. By the following Tuesday, 22 May, a further meeting between Mr Bowden and Sir Keith was announced, for the coming Thursday (*Argus*, 22 May 1973), and, on 25 May, the *Argus* was reporting 'Sir Keith Joseph's decision to set up a Government committee of inquiry into the Maria Colwell case'. The decision was, it said, 'a victory for public opinion'.

Later in the day, the DHSS issued a statement that read:

> Sir Keith Joseph, Secretary of State for Social Services has decided to set up an independent committee of inquiry into the care and supervision provided by local authorities and other agencies in relation to Maria Colwell and the coordination between them....It is expected that the name of the chairman who will be a lawyer, will be announced shortly. The members will include a qualified social worker. The report of the Inquiry will be published. [NA: MH 152/238]

It also made it clear that the work could not begin until matters still *sub judice* were completed. We can safely assume that Sir Keith had been thoroughly briefed on the details of the Colwell case and that he saw some strong resonances with his own particular interests, as we described them in the last chapter. In particular, he may have found an exemplar of the 'problem family', fulfilling its own cycle of deprivation and apparently unamenable to social work as it was currently practised. As we shall see, as well as social work itself coming under scrutiny in the public inquiry, so too was the matter of the 'problem family' to become a matter of concern. Whatever Sir Keith's particular reasons might have been, as far as local interest was concerned, these were subsumed in satisfaction with the form rather than the focus of the public inquiry. A leader in the *Argus* on 24 May said that Sir Keith's decision was 'splendid', and that the Inquiry would have 'all the trappings of a judicial inquiry'. It continued to press, however, for the inquiry to be held in public.

Pressure to expedite the Kepple appeal led to a hearing on 17 July 1973 when the murder conviction was overturned and replaced by a verdict of manslaughter. On the same day, the Secretary of State signed a Minute, confirming the membership of the Inquiry team and its terms of reference. These were made public in the following week although details were brief. The chair was to be Mr Thomas Field-Fisher QC, whose most obvious credential appeared to be that he had been a former vice-chair of the London Council of Social Services. Otherwise, he had been a QC since 1969, a former deputy chair of the Cornwall Sessions and a recorder since 1972. The other two members were Alderman Margaret Davey, described only as 'an Essex County Councillor', and Miss Olive Stevenson, 'Reader in Applied Social Studies at Oxford University'. The *Argus*, giving the announcement prominent coverage (*Argus*, 23 July 1973), could find a picture only of Miss Stevenson. On the following day a few more details, and a picture of a bewigged Mr Field-Fisher, had been found. He had been born in 1915 and called to the bar in 1942. His interests in *Who's Who* included 'social welfare'. It was this interest (together with the absence of any connection to Sussex) that linked the different members of the panel together. Alderman Davey, 'a widow', had 'an impressive record of service in Essex', including chairing the council's health committee. Miss Stevenson was presented as something of a veteran of government work, being the social work adviser to the Supplementary Benefits Commission and a member of the Royal Commission for civil liability and compensation for personal injury (*Argus*, 24 July 1973). A picture of Mrs Davey finally followed, the next day.

The official records are entirely silent on the process through which the members of the Inquiry team were selected. Miss Stevenson recalled being telephoned one evening at home by Joan Cooper,[2]

---

[2] Joan Davies Cooper was born in 1914 and died, aged 84, in 1999, having taken a degree in Arts and History at the University of Manchester and

until recently a member of staff at the University of Oxford Social Work course and now chief inspector at the DHSS (Olive Stevenson, personal communication):

> And she said this thing had happened. And they'd decided to have an inquiry, and would I be a member of it? There was no context, no publicity. I hadn't heard anything about it before the phone call. She thought it might take about three weeks.

On 4 August, the first practical details of the Inquiry were released by Mr Field-Fisher, 'speaking from his London home' (*Argus*, 4 August 1973). The first preliminary hearing was to take place on 28 August, with the first full day of hearing fixed for 9 October. Mr Field-Fisher confirmed that the preliminary hearing would be held in public, but that it would be for that meeting to determine the nature of further hearings. Formal notification of the first meeting was carried in both local and national newspapers on 16 and 21 August, inviting anyone wishing to give evidence to write to the appointed secretary to the Inquiry, Mrs Christine Desborough, at the DHSS's main office at the Elephant and Castle, London.

Local Brighton campaigners, who had kept up their pressure for a public hearing throughout, now joined the call for the oral hearings of the Inquiry to be held in Brighton (see, for example, *Argus*, 20 August 1973).

Then, on 24 August, the *Argus* reported 'Victory! Maria probe will be in public and in Brighton.' The chair of the Inquiry had agreed, in advance of the preliminary hearing, to proceed on this basis. Four months after William Kepple's original trial, therefore, the final outline of the Inquiry into Maria Colwell's death had been determined. The intensity of local opinion, the growing interest of national as well as Brighton-based media and the particular preoccupations of the Secretary of State had combined to overturn the original, private, internal investigation and put in its place a fully independent inquiry

---

qualified as a teacher. She taught in Cornwall and in 1941, at 27, she became, first, an administrative assistant and then, three years later, assistant director of education in Derbyshire. In 1948 she became the first children's officer for East Sussex, and subsequently was chief inspector in the Children's Department of the Home Office and thereafter director of the Social Work Service in the DHSS; in other words, by this time, she was the government's chief professional adviser on social work services. She retired in 1976.

and one to be conducted in an unprecedented glare of national attention.

Setting the tone

At the preliminary hearing the main point at which its otherwise smooth proceedings departed from the script came through an intervention from the secretary of the Maria Colwell Memorial Fund,[3] Robert Beaumont,[4] in which he asked for an absolute assurance (which

---

[3] The Memorial Fund was announced in the *Argus* on 31 May 1973.

[4] Robert Beaumont, eventually the chair of the Memorial Fund, deserves particular mention, albeit in a footnote to this account. Ten years earlier, in one of the most sensational trials of the 1960s, he had himself stood trial for the murder of his 21-year-old wife, Christine. Known, in those days, as Harvey Holford, he had been the owner of a string of Brighton nightspots, including the Whiskey-A-Go-Go coffee bar, the Calypso Club and the Blue Gardenia Club where, in the early hours of 15 September 1962 he shot his wife three times with a .38 revolver. He was discovered, dressed only in a white singlet and cradling his wife in his arms, deeply unconscious from an overdose of barbiturates.

During the summer of 1962, Christine Holford had set off on a European tour where she appeared to have adopted an enthusiastic and ecumenical approach to male members of the then Common Market. In August, she arrived at the Cap Ferrat villa of Conservative MP and barrister, Richard Reader. There she was introduced to millionaire John Bloom, a washing machine tycoon whose own affairs were to end in spectacular and scandalous failure. The relationship between them became known to Holford when he arrived unexpectedly in Nice, taking his wife home to Brighton with him. In August, he seriously assaulted her when she announced her intention to leave him, and set up in a Mayfair flat that Bloom had promised to provide. On 1 September, her 21st birthday, she repeated her intention of leaving him, but was persuaded not to. On 14 September, the couple appeared in public together for the final time at the Brighton Jazz Ball. Later that evening a disastrous quarrel took place, in which Christine Holford again attempted to leave, and declared that the couple's 16-month-old child had a different father.

Before an all-male jury, in March 1963, and aided by a remarkably sympathetic summing up by the judge, Mr Justice Streatfield – 'Can you imagine', he asked the jury, 'any words more calculated not only to sear and cut deeply into the soul of any man?' – a verdict of not guilty was returned on the charge of murder, on the grounds of provocation and diminished responsibility. A three-year sentence was imposed for manslaughter, the judge

the chair declined to give) that all the proceedings would be held in public. Beaumont had come to London with a coachload of other Fund supporters, and had unfurled a large 'REMEMBER MARIA' banner outside the office in which the hearing took place. Their activities were extensively reported on the following day in national, as well as local, newspapers (see, for example, *London Evening Standard*, 24 August 1973, 'Foster girl's death: change law plea').

Thereafter, as the autumn began, the Inquiry shifted to its Brighton location, a former DHSS office, near to the centre of town, at 166–168 Western Road. At its first hearing, on Tuesday, 9 October 1973, the original estimation of a fortnight or three weeks for oral hearings was confirmed.

According to local journalist Adam Trimingham, the Inquiry room was 'large and rather dingy, set above a row of shops. Large mirrors at one end made it appear much larger than it really was. The room was in many ways unsuitable for such an Inquiry. Traffic noise made it essential for windows to be closed all the day, making the atmosphere at times unbearably stifling. The acoustics, despite microphones, left much to be desired and the office facilities were poor.'

The style of the Inquiry was adversarial, essentially that of a trial. At the entrance to the building a notice had been posted, reading 'No Cameras in Court'. Each day began with a procession of the three Inquiry members from a 'robing room' at the rear of the room, to a dais at its other end. Over a quarter of a century later, Olive Stevenson recalled, vividly, that, having gathered beforehand, Mr Field-Fisher always led the procession, conducting proceedings thereafter as if a judge were being assisted by two lay assessors: 'the implication being that you were not being treated on an equal level'. All members of the public, lawyers and others present, stood until the Inquiry formally resumed. Once its business was underway 'witnesses' were 'called' and 'stood down'. Lawyers routinely referred to 'defendants' and even the

---

telling Holford that 'There must be few men indeed who have been subjected to greater provocation than you were.'

On release, in October 1964, Holford returned to Brighton and changed his name to Robert Beaumont. It was in that persona that he headed the Maria Colwell Memorial Fund Committee, firing off letters demanding the return of capital punishment. Most remarkably of all, not a single newspaper in which the Fund's activities were extensively reported ever mentioned his previous life. It was left to his death, in June 2006, for obituaries to recall his double life, as nightclub owner and campaigner (see *Daily Mail* 8 July 2008, for example, for further details).

chair referred to 'the defence'. Witnesses referred to being 'in Court' [see, for example, Dr Franklin, Day Twenty-Six: 12]. When there was a disturbance of any sort (see later), the chair reminded the press and the public that they were in attendance at 'a court of inquiry' [Day Four: 1], with conduct required to reflect such a forum.

Perhaps the most vivid account of the daily proceedings and atmosphere of the Inquiry was provided in the *Daily Mirror* (3 November 1973):

> Listen to the voices. Cool, calm, clear, made metallic by the microphones. They are telling you everything you want to know about the days and the death of little Maria Colwell. Well, everything you can learn by word of mouth....
>
> Every weekday morning for the past month, Authority and the witnesses have climbed slowly up Crown Street in Brighton from Western Street where the shops and cafés give a gaudy impression of London's West End.
>
> They have waved or smiled to cheerful PC Bill Sansom who is always on the door. They turn into the flagged corridors of a building that once served as a Social Security office. They are going to listen, or to speak, at the Inquiry into the handling of Maria's welfare before she died....
>
> SILENCE. The word startles us all for a moment in the large, square room with mirrors at one end, plasticky chairs, trestle tables covered with dark blue cloth.
>
> We stand up from notes, legal papers, newspapers and pay attention. Mr Thomas Field-Fisher, QC, the chairman of the committee has arrived. Now the voices can begin....

It is important, at this stage too, to remind ourselves that the Brighton of October 1973 stood nearer in time to wartime Britain than we stand today in relation to 1973. At the time of writing more than 35 years have passed since the Inquiry took its evidence. Thirty-five years before those hearings, Neville Chamberlain was Prime Minister and the Second World War was still a year away. For many of those who took part in the Inquiry, and appeared before it, these had been their formative years. The headteacher of Maria's last school, Whitehawk Juniors, had begun his teaching career in 1937; the doctor in charge of Brighton's schools' medical service had been in practice since 1938; Bill Kepple had come to Britain, from Ireland, as a 'Bevin Boy', a wartime creation. During the Inquiry, the chair would refer, from time to time, to 'conditions during the war' [Day Nine: 31, for example] as a touchstone for judging social conditions in the Whitehawk Estate of the 1970s. While the Inquiry stands at a turning point in the 30-year fortunes of the welfare state, the formative experiences of many of its participants belonged to an earlier time.

Not only were many of the Inquiry's participants of a common age, but also, among the lawyers and some expert witnesses, at least, there was a commonality of class. Adam Trimingham believed that, as the expected two or three weeks set aside for the Inquiry became two months, 'the Inquiry began to resemble a curious club with its own in-jokes and private language'. Much of that can be traced to a set of male, public school shared experiences on which those who appeared, day after day, in one another's company were able to draw. To take just one example, a good deal of the Inquiry's attention was taken in exploring what Miss Stevenson regarded as the 'rabbit hole' of Maria's height and weight – who should have taken it, where it should have been recorded, how the information should have been accessed and so on. The chair, Mr Field-Fisher, ever interested in the mechanics, put this question to expert witness, Dr White Franklin:

> I remember being weighed incessantly by matron, and measured, every time I went back to Prep School. Has medical thinking moved away from that practice? [Day Twenty-Six: 28]

We draw attention to these points because to understand the ways in which the Colwell Inquiry went about its business, and arrived at its conclusions, it is not only important to locate it in its own time but also to be sensitive to the formative impacts of age, class and gender which were at play beneath the public inquiry's rather polished and urbane surface. Mr Field-Fisher's prep school days were half a century old in 1973. Dr Franklin, with whom the above exchange took place, had just expressed his professional view that Maria's sense of separation would have been diminished in a boy, because boys were so used to being sent away to boarding school [Day Twenty-Six: 27]. If all this seems a distance from the worlds of the front-line workers of the welfare state, then it was, surely, a different world altogether from 119 Maresfield Road where, as Mr Field-Fisher put it, the '"Kepple ménage" were to be found at home' [Day Twenty-Two: 12].

One further, general and contextual point needs to be made here. In common with any trial, Inquiry proceedings were conducted in the knowledge of a certain outcome. Maria's death was an established fact: the challenge was to understand how it had happened. One of the essential tussles between witnesses was between those who believed (as family members and neighbours contended) that the final outcome had been entirely predictable, and those (particularly the social workers) for whom the outcome was unforeseeable until it actually took place. From the outset, however, public perception was shaped, and determined, by the prior knowledge of the events themselves. To take just one example, the *Daily Express* (10 October 1973) headline over its coverage of the opening address of the Inquiry's own counsel, Arthur Mildon QC, read, 'Council let her stay with killer'. Except, of course, that they didn't. Kepple was not a killer then. Nor was there any evidence, in October 1971, to suggest that any such risk might be posed. This sense of Greek tragedy, in which events move, unstoppably, to a known conclusion, is a common characteristic of the way in which social welfare scandals are constructed.

'That is not how it seemed at the time', was to be a regular reply from Diana Lees, Maria's social worker, to barristers who probed what they portrayed as the culpable unwillingness of social workers to draw obvious conclusions from all-too-apparent evidence. An exchange with Treasury counsel, Mr Mildon, makes this clear. He suggested to her that, 'it is right, is it not, that until Maria's death you never considered that you had clear proof that Maria had been physically injured or neglected by the Kepples?' Her reply was designed to expose the way in which the Inquiry reinterpreted everything through the hindsight that it possessed: 'I do not think it was a matter of proof. I never considered that she had been' [Day Twenty-One: 58]. In a sense, however, her reply was to misunderstand a fundamental part of the way in which inquiries operate. They are, by their nature, in the business of *post hoc* rationalisation – a task at which the Colwell Inquiry was particularly adept.

The principal players

Adam Trimingham's pen pictures of the three Inquiry members were typically positive. Mr Field-Fisher was 'an urbane handsome lawyer of great experience' who showed 'a benign control' in difficult circumstances and displayed a phenomenal memory for everything which had been said in evidence. Miss Stevenson was 'a woman of enormous intelligence', a 'formidable member of the Inquiry team'. 'Very little got past her', especially in probing the lack of liaison between the different welfare organisations. Alderman Davey, 'a large plump woman with piercing blue eyes', had 'enormous experience of local authorities' which made her 'invaluable to the Inquiry'.

Miss Stevenson's views were a good deal more uncompromising. Mr Field-Fisher was, she concluded, highly unsuited to his appointment: 'he had *no* previous experience of family issues, or family law. He had only been a judge in the criminal system.... He was not particularly interested or knowledgeable in the field [and] it rapidly became clear that he was basically out of sympathy with those issues.' She believed it would be '*unthinkable*' that someone of that background would, today, be appointed to such a post. As to Alderman Davey, she was 'a very nice county councillor who was very quickly *absolutely* out of her depth ... she actually took very little part in it all'. While Adam Trimingham regarded Miss Stevenson herself as a formidable operator, her own recollection was only of her naivety and lack of preparedness. Neither she, nor Alderman Davey, had been involved at all in the agreement of terms of reference for the Inquiry, nor in such fundamental issues as to whether or not it would meet in public. That had all been predetermined by the chair – 'I was simply given the situation and pulled up in Brighton one day and found an army of lawyers.'

Trimingham also provided brief portraits of the main legal representatives. The Inquiry's own counsel was a Treasury QC, Arthur Mildon, a man with a 'dry manner' who 'seemed to have all the time in the world'. His remorseless attention to detail made him 'squeeze the truth out of witnesses through relentless logic'. The NSPCC were represented by Mr Bernard Hargrove, 'a short, squat barrister' with 'an eye for publicity which constantly gained headlines in the national press'. Brighton County Borough Council were represented by 'a well known local barrister, Anthony Hidden', a man 'with the air of a public schoolboy'. As the finger of blame appeared to swing, during the Inquiry, towards East Sussex County Council, the local authority decided to replace its own lawyer with a QC. Peter Webster, the new barrister was 'one of the most eminent inquiry lawyers in the country', whose 'slow, precise delivery hid an acute mind'. He was 'dull' but tenacious in ensuring that the authority was never criticised unfairly.

Yet the star of the lawyer team was, in Mr Trimingham's assessment, Miss Charlotte Crichton, the daughter of a judge, and the advocate employed to represent Mrs Kepple. Her skilful handing of a very difficult brief, in which 'in the early stages of the Inquiry any derogatory mention of Mrs Kepple's name met with spontaneous applause', resulted, over time, in 'a picture of Maria's mother as a poor, confused woman, who was the victim of circumstances'. She reminded the Inquiry of the hatred which had been directed at Mrs Kepple, reading a selection of letters which had been written to her. One, signed by a mother 'who loves and cares for her children every minute of the day', ended 'I hate you, Mrs Kepple, from the bottom of my heart. All the mothers in England must despise you and feel ashamed you belong to our race.' Miss Crichton's presentation of Mrs Kepple's written statement, very close to the conclusion of the Inquiry, was, for Adam Trimingham, the most 'deeply moving' moment in the whole Inquiry (Trimingham, unpublished).

Hearing the evidence

In this section we wish to give a sense of the order of events as the Inquiry set about its business and to give an indication of the 'atmosphere' in which the Inquiry itself took place. At points, we will introduce further material that is relevant to the judgements that were to be made about how key professionals went about their work but we reserve a detailed account of the evidence of the main protagonists (Daphne Kirby and Diana Lees) until the following chapter.

At the Inquiry's preliminary hearing in Parliament Street, London, on 24 August, the chair made it clear that (Trimingham, 1978), 'This Inquiry is not in any sense a trial. Our task is to seek to establish the true facts involved.' Indeed, this point was repeated in a lengthy opening statement by the Inquiry's own counsel, Arthur Mildon QC. He repeated the chair's earlier contention that the 'sole task' of the Inquiry was 'to establish the true facts', and described his own role as 'neither to prosecute nor to defend', but 'simply to place before you as judicially and dispassionately as I am able all the relevant information' [Day One: 2].

Within a paragraph, however, this simple appeal to judicial objectivity began to break down as the dominant narrative of the Inquiry and the underlying events through which it had come into being was firmly and decisively established. Maria had been 'happily brought up by relatives; Mrs Cooper, a fond and devoted mother' [Day One: 5]; she had been 'taken from them' and then 'left there in spite of repeated reports that she was being ill-treated' [Day One: 2]. In defining the essential narrative of Maria Colwell's life and death in this way, Mr Mildon was also hinting at an underlying dynamic that would be central to the Inquiry's proceedings and to the conclusion expressed in its final report. Implicit in this account of Maria's death was a sense of incredulity and a sense in which, by any standards of reasonableness or common sense, these actions could not be adequately accounted for, justified or defended, ever. Expressed in this way of course, they cannot be, but, as Chapter Two has indicated and as further material presented in this chapter confirms, the actual experience of engagement with the Kepple household was a much more ambiguous and uncertain one. This implicit incredulity in the face of 'the facts', especially when set in the context of plain, ordinary common sense, was to provide an essential frame of reference in which the actions of social workers in particular were to be placed.

Once Mr Mildon's statement was complete, the first set of witnesses was called. All were relatives of the late Raymond Colwell and all, to some degree, hostile to both Mrs Kepple and Miss Lees. The last to be called was Mrs Cooper, Maria's paternal aunt and foster mother. At only 45 years of age, she appeared a broken and elderly woman, over-awed and highly distressed by the ordeal of giving evidence. The daily transcripts, normally a simple, verbatim account of the day's proceedings, contain a highly unusual commentary in describing her entrance – 'Mrs Cooper was assisted into Court [sic] and appeared to be distressed.' Within only a few minutes, devoted just to Maria's very early history, she broke down. Her son intervened, to ask if she might be spared further examination. Mr Field-Fisher agreed. Mrs Cooper was, he concluded, 'very distressed', and in need of attention from a doctor [Day One: 44]. She withdrew and was to take no further part in the Inquiry's proceedings.

With Mrs Cooper indisposed, the Inquiry turned to the evidence of neighbours from the Whitehawk Estate. Mr Mildon had set out the conventional wisdom about the 'mothers of Maresfield Road', as they came to be known collectively. They were the 'salt of the earth' and, as we describe in more detail later, a source (for two at least of the Inquiry team) of solid 'common sense'. Yet Adam Trimingham, otherwise the most generous of commentators, ready to see the best side of every contributor, expressed his scepticism for some of the neighbours. He made an exception for Mrs Rutson of no. 121, 'a concerned and moderate witness', but was less impressed by many other Maresfield Road residents who 'presented their evidence in a rather theatrical manner and it was apparent that the attractions of playing a leading dramatic role in proceedings, coupled with the certainty of publicity in the papers the next day, was more important to them than the life and death of Maria had been' (Trimingham, unpublished). And, in this scepticism about the neighbours, Miss Stevenson, the third member of the Inquiry team, was of the same mind as Adam Trimingham. She had not realised, she said, until the witnesses were in front of the Inquiry, the effect that the lapse of time, and the impact of collusion, had produced on their testimony:

They all came, dressed up to the nines, in their best high-heeled shoes and their shiny handbags. And they had, as it were, constructed a reality by the time they came because they had talked together, and put it together, and conflated and changed it. (Olive Stevenson, interview with author, 1999)

Whereas the chair of the Inquiry and Alderman Davey would appear subsequently to attach considerable weight to the testimony of members of the Cooper family and the Kepples' neighbours on the Whitehawk Estate, Olive Stevenson's less than favourable impressions influenced her judgement as to the weight she would give to the evidence that they provided. This is reflected in particular in her view of the Coopers and the wider Colwell family set out by Stevenson in her dissenting chapter of the Inquiry's final report.

On the third day of the Inquiry, the original group of neighbours having given evidence, it was the turn of the first group of professionals. Miss Dean, the first such witness, had been a teacher since 1941. She had no difficulty with one of the core concerns of the Inquiry. Whitehawk was, she said, a 'very robust area' with 'a fair number of problem families and problem children' [Day Three: 17] (see Chapter Five, this volume, for a full discussion of the 'problem family'). Her evidence contained a number of vivid phrases which were to enter the narrative of the Inquiry, describing Maria as 'the Cinderella of the family' who was 'used as a little drudge', and who came to school 'as a place of refuge'.

The third day was most memorable, however, for the evidence of Mrs Turner, Maria's class teacher at the time of her death. Looking back many years later, both Adam Trimingham and Olive Stevenson were in relatively rare agreement in their recollection. For Trimingham, she was, 'perhaps the most impressive of all the Inquiry's witnesses', while, for Olive Stevenson, Mrs Turner's evidence was 'very, very important. She stays with me as a manifestly sincere woman.' In terms of scandal construction, as we have seen from the decisive effect of her account in the *Argus* when the form of the Inquiry was still at issue, Mrs Turner was a significant figure. She had arrived at Whitehawk Juniors a married woman with five children of her own. She was also a state registered nurse. This was, however, her first post in teaching and, as such, she was employed as a probationary teacher. In her evidence, she told the Inquiry of her early concerns at Maria's repeated lateness for morning school, and of the reassurance she received that, 'there almost seemed to be a tradition for children to arrive late at the school' [Day Three: 37]. Her attempts to make her concerns known to the school authorities met with little success. Complaints to the school's welfare assistant about Maria being sent to carry coal up a steep hill to her home were met with the suggestion that, 'if she pushed it in a push–chair it must not be such a terrible thing to ask the child to do' [Day Three: 41].

Later in the Inquiry, it became clear that, as Mrs Turner's concerns mounted, so they came to be more and more discounted by the school authorities as the product of an over-anxious, under-experienced, rather obsessional individual who judged against standards which simply did not apply in the Whitehawk context [Day Twenty-Nine took the evidence from the school authorities, on which this account is based]. Mrs Turner was to complete her probationary year at Whitehawk, but did not teach there again after July 1973.

Mrs Turner's very positive impression, as a witness, was reinforced by the absence of partisanship in her evidence. She made no attacks on social workers. She reported a letter which Mrs Kepple had sent to her, about seeing Maria's school work, and agreed that Maria was 'certainly not the worst dressed child in the class. She was superficially neat and tidy in appearance' [Day Three: 49]. Nevertheless, as the school term had gone on, her anxieties about Maria had mounted. She summed them up in an image that was reproduced in the Inquiry report, and used in the daily accounts of every national newspaper [Day Three: 36]:

> When I took her on my knee the first thing that happened to me was a shudder went through me because I could feel her bones sticking into me, and the way I describe it is if you have ever held a bird in your hand you can feel the bones and you are frightened to hold it too tight in case you squeeze the life out of it, and this is how I felt about Maria – I was frightened almost to hug her because she felt so thin.

In addition to Mrs Turner's evidence, the first week also heard from the school's education welfare officer, Mrs Dickenson. In later years, Miss Stevenson was to remember her mainly as 'ineffectual', but to the majority of the Inquiry team, and in contemporary reporting, she emerged more positively. Mrs Dickenson was, like Mrs Turner, in her first job as an education welfare officer. She too had qualified as a state registered nurse and state certified midwife and had 14 years' experience in that capacity. Despite being responsible for seven different schools, she recounted how she was soon spending a significant amount of time and attention on Maria, pursuing her with a determination described in detail in Chapter Two (this volume).

Mrs Dickenson's evidence also illustrated a number of critical weaknesses in the professional responses that had been made to Maria since returning to the care of her mother. First, her evidence highlighted the invisibility of Maria, despite the strenuous efforts made to contact her. Mrs Dickenson made, in total, over 14 numerous recorded visits to Maresfield Road in a three-month period, prior to Maria's death, together with a number of other unannounced calls, when travelling through the area. As we have indicated, however, on only one occasion did she physically see Maria and that was in July 1972, during one of her very first attempts to make contact. Second, she highlighted the haphazard and unpredictable nature of contact between different professional workers with an interest in Maria's case. Taking her own example, Mrs Dickenson's first point of contact came through Miss Dean, Maria's former class teacher. She had warned Mrs Dickenson of her concerns in terms that the education welfare officer was to remember as especially troubling. Over the summer of 1972, Mrs Dickenson contacted the Kepples' health visitor, Miss Bodger, who, at that stage, nine months after she had moved to Maresfield Road, was not aware of Maria's presence in the family. Mrs Dickenson and Miss Bodger were known to one another personally. Professionally, they occupied the same office building, but they were never to meet face to face to exchange impressions of the case. Mrs Turner, with whom Mrs Dickenson was to share an escalating set of concerns during the autumn of 1972, she was never to meet at all.

The second week saw the end of Mrs Dickenson's evidence, the appearance of a further clutch of neighbours and more evidence from teachers. On Day Seven, the Inquiry heard from Inspector Curran of the NSPCC. Inspector Curran's evidence could only deal with Maria's very early history, and the wider early circumstances of Mrs Kepple. The chair was wary of opening the Inquiry to this contextual material. In his opening remarks, at the Committee's preliminary hearing on 24 August, he had specifically identified the date of Maria's birth as the starting point for the Inquiry's investigation [Day One: 2]. Now, he repeatedly urged counsel to keep the inspector's evidence 'as brief as possible' [Day Seven: 35] and 'as short as you can' [Day Seven: 36]. On this, he and Olive Stevenson were to take a very different view. She consistently argued that later decisions by social workers could only be understood against the wider background, for which the inspector's evidence was critically important. For Olive Stevenson, it demonstrated the considerable improvement that could be traced between Mrs Colwell's circumstances at Maria's birth and early life and the circumstances of the Kepple household from 1970 onwards.

The main witness of the second week, however, was Professor Cameron, the forensic pathologist who had carried out Maria's post-mortem examination. His early evidence was distressing, providing the Inquiry with details of his autopsy findings. Much had already been made about Maria's loss of weight; so visible to Mrs Turner, so emphatically claimed by neighbours. Newspaper reports of Professor Cameron's findings had also concentrated on the same point. Yet, medical as well as social welfare professionals, examining the child within weeks of her death, had found nothing remarkable in respect of Maria's weight. Under pressure from counsel for the NSPCC and Dr Barley, Professor Cameron therefore appeared to temper his position. He agreed that Dr Barley's assessment that Maria was 'thin but not remarkably thin' was 'quite fair'. She was 'malnourished' but not 'emaciated' [Day Eight: 31]. Professor Cameron's analysis had suggested that Maria was 30 per cent under weight. Mr Hidden, the barrister representing Brighton County Borough, produced earlier medical records that demonstrated that, while under the care of Mr and Mrs Cooper, Maria's weight had been exactly 30 per cent below what her age and height would have anticipated. The final impression made was that Maria's appearance was that of a 'light' child, rather than anything more alarming. Even such 'facts' as Maria's weight were susceptible to competing interpretations, which is simply to re-emphasise the inescapably interpretive nature of any public inquiry.

On the final day of the second week, the Inquiry team made a visit to the Whitehawk Estate, and to Maresfield Road. When it reassembled on the following Monday, members were better placed to follow the evidence of that week's first main witness, Mrs Kirby of the NSPCC. In the following chapter, we will examine in more detail Mrs Kirby's evidence and how it came to represent a particular view of what social work was and what it should be. We wish only to note at this point that, as a witness, Mrs Kirby was, in the view of Adam Trimingham, 'a hardworking woman who made a good impression'. Over three days of cross-examination she emerged as a dedicated, grass-roots practitioner. A brief extract from a note made by Diana Lees of a telephone conversation between the two social workers, early in September 1973, perhaps best captures that impression [Day Thirteen: 15]:

> Phone call from Mrs Kirby. She has been seeing Maria very frequently during the summer, passing up Maresfield Road almost every day and seeing Maria playing outside on most occasions. She has also called at the house with clothing and other goodies.

As an organisation, however, the NSPCC itself appeared to Miss Stevenson as a 'bloody shambles', utterly amateurish in organisation and characterised by claims far in excess of its ability to deliver. The final Inquiry report was to reflect both these impressions: critical of the NSPCC as a body, but positive about Mrs Kirby as an individual.

The third week ended with a further set of important witnesses, Miss Bodger, the health visitor, Miss Martin, the receptionist at Dr Barley's surgery, and Dr Barley himself. Much of the substance of their evidence has already been captured in Chapter Two and we do not discuss it in any further detail here.

Week Four began with a further round of education and social services witnesses, concentrating now on the minutiae of interagency working. Matters, however, again set off in a new direction when further members of the Cooper family took to the stand, bringing the long-established tensions between them and Mrs Kepple to the surface. Mrs Kepple's possible participation in the Inquiry had, from the outset, been a matter of much speculation. In the first week, her barrister, Miss Crichton, had announced that Mrs Kepple would *not* be giving evidence orally. She would provide a full written statement, but Miss Crichton had decided – not Mrs Kepple – not to call her to give evidence in person [Day Three: 12]. At the start of the third week, however, Mrs Kepple unexpectedly turned up at the Inquiry building for the first time. She met Miss Crichton, but otherwise waited outside, talking to newspaper reporters and the policeman on duty. The *Argus* reported that, 'Mrs Kepple said she had still not decided whether to speak. She had intended originally to give evidence but the number of people attending the Inquiry had changed her mind' (*Argus*, 24 October 1973). On the final day of the third week, Mrs Kepple attended again, this time going into the public gallery where she sat next to the door and close to a police officer. The reason why was to become clear two days later, when she arrived in time to hear the start of proceedings, only to become involved in a tussle in the main entrance, in which Mrs Betty Brashill, a neighbour, was thrown to the ground. The event was widely reported in national newspapers. *The Sun* (1 November 1973) recorded a 'street shouting match', while the *Daily Mirror* (1 November 1973) reported events in this way:

> The incident happened as Maria's mother ... arrived for the hearing. With her was a man friend ... and a relative, 18 year old Sandra Tester. As they entered the inquiry building in Brighton, the woman witness, Mrs Betty Brashill, called Mrs Kepple, "a witch". .... Police constable Bill Sanson rushed in

and tried to separate them. In the struggle, Mrs Brashill was knocked to the ground and the two men fell on top of her.

Inside the Inquiry, Mr Field-Fisher began the day by warning that it was intolerable that anyone should be threatened in this way. 'I appeal', he said, 'to everyone to keep their cool, if I can use that disgusting expression, and not to allow themselves to get over excited' [Day Eighteen: 2].

By now, the public gallery was full every day, with over 100 people attending and queues forming each morning to obtain seats. Some attendees were regular fixtures. Mr Beaumont, of the Maria Colwell Memorial Fund, maintained a continuous presence that remained very clearly in the memory of Olive Stevenson, more than a quarter of a century later:

> One of the worst things was having a night-club owner there everyday, who was obsessed with the whole case and wanted to set up a Maria Colwell Museum in the house in which she died! And we found him prowling round, pinching our name plates so that he could use them in the museum. He bought an enormous teddy bear and got pictures taken of the foster mother standing at Maria's grave. Sick, sick, sick. The presence of people like that I found it very off-putting.

On the day after the main entrance scuffle, the 18th day of oral hearings and with Mrs Kepple again in attendance, the chair had, more than once, to threaten to end the public session as the gallery cheered and clapped during the hostile evidence of Mrs Cooper's sister, Mrs Shirley. On the following day, 2 November, the national press again covered the events. *The Sun* (2 November 1973), under a headline, 'I'm so scared, says Maria's Mum', reported that Mrs Kepple and Sandra Tester had been unable to leave the Inquiry building until 7 o'clock on the preceding evening, because of threats of violence against them. She told reporters, 'I am frightened but I'm determined to be here to hear what they are saying about us.' The *Daily Mirror* (2 November 1973), covering the same story, under the headline, 'I have nothing to hide', reported Mrs Kepple as saying, 'nobody will keep me away. I have a right to hear all the wicked things people are saying about me. They are all untrue – I have nothing to hide.' Again, the chair called for calm. 'Everybody is entitled to come here, and in particular, Mrs Kepple is entitled to listen to what takes place', he told the Inquiry.

These disturbances were only a taste of what was to come, however, when, on Day Twenty of the Inquiry, social worker Diana Lees was called to give evidence. Adam Trimingham describes her as 'a dark haired, composed, concerned young woman' who 'business like and efficient', made an excellent witness (Trimingham, unpublished). Press photographers were already gathered to record her arrival, as they were to take photographs of her arriving and leaving from every session in which she gave evidence. A 'minor disturbance' took place before she began to speak, and a woman was escorted from the Inquiry. The session began with another warning from the chair that the 'slightest indication of public disorder' would result in the rest of the day's proceedings being held in private [Day Twenty: 2]. Despite this, Miss Lees continued to be interrupted from the public gallery. On the second day of her evidence, queuing for seats intensified, with 65 people turned away without gaining access. Angry shouts from the public gallery greeted her, as her evidence began. A shout of 'She ought to get the sack!' from the gallery led to a woman being escorted away by the police and a further warning from the Inquiry chair that he would clear the room if interruptions persisted.

Then, during the lunch interval, matters deteriorated further. The *Daily Mirror* (6 November 1973) reported that, 'Fury erupted at an inquiry yesterday over the heart-rending ordeal of tug-of-love girl Maria Colwell.... When 29 year old Miss Lees left during the lunch break, she was followed by thirty women who booed and chanted, "Liar" and "Get out!" Police escorted her for 100 yards before the crowd broke up.' *The Sun* (6 November 1973), on the same day, told readers that, 'A crowd of booing, fist-waving people chased social worker Diana Lees along a street yesterday after she gave evidence at the Maria Colwell inquiry.... Even as Miss Lees gave her evidence, there were cries of abuse from the public gallery.' At the end of day, a crowd of 20 people, almost all women, was waiting again. Police surrounded Miss Lees as she hurried to a waiting taxi.

Nor were reports of this sort confined to the mass circulation newspapers. *The Times*, *Telegraph* and *The Guardian* all covered events in similar detail. Soon, the *Daily Express* (14 November 1973), among others, was bringing readers up to date with new details that verged on the surreal. Under the headline 'Maria social worker gets bodyguard', it reported:

> Social worker Diana Lees, the woman at the centre of the storm over the death of seven-year-old Maria Colwell, has been given a squad of bodyguards. The move follows

harassment from the public, threats and "vile letters". The squad, set up by East Sussex Social Services Department, includes ex-Brighton police superintendent, Alan Probyn, and 16st former Nigerian police chief, Leonard Oliver. They chauffeur Miss Lees to and from the Inquiry into Maria's death, and take her away at lunch. Miss Lees, 29, has been booed and shouted at during her six days of evidence. Yesterday she dashed through the public gallery when the inquiry adjourned. She was escorted downstairs by Mr Oliver and swiftly entered a car with its engine running.

Miss Lees continued to give evidence over five consecutive days, with 25 hours of cross-examination. (We will return to the substance of her evidence in the following chapter.) She faced some of the most challenging questioning of the whole Inquiry. Gradually, however, her composure wore down both the Inquiry and the gallery. As a witness she proved uncompromising. Her strengths were her obvious integrity and her ability to know her own mind, and to stick to it. Her weaknesses were what appeared to be a certain lack of sympathy, or shared understanding of the enormity of what had taken place.

The end of Miss Lees' evidence marks a cathartic point in the Inquiry's proceedings. On the following day, it turned to a set of expert witnesses, none of whom had had direct contact with Maria or her family. The first, the bowler-hatted Dr Alfred White Franklin, took the stand with only nine people in the public gallery, a reduction that was at least partially explained by the rival attraction of a Royal Wedding on the same day. Interestingly, Olive Stevenson was ill on the occasion of Dr Franklin's evidence, but the chair decided to go ahead regardless. Miss Stevenson, he explained, was 'the person appointed to assist us with social work', and as Dr Franklin's evidence was 'basically medical in nature', her absence could be overlooked [Day Twenty-Six: 2]. By and large, the excitement of the Inquiry was over. More experts and senior staff from East Sussex County Council gave evidence. Earlier witnesses were recalled to confirm or clear up points of detail provided earlier.

Only one real day of drama remained. In the early days of the Inquiry, any derogatory mention of Mrs Kepple's name was met with spontaneous applause. She, herself, had stayed away from the oral hearings since her appearance had provoked public disorder. Now, on Thursday 6 December, in the final week of the Inquiry's oral hearings, her barrister, Miss Crichton, presented Mrs Kepple's statement. It portrayed her as a poor, confused woman, who had been the victim of circumstances. The *Daily Mirror* (7 December 1973) led its coverage under a headline 'THE AGONY OF MARIA'S MOTHER – by a woman barrister', telling readers that, 'A woman barrister choked back tears yesterday as she described the agonies that piled up for the mother of little Maria Colwell.' *The Sun's* (7 December 1973) variation followed closely along the same path: 'THE TORMENT OF MARIA'S MOTHER – tears as inquiry hears of poison pen campaign'. The *Daily Telegraph* (7 December 1973), along with other broadsheets, reported Miss Crichton as saying that 'Mrs Kepple has lost her child, her husband and her home. She has been turned away by shopkeepers. She has lost her job.'

Thus ended an Inquiry that was meant to last two or three weeks but took nine weeks to complete. It had dominated newspaper and other media headlines throughout its length, a period which it is almost impossible to parallel in terms of sustained media attention. In its public phase it had taken 41 days of oral hearings, heard from 70 witnesses, accumulated 1,350,000 words in written evidence and cost, in 1973 terms, £100,000 (*Daily Telegraph*, 7 December 1973).

Common sense

As we will describe fully in the following chapter, it is not only the practice of individual social workers that came to be at the heart of the Inquiry's efforts to set out the 'facts' of the Colwell case. It was also the practice of social work itself. Very early on, the majority report of the Inquiry makes this clear. Specifically referring the decision to return Maria to the care of her mother in April 1971, the report notes (DHSS, 1974a: 45):

> An Inquiry such as this should be very chary of criticising [the contemporary standard of practice itself] but it is our view where any particular aspect of that practice may offend against ordinary standards of social or moral concern or even appears to go against accepted tenets of commonsense it would be wrong not to do so.

The general application of this approach is made clear in the next sentence:

> Two of the older professions, law and medicine, are not immune from criticism from outside sources and are probably the better for it.

The essential difference between the majority report of the Inquiry and the minority report, written by Olive Stevenson, lies in the significance attached to the self-evidently critical decision to return Maria to the care of her mother, behind which lay a considerable degree of difference in understanding the nature of social work practice among the members of the Inquiry team. Olive Stevenson's precise purpose in writing her minority report was to provide a detailed account of the circumstances in which that critical decision was made with the explicit intention of showing 'that the problems confronting the social workers, in the network of relationships with Maria at the centre were less clear cut than my colleagues appear to suggest' (DHSS, 1974a, p 316). In this way, she seeks 'to be fair to the East Sussex social workers' by setting out the legal, moral and professional complexities that surround those situations where the judgement of Solomon is required (see DHSS, 1974a, p 316). However, what is clear from both the majority report and the minority report is that more straightforward views, untrammelled by professional perspectives, were perfectly possible. The 'accepted tenets of common sense' would also prove a powerful lens through which to view what had happened to Maria Colwell.

In fact, throughout the Inquiry, social work practice fell under the microscope of 'common sense' at very regular intervals. One of the most important of these was precisely in relation to the decision to return Maria to the care of her mother and the evidence heard from Mrs Pearl Shirley, the youngest sister of Raymond Colwell. Her evidence was typical of that offered by other members of the Cooper family, for whom the decision to return Maria to her mother defied all sense of ordinary reasonableness. Mrs Shirley's evidence was given on the 17th day of the hearings. It was to be a day of high drama. It will be recalled that Pauline Kepple attended the hearing herself, creating an even more than usually intense atmosphere, with interruptions from the public gallery at different points in the day, and a physical attack on Mrs Kepple at the end of the day's proceedings. In an excitable, and aggressive, evidence giving – 'I am highly strung, anyway, I admit it' [Day Seventeen: 42] – Mrs Shirley repeatedly claimed that she had provided evidence to Miss Lees of the unfitness of Mr and Mrs Kepple to take over the care of Maria, particularly focusing on their appearances, 'paralytic drunk' during the daytime outside different Brighton public houses. She recounted, for example, having seen Mrs Kepple coming out of the City of York public house during the afternoon, much the worse for drink. In her evidence, Mrs Shirley said that she urged Miss Lees – whom she had met, by chance, at the Coopers' house immediately after seeing Mrs Kepple – to get in her car and see for

herself what she had just witnessed. Asked about Miss Lees' response
to this suggestion, she said [Day Seventeen: 43]:

> Naturally she declined.... To be honest, she did not look
> interested, but she did tell me it was none of her business,
> their personal life was none of her business.... She said
> something like, that was not her duty; it was her duty to
> see to Maria.

By contrast, Mrs Shirley thought and acted very differently. As she put
it to the Inquiry: 'I made their background my business and I felt so
should she have done.'

Mrs Shirley's refusal to separate the child's interests from the conduct
of the parents is presented by her as an 'ordinary' person's 'commonsense'
understanding and one which she thinks social workers would have
done well to share. The difference between lay and professional
expectations was further illustrated by Mrs Shirley in her reference to
what she regarded as the intolerable position that had been created for
the Coopers, especially when compared to the demands made on the
Kepples. The Coopers were expected to assist in Maria's reintroduction
to her mother, despite her very evident objections – 'That kid, I cannot
tell you what she did not do, she ran under the bed, we pulled her out
from under the bed, she ran behind the suite, she was screaming, she
nearly went hysterical' [Day Seventeen: 41]. The expectations of Mrs
Kepple, by contrast, were very modest. Asked by Miss Crichton, Mrs
Kepple's barrister, whether her client had made visits to Maria during
the trial period prior to her going home, Mrs Shirley replied: 'Of course
not. Pauline never bothered to come and see her' [Day Seventeen: 51].

In her minority report, Olive Stevenson makes it clear that the
Coopers are entitled to 'respect and sympathy as human beings, not as
saints' (DHSS, 1974a, p 316), and the account provided by members
of the Cooper family did not go entirely unchallenged during the
conduct of the Inquiry. Mrs Shirley's evidence was put directly to
Diana Lees during her own cross-examination and roundly rejected.
Anything that Mrs Shirley said ought, Miss Lees advised in a very
commonsense phrase, to be 'taken with a pinch of salt' [Day Twenty-
Two: 23]. The evidence on which Mrs Shirley relied for her view of
Mrs Kepple's suitability was discounted because it was tainted by the
wider family tensions in which all the relatives, from whichever camp,
were caught up:

I think the impression I got was that many of the allegations
made, particularly by Mrs Pearl Shirley, but in general by
Mrs Cooper's relatives, seemed to me to refer back to Mrs
Kepple's life at the time the children went into care and
fairly immediately after. I believe this was interspersed in
fact with particular references to things that had happened
some years previously and I think this could, perhaps, explain
why I did not take Mrs Shirley's allegations, if you can call
them that, as being serious and applying at that particular
time. [Day Twenty-One: 25]

Mrs Shirley's account, far from being the product of common sense,
was, Miss Lees suggested, likely to be the product of malice [Day
Twenty-One: 48]:

It seemed to me that most of what Mrs Shirley said, in fact
related not to recent years but to the past and that she was
bringing this up again in a malicious way.

It is important to note one further ground on which the battle of
common sense was conducted in relation to the wider Cooper family.
Mrs Shirley's case can, once again, stand for the others. Towards the
conclusion of her evidence, she was asked whether she had ever
seen Maria after she had been returned to the Kepples, replying,
'heartbreakingly, no' [Day Seventeen: 44]. This immediately raises the
more general question of why, having been so very concerned about
Maria's welfare prior to her removal, no single member of the Cooper
family ever contacted her again, once the switch to Maresfield Road
had been made. The rapidity with which the Coopers ceased to be a
feature in Maria's life is one of the unexplored territories of the Inquiry.
In January 1972, within three months of Maria's removal to Maresfield
Road, Miss Lees' case note summary recorded her intention 'to keep
in mind the possibility of eventual renewing of contact between Maria
and the Coopers' [Day Twenty-Four: 9]. In this phrase, the six-year
relationship with the Coopers is relegated to being 'kept in mind' as
an 'eventual possibility' for resumption.

By the time her cross-examination, and that of Miss Lees, was at an
end, Mrs Shirley's standing had been tainted, at least in some degree,
by the residual ambivalence which attached itself to the Cooper family
in the eyes of at least some Inquiry participants, although to judge by
Olive Stevenson's decision to write a minority report, clearly not by
her fellow Committee members. A quality of self-interest and self-

justification emerged from Mrs Shirley's account that suggested that, robustly commonsensical as they claimed to be, social workers were not entirely wrong to regard her views as open to question. For those charged with defending the actions of the authorities, the same sense of ambivalence needed to be created in relation to the second source of common sense to be investigated in this chapter – that of the neighbours of Maresfield Road. That task began at the very start of the Inquiry.

What did the neighbours say?

The daily hearings of the Inquiry team featured the first of the neighbour witnesses on its opening day. Mrs Cooper, Maria's aunt, it will be recalled, had been taken ill during her evidence giving, overcome by the stress and distress of the occasion. On the intervention of her son, the chair – already ill at ease with interventions from the public gallery – agreed to adjourn her appearance and called, instead, the Kepples' next-door neighbour, Mrs Shirley Jean Rutson. She lived at 121 Maresfield Road, immediately next door to the Kepples, and separated from them by only a narrow gap that ran between their two houses.

Mrs Rutson was to prove the key witness from the Whitehawk Estate. The Inquiry report described her evidence as 'of the utmost importance' (DHSS, 1974a, p 82). Socially, the family summed up a set of familiar, contemporary characteristics. Mrs Rutson had been born at the address and, other than a gap of some 18 months of marriage, had lived there all her life. In the early 1970s, she lived with her mother, father, husband and young son, intimately linked to a wider network of family members all of whom lived in the immediate locality. Mr Rutson was in full-time employment as a butcher, while his wife worked on a part-time basis at a local shop. The family shared a material prosperity that set them apart from the Kepples, owning a car and having access, through her sister, to a telephone. In sociological terms, the Rutsons belonged to the white, respectable, aspirational and highly stable working class that largely populated the Whitehawk Estate.

Mrs Rutson is described in the final report as 'an honest and concerned person with the welfare of Maria very much at heart' (DHSS, 1974a, p 82). And, reading the daily transcripts of evidence, more than 30 years later, Mrs Rutson indeed emerges as an impressive witness. The atmosphere of the Inquiry, which had proved so upsetting to Mrs Cooper, was no less adversarial for Mrs Rutson. Yet she proved wholly equal to it. Her grasp of specifics was secure and confident. For example, in her evidence, Mrs Rutson described an incident at an ice cream van. It was a variation of a theme that many neighbour witnesses recounted – that of Maria being left out of family treats. Mrs Rutson's grasp of specific detail, however, is what makes her version both compelling and telling [Day Two: 25]:

> On one occasion Mrs Kepple bought a treat. [Maria's sister] came in and said, could she have an ice cream, and Mrs Kepple said, "Get four", and [Maria's sister] said, "I am not going to get four." Mrs Kepple said "F—king get four or he next-door will only go and buy her one."

In introducing Mrs Rutson's evidence, the final report of the Inquiry specifically rejects suggestions that 'there was any unfriendliness towards or dislike of the Kepples on the part of the Rutsons in the early days after the Kepples became their neighbours' (DHSS, 1974a, p 82). The tone set by Mrs Rutson at the start of her evidence, however, strikes a cooler note. Asked if she recalled her new neighbours moving into their home, she replied, 'I remember the people moving in there; I did not speak to them at the time.' Mr Mildon, the counsel to the Inquiry, no doubt aware of the line to be pursued by lawyers representing other interests, worked hard to establish the good relations which were claimed to exist between the two families. Mrs Rutson's own reply reduced his enthusiasm several notches:

> Mr Mildon: "So that really, at one time relations between you and the Kepples had been very friendly?"

> Mrs Rutson: "Well, yes, quite friendly. I did not go into Mrs Kepple's house and she did not come into mine." [Day Two: 5]

In the final report, Mrs Rutson's own reservations and careful calibrations of her views were overlooked in favour of an account in which she represented a source of solid, common sense: as acute in her judgement of danger as social workers were naïve in theirs; persistent where they were too easily shrugged-off; as determined that action needed to be taken, as they were anxious to avoid it. The focus of these contrasting assessments revolved around what became known, in the Inquiry, as the 'April incident' of 1972. This was, in fact, a linked sequence of events that had taken place during the Easter holidays of that year and which marked the point at which Mrs Rutson's general concern for Maria's welfare led to her first contacting the NSPCC.

Given the pivotal importance that the Inquiry came to attach to these events, the prominence that it receives in the Inquiry report and the dispute between Inquiry members as to its significance, what took place needs to be briefly examined here. Our immediate purpose, however, is not to provide an exhaustive account of the events themselves, which are, in any case, fully set out in the Inquiry report. Rather, we are concerned here only with what the events can tell us about social work and the differences between lay and professional understanding of the 'incident'.

By April 1972, Maria had been living at Maresfield Road for more than six months and, in her mother's account at least, had settled well. On Thursday 13 April, at 4 pm, the NSPCC received a lengthy telephone call from Mrs Rutson. It contained a complaint that Maria had been slapped by her mother – 'she is always screaming and shouting at the children' – leaving her with bruising which was already fading, and a black eye. The note taken concluded that, 'Mrs Rutson seemed a very sensible sort of person and was not being vindictive' [Day Eleven: 31]. Mrs Kirby received this lengthy message on the following day. She then contacted Miss Lees and they carried out a joint home visit to 119 Maresfield Road that afternoon.

We have already indicated something of the favourable impression that the Inquiry report presents of Mrs Kirby. One of the more remarkable omissions of the report lies in the decision of its authors to leave out all of her previous history of involvement in the Colwell case. To a reader of the report, Mrs Kirby arrives at the April incident armed only with the note of Mrs Rutson's telephone call. Her tenacity, and determination to do her duty, stands out in even sharper relief against her status as newcomer to events. In fact, the oral evidence makes it clear that she was already acquainted with a good deal of Maria's history. As a trainee NSPCC inspector she had accompanied Inspector Curran to the court hearing where the original Care Order on Maria had been granted. Less than a year before the April incident, she had held a meeting, in her own home, with Mr and Mrs Cooper, where they had set out the whole subsequent history of the dispute between themselves and Maria's mother, asking the NSPCC to intervene on their behalf in any new court hearing. While Mrs Kirby had no direct involvement in the case, of the sort that was well known to Miss Lees, she was quite certainly no ingénue in the whole matter.

As the two social workers made their visit, a good deal of difficulty was experienced in getting to see Maria. Both Mrs Kepple, and her husband, made up stories about her whereabouts that were easily exposed as completely untrue. It was only later in the evening that

Mr Kepple offered an explanation for what might have been seen: 'Maria had fallen off her scooter down the steps and ... the scooter was produced during the afternoon with buckled wheels' [Day Eleven: 34]. In the process, she had suffered what Mr Kepple termed a 'little bruise on her face' [Day Eleven: 36]. As the afternoon wore on Miss Lees had to leave for other duties. Mrs Kirby remained with Mr Kepple for more than another hour. As she told the Inquiry, 'I made it quite clear to him that if I sat there all night I would see Maria because that was what I had come for' [Day Twelve: 49]. During that wait she had an opportunity to observe Mr Kepple in interaction with the two younger children – 'he was patient with them ... he was kind to the children and patient' [Day Eleven: 35]. When, eventually, Maria was seen, Mrs Kirby found that 'her eye was very black, and the pupil was bloodshot. She had a black eye on one side and on the other side her face was bruised. It was in the region of the eye, but the eye was all right' [Day Eleven: 38]. Questioned closely about the explanation offered, Mrs Kirby told the Inquiry that she had accepted what she was told because she had an opportunity to question Maria directly, and without interference and that, in answering 'She did not hesitate and she did not look at her parents to see whether or not she should be answering me' [Day Eleven: 38]. The answers that Maria gave confirmed the story of the scooter and her fall from it. More definitely, the signs of physical injury which Mrs Kirby was able to view, however they had been caused, did not support the view which Mrs Rutson had adamantly expressed, that Maria had been smacked.

However, the business of the April weekend was not yet over. On the afternoon of Sunday 16th, a Public Order incident took place at Maresfield Road, involving the Kepples, the Rutsons and other neighbours, during which Mrs Rutson informed Mrs Kepple that it was she who had called the NSPCC earlier in the week. The police were called to restore order, whereupon Mrs Rutson tried to call at Mrs Kirby's home where, finding no one at home, she 'left a message to say that there had been further troubles' [Day Eleven: 42].

On the Monday morning, Miss Lees took a telephone call from Mrs Kirby, bringing her up to date with developments. Together they now visited Mrs Rutson who told them of overhearing Mr and Mrs Kepple openly quarrelling about which of them had hit Maria. Mrs Kirby's contemporary notes record the outcome of the discussion in this way [Day Twelve: 54/55]:

> It is quite apparent one of them is the culprit. This could
> easily be Mrs Kepple, she is said to go into the most

outrageous frenzies and can be heard screaming and swearing. Maria is not in school today, but Miss Lees intends to have her medically examined, first warning the Dr why she is bringing the child and she hopes to take Mrs Kepple with her.

On the following day Miss Lees succeeded in making a home visit and finding Maria at home. She recorded that:

> I visited the Kepple household and saw Maria who had very faint traces of a bruise (barely discernable) and a rather bloodshot eye. I was given an explanation identical to that given to Mrs Kirby.

And there, until the Inquiry itself, the 'April incident' largely rested. Two days later, Mrs Kirby went on leave and was away for the rest of the month. Miss Lees discussed what had taken place with Mr McBurney, her Brighton social work contact, but took no further action.

Eighteen months later, and under the examination of the Inquiry, things were treated very differently. There was little use in Miss Lees' protestation that the whole event had attracted far less attention at the time. Her cross-examination began with a warning aimed directly at her from Mr Mildon that has resonated with a folk horror through social work ever since [Day Twenty-One: 54]:

> What I am going to do is to suggest that Maria's death occurred because of the failure to seize an opportunity to retrieve the situation which occurred in April, 1972, and for that you were primarily responsible.

Fobbed off by a demonstrably false story, faced with clear evidence of collusion in fabricating an alternative account, the professionals in this case nevertheless preferred what the Kepples had told them, rather than the evidence which neighbours were able to provide. The determination with which Mrs Rutson pursued her concerns of the April weekend, and beyond, was contrasted with the less-than-urgent way in which Miss Lees, in particular, was said to have reacted. Accepting that she was unable to remain at the Kepple home on the original Friday afternoon, Mr Mildon pursued the way in which she kept in touch with events over the weekend. Had Diana Lees alerted the Brighton duty officer? She had not. Had she contacted Mrs Kirby on the Friday night to find out the outcome of the visit? She had not.

Had she given Mrs Kirby her telephone number, so that she could be contacted? She had not. Had she tried to speak to Mrs Kirby on the Saturday? She had not. Miss Lees' suggestion that she had relied on an understanding that 'no news meant good news' was used to convey a gap between the urgency of those living on the spot, and the irresolution and lack of importance apparent in the actions of the social workers.

Finally, Mrs Rutson's demand for action was contrasted with the wish of Miss Lees to allow things to continue as before, or, as Mr McBurney put it in his record of a contemporary conversation with her, to 'keep child at home despite apparent set-back' [Day Seventeen: 18]. The following chapter deals in more detail with the accusation that social workers were in thrall to a single-track theoretical approach, in which a linear course of action was being pursued, regardless of evidence to the contrary.

The preference which the Inquiry shows for the common sense of lay people is reflected in its portrayal of Mrs Rutson as a concerned, determined and essentially disinterested person, who did her very best to communicate to the reluctant authorities the seriousness of the problem presented by the Kepples' malign neglect of Maria. Yet, the fine detail of her evidence, none of which found its way into the final report of the Inquiry, suggests a more compulsive interest than simple 'good neighbourliness'. She repeats, at regular intervals that her concern had reached a pitch where 'my husband threatened to leave me if I kept on about Maria' [Day Two: 5]. He had 'packed his case' [Day Two: 19] and was going to 'go to live with his mother' [Day Two: 25]. 'My little boy was becoming a nervous wreck because my husband and I were arguing between ourselves' [Day Two: 9]. 'There was terrible friction' [Day Two: 25] over it all.

Indeed, such was Mrs Rutson's concern for Maria that she tells the Inquiry that, during her first interview with Miss Lees and Mrs Kirby, she offered to look after Maria herself – 'I said could I have Maria if I moved away from my present address' [Day Two: 16]. It will be remembered that Mrs Rutson had lived all her life at Maresfield Road. Her husband, son, mother and father all lived there with her still. Even if her offer to look after Maria was made on the spur of the moment, the willingness to contemplate such a major upheaval does suggest less of the 'concerned neighbour' as the report characterises her, and something less disinterested and more personally engaged.

Cross-examined by Mr Hargrove, [Day Two: 10] for the NSPCC, it emerged, within their first exchange, that during the April incident, a wider imbroglio had ensued, in which Mrs Rutson's father had been struck on the head by Mr Kepple; Mrs Rutson's father then died of a heart attack two or three weeks later. There is no suggestion in the evidence that the two events were directly connected, but the matter is omitted entirely from the report. Nor does the report include the fact that, in a further incident between the two families that followed that heart attack, it was not Mr Kepple, but Mrs Rutson's brother-in-law, who was arrested by the police and dealt with by the courts a week later [Day Two: 18].

Indeed, one of the more florid disputes between the Kepples and their neighbours came when Mrs Rutson identified herself as the source of the complaint to the NSPCC about Maria's treatment. In his cross-examination, Mr Hargrove, for the NSPCC, attempted to probe the reason why Mrs Rutson had chosen to reveal herself as the source of the complaint in this way. Her reply, that 'I was doing my duty as a law-abiding citizen by reporting Mrs Kepple to the NSPCC. I had nothing to hide, nothing to be worried about', missed the point which he was attempting to make about the deliberately provocative nature of the disclosure.

Some of the same ambiguities, present in the evidence, but absent in the report itself, can be seen in relation to the petition which, at the same time as the April incident, had been presented to the Whitehawk housing office, setting out complaints about the Kepples and pressing for them to be re-housed elsewhere. In his cross-examination of Mrs Rutson, the NSPCC barrister emphasises the point, to which she agrees, that the petition makes 'no mention in it anywhere of ill-treatment of the children' [Day Two: 12]. Rather, it concentrates entirely on what would, today, be referred to as 'anti-social behaviour'.

What emerges most strikingly, however, is the extent to which the petition was the work of a relatively small group of neighbours and the extent to which the Rutson family were the moving spirits behind it. It contained signatures from nine different properties, fully four of which were occupied either by the Rutsons themselves or their blood relations [Day Seventeen: 35]. Of those neighbours who visited the housing office in order to present the petition in person, the largest group was made up of Mrs Rutson, her mother and her husband. On the following day, Mr Kepple made a counter-complaint against the Rutsons, including an allegation that Mrs Rutson had broken his back door window. When the point was put to her by the barrister acting on behalf of the Brighton Local Authority, she replied simply, 'Yes, I did break his back door window' [Day Two: 21].

At this point, the characterisation that the report makes of Mrs Rutson as 'fair and unbiased' becomes hard to sustain in the undifferentiated way in which it is presented within its pages. Certainly, it casts some new, and more complex and conflictual light on the idea that solid common sense was the property of only one party.

Characteristically, Dianna Lees refused to offer an uncritical endorsement of all that the Rutsons and the other neighbours had had to say. Asked whether she believed that the picture Mrs Rutson had provided was accurate, she responded with the strikingly post-modern observation: 'I believe that she saw it as accurate' [Day Twenty-One: 47]. Her contemporary notes suggested a rather different picture. Her Brighton counterpart, Mr McBurney, made a detailed note of his face-to-face discussion with Miss Lees of the April incident, which took place at his office on 24 April. He concluded that the complaints made by Mrs Rutson were 'not justified on this occasion' [Day Eighteen: 6]. The basis for this conclusion was largely that 'Miss Lees feels that the Kepples' neighbours have not Maria's well being in mind when complaints are made.'

Conclusion

> ... there are few, if any, situations of the kind in which Maria was involved which are "black and white". The harsh lesson which social workers in the child care service have had to learn is that, so far as children in long-term care are concerned, there are very few situations in which choices are clear cut and outcomes predictable. Unhappiness in children is something which the ordinary humane person finds very difficult to bear and, in consequence, of this frequently seeks simple solutions or suggests that they are attainable. (DHSS, 1974a, p 316)

Although referring specifically to the decision to return Maria to the care of her mother in April 1971, these words by Olive Stevenson in her dissenting, minority report, speak to a larger truth. In circumstances such as Maria's, perhaps most of us seek to find explanations as absolute and certain as death itself. The Cooper family, the residents of the Whitehawk Estate and their representatives, the general public in the gallery and those reading their newspapers at home and even the members of a public inquiry, needed to know what had happened to Maria at some very fundamental, visceral, human level. It may have been this that inflamed the angry demands for a public inquiry into Maria Colwell's death. Any attempt to frustrate these demands, or so it appeared, could only be self-seeking or to suggest that there was indeed something to be discovered.

By bringing the 'facts' of Maria's death before the public gaze, however, the practice of those whose job it was to protect Maria were also exposed in a climate of anger and suspicion. As well as located in the inexplicable wickedness of the Kepples (who perhaps were capable of no better), some of the explanation for Maria's death might be found in the failure of the social workers responsible for Maria to carry out their duties properly. These duties might be poorly understood outside of the profession, despite Seebohm's populist vision for the 'fifth social service' but, judged by the standards of common sense, a common sense with the Olympian advantage of hindsight, there were those prepared to say that this was indeed the case. Here might be somewhere to fix the blame and so provide an explanation for what happened to Maria in understandable terms. Someone had let this tragedy happen.

We turn now to look in more detail at the practice of those social workers on whom so much blame was placed.

FIVE

Social work on trial

The Colwell Inquiry had established early on that it was prepared to criticise 'the contemporary standard' of social work practice where it offended against 'ordinary standards of social or moral concern' or went 'against accepted tenets of commonsense' (DHSS, 1974a, p 45) (see p 115). Far from being an established profession that might have regarded any such criticism as an affront, on principle, we have argued in Chapter Three that social work, neither in function nor administrative form, was in any sense established within the contemporary welfare state of the early 1970s. Nonetheless, within social services departments, despite the bureaucratic frustrations and ever-increasing demands, there was at least a sense of forward momentum. Those who expressed some regret 'that something had been lost' (see p 63) in the post-Seebohm world appeared in the minority, as the discussion had turned decisively to focus on what social work could and should be in the future, both as an occupation and as an institutionalised form of welfare practice.

Those discussions were very largely taking place, however, within the narrow confines of the town hall, the profession and its trade press. Neither the popular press nor the wider public had taken very much notice of the rushed legislation at the end of the most recent Parliament, and other than in relation to the advertising of changes to local services, the implementation of the Local Authority Social Services Act 1970 may have appeared to be very little more than an administrative reform, even as the name suggests. Outside the new social services departments, others may have retained a much older conception of what social work was and what it should be than even Eileen Younghusband had described, let alone Frederic Seebohm. The Colwell Inquiry would provide an opportunity for a much wider audience to see and to judge 'the contemporary standard of practice' in the light not only of their own 'common sense' but also in the light of their own experiences, many of which would have been formed, as we have suggested, in the pre-welfare state Britain of less than 25 years previously. For others, of course, that pre-1948 experience offered a prelapsarian prospect, not back to the past but onto the future and new designs for the provision of services for those who seemed unwilling or unable to look after themselves.

In this chapter we look in detail at how the practice of social work was judged during the Colwell Inquiry and focus particularly on the tensions that existed between competing understandings of its nature and purpose. First, we establish the local context for the reorganisation of services that had followed from the implementation of the Local Authority Social Services Act 1970.

East Sussex Social Services Department, 1973

In Chapter Three we explored the wider debates that had led to the passage of the Local Authority Social Services Act 1970, and the policy and practice ambitions that it embodied. In Chapter One we also noted how variable the Act's implementation seemed to be as its provisions were mediated by particular local social and political circumstances. The most informative account of the way in which social services organisation, and reorganisation, had impacted on the work of the East Sussex Social Services Department was provided to the Inquiry by Denis Allen, its director of social services. He had been the director since it was created, in shadow form, in October 1970, and was, in 1973, president of the Association of Directors of Social Services (ADSS). Mr Allen spent a great deal of time listening to the evidence provided by others to the Inquiry before taking the witness stand himself, late in proceedings. For much of his evidence, he drew on an internal document, prepared for the Social Services Committee of East Sussex Council, *The social services department – The effects of re-organisation*. It noted that the Seebohm Social Sevices Department, which came fully into being on 1 April 1971, was the result of the merger of four existing departments, but that this was only the culmination of a process which, just over two years previously, had begun with 10 separate departments.

As far as childcare social work was concerned, the legacy departments had carried a heavy and increasing workload, but had been able, predominantly, to allocate that work to qualified childcare staff, over 80 per cent of whom held professional certificates of one sort or another. The effect of reorganisation, and the need to distribute qualified staff across a wider range of activities, meant, Mr Allen told the Inquiry, that on establishment, the social services department had the proportion of qualified staff immediately reduced to 45 per cent [Day Thirty-Three: 6]. At the same time, the department was provided with a new mission which, drawing directly on the language of the Seebohm Report, the director described as, 'embodying a wider conception of social service, directed to the well-being of the whole of the community, and not only of social casualties' [Day Thirty-Three:

7]. Unsurprisingly, as elsewhere, the new universalist approach, and the publicity that attended the creation of the new departments, produced an increased public expectation of the service on offer, which in turn led to a rapid upsurge in referrals to the department. East Sussex's own figures demonstrated, for example, an increase in case referrals of 12 per cent in the first six months of 1973, as compared to the same period in 1972 [Day Thirty-Three: 10]. In this south coast county, the increased demand came primarily from older people, with 60 per cent of all referrals and 80 per cent of all active cases being drawn from that category [Day Thirty-Three: 8].

Against this background, responsibility for the approximately 1,000 children in care in the new East Sussex area fell to social workers with rapidly increasing caseloads, and those with qualifications and experience tended to be allocated those cases which were likely to be the most difficult and demanding. Questioned about priority setting and decision making about the time to be invested in particular cases, the director suggested that, in the circumstances he had outlined, 'such judgements had to be made by individual workers as to which cases, at any one time, were their priorities' [Day Thirty-Three: 6/7], rather than being the subject of county-wide standards. However, this must not be taken as suggesting that East Sussex was anything other than a well-regarded social services department. Not only was Mr Allen the current president of the ADSS but also Joan Cooper, a recent colleague of Olive Stevenson at Oxford and now a senior civil servant, had recently worked there.

This was the immediate and local background against which the two social workers most directly concerned with Maria's care operated. Daphne Kirby of the NSPCC and Diana Lees of East Sussex Social Services Department were the literal embodiments of the social work practised in the Colwell case. The fine details of their practice were to be forensically examined by the Inquiry and the greater part of this chapter follows the account that the Inquiry heard, but first, we wish to describe something of these two central figures' background and the impression that each of them made during the process of the Inquiry as these have a direct bearing, we believe, on the judgements that later came to be made of them and their work. It is important that we develop a sense of them not only as representatives of sharply differing conceptions of social work, but also as individuals.

The social workers

Mrs Kirby

Mrs Daphne Josephine Kirby had worked for the NSPCC since January 1965. Having completed its 12-month training course, she was appointed to Brighton on 1 January 1966, as a woman visitor [Day Eleven: 25], moving with all other women visitors to the rank of inspector in 1972. During 1972, the year in which her direct involvement with Maria took place (although she had come across the Kepples previously; see p 121), she worked with 50 new cases and held an average number of 51 cases open at any one time. Over the 12 months of 1972, she had made 681 home visits and 373 other visits to children and families on her caseload. She also made 71 agency visits and held 15 interviews in her office, which was located in her home [Day Eleven: 26]. When it was put to her, that with such a workload, 'it is not really possible or practicable for you to do very much in the way of "supportive" work', Mrs Kirby denied the proposition emphatically: 'It certainly is. I do a great deal of "supportive" work' [Day Twelve: 23].

There can be little doubt, from reading the report of the Inquiry, and from the contemporary media accounts, that Mrs Kirby made a more favourable impression than that conveyed by Miss Lees. She was, as the counsel to the Inquiry noted approvingly, 'by some extent the older woman of the two' [Day Eleven: 32]. She also appeared to practise social work in ways that came closer to at least two members of the Committee's conception of how it should be practised. To begin with, she spent a good deal of time 'on the patch', with ample opportunities for informal as well as formal observation of families known to her professionally. Her underlying attitude to social work was evident in the defence she made of working from home [Day Twelve: 25]:

> I do not work office hours; I work whenever I am at home, and my telephone rings whether it is early morning, evening or weekend....When my families want to see me they just come to my home irrespective of the time of day or the actual day.

Mrs Kirby's mother lived very close to Maresfield Road [Day Eleven: 54] and, for that reason, as well as for work, she passed almost daily through the area. From the April 1972 incident to mid-August, for example, she estimated that she 'saw all the children frequently – three or four times a week, in fact. This included Saturday and Sunday' [Day

Eleven: 44]. These sightings varied between simply waving to the children as they played in the street or stopping to talk to them. At less regular intervals, she also called at the Kepple home, being 'invited to return at any time' [Day Eleven: 46] and, indeed, being waved down by Mrs Kepple as she drove down Maresfield Road in order to go into the house to view a new item of furniture.

A second reason why Mrs Kirby's *modus operandi* appealed to the Committee was her emphasis on practical help. She called with shoes and clothes. She stopped her car to hand out sweets to Maria and her brothers and sisters. She provided lifts to appointments. On learning that Mrs Kepple was pregnant again, she offered her a cot. Mrs Kirby was and did what the Inquiry thought social workers ought to do and be – a locally based figure of some authority, keeping a close eye on what went on inside a family, while helping out in tangible ways which improved conditions for the children. Her focus was on what the chair described as 'practical work on the ground' [Day Twelve: 24].

In both dimensions, Mrs Kirby's practice came closest to matching what had been one of the most radical aspects of the Seebohm Inquiry's conclusions – its emphasis on the *community* dimension of social work (see p 64). In its own final report the Colwell Inquiry, too, devoted a short section to 'Social workers and the local community' (DHSS, 1974a, pp 199-208), calling for new investment in the 'time-consuming process' of building up trust between social workers and the communities within which they operated. However, the rather abbreviated account of the potential for community work provided by the Inquiry report acknowledged that such work was likely to be accorded a 'low priority' (DHSS, 1974a, p 207) by 'the average caseworker in a social services Department' until such time as 'crisis pressures diminish and resources increase'. They never did, of course, and, as we noted earlier, in the minds of some later commentators, the failure of community social work to develop was 'one of the great failings of social services departments' (Holman, 2005, p 23).

Yet, even here, there was some ambivalence in the report's overall conclusion. Below the surface of the text, and closer to the surface in the oral evidence, was a far darker and more fundamental critique of the contemporary welfare state. Cumulatively, the Inquiry learned how adept Mrs Kepple had been at obtaining practical help from almost every source. The arrival of yet another child was, in many ways, it appeared, the sign for welfare agencies to rally round with a further supply of cots (from the health visitor), baby clothing (from the NSPCC), rubber sheets (from the social services department) and blankets (from the WRVS), in order for the state to assume responsibility for what, in Sir Keith Joseph's terms at least, was a self-inflicted calamity in a family where resources were already stretched well beyond reason. And, while all this was going on Mr Kepple continued, at irregular intervals, to go on working under different names while continuing to claim state benefits. Much of this was to surface in the Inquiry's ultimately fruitless attempts to classify the Kepples as a 'problem family', discussed later. It also provided a subtextual commentary on the surface appreciation that the Inquiry expressed of Mrs Kirby's efforts. While she may have tried to help, there is an implication that for families such as the Kepples, such help merely sustained what was, in fact, a hopeless situation.

Miss Lees

Miss Diana Lees began, as did all witnesses, by confirming her (substantial) credentials. A graduate of the University of St Andrews, where she had also taken a post-graduate degree in Social Administration, her specific social work qualification came from a further one-year course at the University of Southampton. Her first job, for two-and-a-half years, had been as a medical social worker at the Radcliffe Infirmary at Oxford. Her basic approach to social work, she said, was one of 'sympathy tempered by objectivity' [Day Twenty-One: 7].

Miss Lees moved to work in East Sussex on 1 April 1970 where the Colwell and Cooper families had been one of the first 12 cases carefully transferred to her [Day Twenty: 17/18]. Her caseload rose rapidly. When a county-wide census was taken mid-way through 1972 she was recorded as having 57 active cases, compared to an average of 59 for members of the Hove Office and 51 across the county as a whole [Day Thirty: 61]. In the months leading up to Maria's death her caseload averaged around 70, of which 50 related to children. Of those 50 cases, some 35-40 were long-term cases, and included six identified as children at physical risk. Of those six, two were relatively quiet, two active and two new cases, both of which were, in Miss Lees' words, 'very active' [Day Twenty: 19]. Maria Colwell was not one of the six. When Miss Joan Court, DHSS social work adviser on child abuse, was asked about the effect of caseloads of this magnitude, she replied: 'If she truly had four battered babies, and two potential battered baby cases, plus a caseload of 64, I would have thought it was inhumanly possible to give the amount of time and devotion to each case as I am sure she would have liked to have done' [Day Thirty: 16]. Miss Simpson, the department's assistant director, described it as 'a workload which will inevitably keep the social workers at very full stretch and will leave them inadequate time to do all the things they would like to in relation to their ongoing cases and respond appropriately to crises' [Day Thirty: 61].

When Miss Lees took the witness stand during the 20th day of the Inquiry's hearings, the Committee had already heard extensively from the NSPCC and from Brighton Social Services Department. This was the first time on which evidence was to be taken directly from anyone from the East Sussex Social Services Department and, at four days of solo evidence giving, was to represent the longest any witness appeared before the tribunal. In contradistinction to Mrs Kirby, the impression that is left by reading the Inquiry report and, especially, the four days of Miss Lees' oral evidence, is of someone mistrusted because of her youth and because of her qualifications.

On the surface the Inquiry pays due regard to her 'impressive' credentials. Just beneath the surface, however, lurk suggestions that (a) such qualifications were unnecessary for the job of a social worker; (b) that they were no substitute for 'common sense'; (c) that they probably undermined whatever common sense a person as young as Miss Lees might be expected to have acquired; and (d) that, whatever else might be said about them, they manifestly had not worked in providing a proper level of care and oversight in the case of Maria Colwell. These themes are explored more fully below, but in relation to Miss Lees, personally, such impressions were compounded by the unbending nature of her testimony as a witness (see p 114). In settings where the allocation of blame was an explicit part of proceedings, she resolutely refused to accept that the conduct of the case, in which she had been the principal protagonist, was flawed in any of its fundamentals. In the immediate aftermath of the arrest of Mr Kepple, and his being charged with Maria's murder, she gave the first of what were to be many statements, this time to the police. It was brief, to the point, and made no concessions whatsoever to any suggestion that responsibility for what had taken place might be laid at her door [NA: DPP 2/5197/1]. In the final dénouement of the Inquiry process, when its report was finally made public in September 1974, she appeared at a deeply hostile press conference, her self-possession and belief in the essential rightness of what had been done unshaken by the criticisms of her that it contained.

Between these two outer limits of the Inquiry process she remained a figure of uncompromising composure, as we have noted. While her steadiness under fire earned her some grudging approval, the impression which the Committee as a whole formed was of someone whose willingness to defend her practice of social work amounted to a lack of respect for other professions and a culpable readiness to operate from some highly contentious assumptions. The general problem, the counsel to the Inquiry suggested, was one of social workers (and, by implication, social work as a profession) becoming 'too self-confident' [Day Nineteen: 22], perhaps like Miss Lees herself.

Social work on trial

The charges laid against the social workers involved in the Maria Colwell case fall into four broad categories: simple incompetence in carrying out their duties properly; the flawed nature of some of their fundamental assumptions about children and families; failures in the exercise of professional judgement; and a lack of awareness of the proper boundaries of social work. Taken together, these charges also constituted a powerful critique of social work itself. We now examine each of them in turn.

Incompetence

The first, and in some ways the most straightforward accusation levelled at social workers in the majority report was one of incompetence: they had failed to discharge their duty adequately, even where that duty was plain and undeniable and defined in its own terms. Thus, for example, much is made of Miss Lees' failure to provide Brighton with the promised six-monthly case summaries. The majority report concluded that this was a failure which, had it been rectified, would have undoubtedly led to more focused attention on the progress being made in the case. In particular, the report argues, the obligation to provide a six-monthly report, if honoured, would have addressed Miss Lees' failure to carry out an 'effective' visit between 1 June and 1 December 1972. The report describes this as 'a complete failure to supervise over this period for which Miss Lees' seniors must share her responsibility' (DHSS, 1974a, p 107). In instances such as this, where there was a conflict between the available written evidence and personal recollection, the majority report generally takes the harsher of interpretations available to it. Miss Lees' records did indeed show only two visits to Maria from her relocation to Maresfield Road, on 20 October 1971 and the end of February 1972. However, in her oral evidence, Miss Lees was adamant that she had made 'several' visits during this period. While 'not prepared to reject Miss Lees' oral evidence on this point, since there is a pattern of inadequate recording of certain events in her case notes', the report concludes that, 'there is not enough evidence to satisfy us that Maria's general wellbeing was being watched by East Sussex with sufficient care' (DHSS, 1974a, p 76). Although agreeing that Maria had not been adequately supervised (DHSS, 1974a, p 333), Olive Stevenson, in her separate minority report, was compelled to remark that the analysis that the Inquiry had conducted 'would not have been possible had it not been for the full records made available to us' (DHSS, 1974a, p 312).

In developing this general theme of social work incompetence, the majority report includes a number of examples where it applies a selectivity that Olive Stevenson repeatedly felt obliged directly to correct. Almost the final word which the majority report provides about the Coopers, for example, comes at the point where Hove Juvenile Court revoked Maria's Care Order thus, effectively, sealing the decision to move her to Maresfield Road. The whole issue of representation at such hearings was one that was to preoccupy policy makers in the aftermath of the Inquiry (see Chapter Six, this volume). The report makes the factual point that the Coopers were not told the date of the hearing, had no right to be so notified and that they were therefore not present during proceedings to articulate their point of view. The report also suggests that, 'they were not told the result', before concluding that, 'we think the Coopers should have been kept in the picture and that there was at this time a lack of tact, sympathy and help which we had indicated might reasonably be expected in such cases' (DHSS, 1974a, p 68).

However, as early as the second day of the Inquiry hearing, Mr Mildon, the Inquiry's own QC, in his lengthy opening statement, had gone out of his way to emphasise that, 'immediately following Maria's return to Mrs Kepple, Miss Lees kept in very close touch with Mrs Cooper', providing her with regular reports of Maria's progress [Day Two: 13]. In her minority report Olive Stevenson takes up the same issue. She makes a point of noting Miss Lees' attention to the Coopers, early in her contact with them, visiting 'much more often than the *Boarding Out Regulations* required' (DHSS, 1974a, p 276). The Coopers, she concluded, 'are entitled to respect and sympathy as human beings, not as saints' (DHSS, 1974a, p 316). In relation to the aftermath of the court hearing, Olive Stevenson points out that Miss Lees had been sure, in her evidence, that the Coopers had been told the outcome. The Coopers had been equally adamant that they had not – but only one of these perspectives was quoted in the majority report. Nor had that report included any reference to the letter that Miss Lees had immediately sent to the Coopers, arranging to visit them. Nor did the report mention the three attempts that Diana Lees had then made to find the Coopers at home, nor the fact that she continued to visit them for many months after Maria had been moved to Maresfield Road (DHSS, 1974a, p 310).

The general theme of incompetence is one that encompasses more than matters of professional practice, it must be acknowledged. The seemingly unending catalogue of missed messages, lost documents, conflicting accounts, ambiguous recordings and competing recollections is one which runs right through the report, and implicates all agencies. Yet, a different standard appears to be applied when assessing the performance of social workers. One example must suffice to illustrate this general conclusion.

In September 1972, Maria moved from Whitehawk Infants to Whitehawk Junior School. Both schools occupy a single continuous site and Miss Lees was judged to have failed in the exercise of her duty when she did not realise that they were, nonetheless, two separate schools. She was not alone in doing so, because Mrs Kepple shared the same misapprehension. Because Miss Lees failed to understand that the Whitehawk Juniors was a different school, she did not make fresh contact with school staff at the start of the autumn term, a failure for which she is specifically criticised in the majority report. Yet, the school's own record card for Maria, passed from Infants to Juniors, made no reference to the involvement of social services, despite the contact which Miss Lees had made with the head of the Infants school, and Maria's class teacher. For the majority report, at least, the responsibility was one-sided, and it was the social worker who was at fault.

In her dissenting chapter, Olive Stevenson notes rather sharply in relation to the myriad examples of poor communication, that she was:

> ... perturbed by the implicit assumption on the part of some of those who gave evidence to us that the responsibility for efficient communication lay solely with the social workers rather than with all the official persons concerned with Maria's welfare. (DHSS, 1974a, p 332)

In her letter to the Secretary of State explaining her dissent from the majority report, Olive Stevenson notes even more directly (DHSS, 1974a, p 8):

> The social workers who bore the ultimate responsibility for Maria's care and supervision had a right to receive information from their colleagues in other disciplines as well as a duty to convey it. Neither can such responsibility rest only with professionals and officials. Of the many

residents of Brighton who came forward at the inquiry, very few had voiced their anxieties to the appropriate persons at the material times. It is most disturbing to contemplate the amount of anxiety about Maria which never reached Miss Lees.

In locating the several failures in practice that emerged before the Inquiry, it is not simply that social workers made mistakes; many others made mistakes too, not least in communicating their various concerns to each other. However, it is clear that in the view of the majority report, the burden of responsibility for *any* mistake rested with the social workers. In its conclusions, while accepting that it would be 'quite impossible, and indeed, unfair, to lay the direct blame for ... inadequacies in the care and supervision of Maria upon any individual or indeed any small group of individuals' (DHSS, 1974a, p 241), the majority report has no difficulty in placing the social workers at the top of their 'hierarchy of censure' (DHSS, 1974a, p 334). Olive Stevenson, in declaring her sympathy for Miss Lees, also expressed her undoubted ambivalence to the role played by the 'neighbours' and other professionals involved in Maria's care. As we have noted, in this, Olive Stevenson was indeed squarely in the minority.

Fundamental assumptions

Even if all the practical and professional responsibilities had been impeccably discharged, however, as Olive Stevenson notes, the view of the majority report was that 'painstaking work is of no avail if its fundamental assumptions are mistaken' (DHSS, 1974a, p 313). First among those assumptions to be questioned by the Inquiry were those made concerning the proper place of children in families who were deemed unfit to look after them.

The blood tie

One of the key assumptions that the Inquiry sought to challenge was that the social workers, Miss Lees in particular, had over-valued the claims of birth parents as against those of foster or other substitute carers. In the language of the times, this was the 'blood tie' argument around which the decision to return Maria to her mother's care, and to keep her there, was said to have revolved. Throughout the 1960s there had been considerable public debate in the media that had focused on so-called 'tug-of-love' cases. Such cases typically involved the competing claims of 'natural' and (usually) long-term foster parents (see Howells, 1974, pp 17ff) over the care and, crucially, the placement of a child. To some degree, this reflected a larger debate on adoption, the law on which had lain largely unattended since the Adoption Act 1958. Despite Hendrick's view, that 'most of the amendments to adoption law' in the 1950s had 'favoured the adopters' (2003, p 156), the law was generally regarded as unsatisfactory and public sympathy was increasingly aligned with substitute carers. This was reflected in the newspaper campaigns that emerged, which argued for a change in the law to make the interests of substitute carers, including foster parents, more secure. The framing of the Colwell story as part of the 'blood-tie' and 'tug-of-love' narrative continued throughout the period, in both national and local coverage (see, for example, *Daily Express*, 17 April 1973; *Argus*, 2 May 1975). Accordingly, under pressure, from among others, Leo Abse, who 'vigorously lobbied Home Secretary Callaghan and his wife', promising Callaghan that he would go down in history as 'the man who had revolutionized Britain's Child Law' (Abse, 1973, pp 243-7), the Department Committee on the Adoption of Children (the Houghton Committee) had been established in 1969. The Committee was appointed to 'consider law, policy and procedures on the adoption of children and what changes are desirable' (Houghton, 1972, p 1). It noted early, however, that, 'at the time of our appointment concern had been expressed about a number of children who had been reclaimed by their natural parents after many years in foster homes' (Houghton, 1972, p 139). Members of the Committee regarded the making of 'recommendations about the position of long term foster parents who wish to keep a child permanently, by adoption or otherwise, against the will of the natural parent' (Houghton, 1972, p 1) as one of their key purposes. The Colwell Inquiry report consciously picked up this debate, using the term 'tug-of-war' (DHSS, 1974a, p 60) to describe the position between Maria's natural mother, Mrs Colwell, and her long-term foster carers, the Coopers. It drew attention to the way in which social workers acted in such circumstances. It had become, as civil servants were to advise the then Minister, Sir Keith Joseph, the issue which 'attracted most public concern' [NA: MH 152/198].

The charge against the profession was articulated very clearly by Dr Alfred White Franklin, an expert witness closely associated with the Tunbridge Wells Study Group. This was a self-appointed, *ad hoc* group, established to highlight the existence of child abuse and to encourage interprofessional cooperation in dealing with it. The Study Group consisted of leading paediatricians, psychiatrists, social workers, health visitors and the police, and was chaired by the prominent paediatrician,

Dr White Franklin. The Study Group had taken a particular interest in the work of the Children's Division of the American Humane Association, and in particular the work that was sponsored by Dr Henry Kempe. In 1961 Kempe and his colleagues had published the results of their research into the growing frequency with which children were turning up on radiographers' records with sub-dural haematomas (a swelling of the tissue around the brain, often caused by violent shaking of an infant by an adult) and long bone fractures that could not be attributed to any known disease. Kempe and his colleagues subsequently accounted for these injuries as being the result of physical abuse, the 'battered baby syndrome'. By describing it as a 'syndrome' ('a group of concurrent symptoms of a disease', *Oxford English Dictionary*), child abuse was identified as an aspect of personal pathology in the manner of other medical conditions.

Kempe's ideas had been imported into Britain through the founding, in 1968, of the NSPCC's Battered Child Research Unit, which was set up as a direct result of contact between the then director of the NSPCC and Dr Kempe. Sir Keith Joseph had specifically linked the work of the NSPCC Research Unit, the Study Group and the work of Henry Kempe in a speech he made on the day the Colwell Inquiry opened and which was reported in *The Sunday Times* on 11 November. Just how much of Sir Keith Joseph's understanding of intergenerational transmission of deprivation had been based on the pathological model of abuse that was of such interest to the Study Group cannot be determined precisely but, as Dr White Franklin was later to say, 'While the timing of Maria Colwell and Tunbridge Wells was coincidental the combination was explosive' (Parton, 1985, p 77).

Dr Franklin's conclusion was that the only explanation which made sense of social workers' failure to remove Maria from Maresfield Road, at successive opportunities from April 1972 onward, was 'their belief that the mother had an absolute right to possession of her child regardless of anything which happened' [Day Twenty-Six: 18], that is, that blood ties rather than affection were paramount and outweighed any other consideration, including the degree of emotional distress suffered by Maria.

The Inquiry report focused on the 'blood tie' question at several points in Maria's history. The first of these was occasioned by the case conference that took place on 26 April 1971. This had been convened to agree a response to Mrs Kepple's increasing threats to return to court to challenge the local authority's Care Order. The meeting was attended by Miss Lees, her senior social worker, Mr Bennett, and the assistant director for children's services, Miss Simpson. It marked the point,

Miss Simpson told the Inquiry, at which the 'academic' problem of the longstanding feud over Maria's future had finally become 'a practical one' [Day Thirty: 53]. The meeting took the fundamental decision that, 'it would be better for Maria in the long term to be returned to her mother....The conclusion we came to was that we should try to work towards this' [Day Twenty: 26].

For the Inquiry, the fundamental question was how far the April decision, and the actions which flowed from it, were predicated on a belief in Mrs Kepple's overriding claims to a blood tie with Maria. The position taken by Miss Lees, and that of other social workers from the department, was that the blood tie was an important but not a determining factor in their thinking. It represented a re-levelling of the playing field, against previously prevailing orthodoxies that had placed little store by the rights of birth parents, or the needs of children to be aware of their own histories. In the view of the Inquiry, the playing field appeared not so much to have been levelled as tipped in the opposite direction, with the slope now running towards the family of origin, or 'natural' family, and against, for example, foster care of the sort provided by the Coopers. An exchange that illustrates this difference took place on Day Twenty [10] of the Inquiry, when Mr Mildon attempted to sum up Miss Lees' position in this way:

> Your training and experience had convinced you that where
> a mother had established her fitness to have her child it was
> in the child's best interests that she should be returned to
> her mother.

Miss Lees replied 'I would not say that unconditionally like that.'

The debate here, therefore, was a very basic one, about how children should be cared for when their own family care breaks down. Put most simply, for those who located responsibility for such breakdown within the family, then 'rescue' into substitute care provided children with the best chance of escaping their inheritance. For those who regarded family breakdown as shaped by wider social forces, then preventative work, and services to shore up struggling families were preferable. The 'blood tie' represented a shorthand way of evoking this debate. It was used as a means of throwing onto the defensive the sort of social work practice that owes its origins to the Act of 1963, Ingleby and even earlier, but that had really begun to take root in the Seebohm social services departments.

Mr Mildon, in cross-examining Mrs Kirby, put the case which most closely reflected an intergenerational transmission perspective when he suggested that 'the only really safe course where you have young children in a problem family is to put those children in care, is it not?' [Day Twelve: 38]. Mrs Kirby rather hesitantly agrees. However, she confirmed, far more readily, Mr Mildon's second-best solution. He conceded that, 'where inadequate natural parents want their children, you cannot take them away simply because they are less adequate than you would like them to be'. The result was, he suggested, that 'current thinking is that an inadequate home life may be preferable for a child than an institutional life'.

That conclusion was not only endorsed by Mrs Kirby. It was set out in more detail, and as a policy of first choice by the director of East Sussex Social Services Department, Mr Allen. Reminding the Inquiry that his authority had 1,000 looked-after children, he argued that the only way to provide for the 500 children in foster care, and the further 500 accommodated in a variety of specialised community homes, was to develop 'preventative services to stem the flow of crisis work' [Day Thirty-Three: 8]. Dealing with an issue at the heart of the Inquiry, he provided direct support for the general approach taken by the social workers of his department, rejecting the 'rescue' model of child protection:

> Perhaps I should explain that whereas some 20 or so years ago it was generally thought that children could be helped by being removed from what were considered to be "bad homes" and prepared for adult life by being brought up in some other environment, and the evidence of research and the experience of the intervening years have shown that this is not generally true.

The corollary of this approach was that social work should aim, as much as possible, to keep families together [Day Thirty-Three: 6]. This conclusion was echoed, for a different reason, by Miss Simpson, Mr Allen's assistant director for childcare, when she, too was questioned about the influence of the 'blood tie' in the decision to return Maria to her mother. Her response was to emphasise not biology, but social responsibility. Parents, she said, should carry the 'expectation that they can and should care for their own children unless it is proved that they are incapable or unsuitable to do so' [Day Thirty-One: 13]. There should be no easy evasion of that responsibility. A sensible system would look for ways of returning responsibilities to the Kepples, once they were capable of being assumed, not relieving them of such obligations.

It was this general approach that, social workers attempted to argue, had been put into practice in the Colwell case. The fundamental choice that, in their view, faced them was not one between blood ties on the one hand, and the ties of affection on the other. The choice was of a return, either on the basis of some agreement and continuing ability to safeguard Maria's welfare, or a return with the already fragile relations with the Kepples broken beyond repair and with possibly fewer grounds or opportunities to work with the family in Maria's interests in the future. In either case, return was inevitable. Mrs Colwell's interest in Maria may have been sporadic, but when aroused, it had always been vehement and almost always accompanied by recourse to legal advice. Since her move to Maresfield Road her physical circumstances had improved considerably, and, under her care, the Kepple children were 'thriving' [Day Twenty-Two: 2]. The chances of a Care Order being overturned, social workers argued, had been judged practically and pragmatically, not ideologically.

For Miss Lees, however, this was, at times, a fine line to tread. Her records and her oral evidence contained assertions that could be portrayed, at least, as pointing in the other direction. She told the Inquiry that: 'I have said before, that a child has certain feelings about the natural family that are unique' [Day Twenty-One: 41]. On Day Six, Mrs Locke, Maria's class teacher during the period when her transfer to Maresfield Road was being completed, reported a disagreement with Miss Lees about the policy, when the social worker was said to have been 'adamant' that the child should be returned to her 'rightful mother' [Day Six: 26]. Much later in Maria's story, during the gathering storm of December 1972, the head of Brighton's Education Welfare Service, Mrs Tattam, became involved, and contacted Miss Lees. She, too, questioned the strategy of leaving Maria with the Kepples. Her notes of the conversation recalled a sharp interchange, in which the social worker insisted that the placement at home 'had to be made to work', to which Mrs Tattam had replied, 'Well, at whose expense, the child's?' [Day Five: 33].

When it came to completing the final report, Olive Stevenson summed up the official position accurately, in this way (DHSS, 1974a, p 315):

> ... [if the 'blood tie'] means an emotional relationship, which in some way takes precedence over others, exists simply because of consanguinity, then this is not generally accepted by social workers and was explicitly rejected by the East Sussex social workers at the hearing.

Too much ambiguity remained, however, to convince others that this told the whole story. Mr Mildon, the Inquiry's counsel, for example, told Miss Lees that he regarded her failure to remove Maria from Maresfield Road, despite evidence of harm to her there, as [Day Twenty-One: 54]:

> ... virtually inevitable having regard to current thinking that children should not be removed from the care of the natural parents, unless there is clear evidence that they will suffer serious harm if they are not.

Throughout Miss Lees' evidence, newspaper reports focused on the same issue. The *Daily Mail* (6 November 1973) for example, headlined its account of her cross-examination, 'How Maria was torn between two families'. *The Guardian* (8 November 1973) suggested that the 'tragedy of Maria' had been caused by the 'code' that social workers had followed in relation to the rights of natural parents.

The 'problem family'

If the fundamental assumption about the proper place to bring up a child when there were evident failures on the part of the birth parents to do so proved difficult to resolve, the degree to which the Kepples were to be understood as a 'problem family' was also difficult to fix accurately. Even if it could be accepted that there was a reasonable case to be made for returning a child to the care of her mother, what possible case could be made for returning this particular child to the Kepples? Not only did this seem to fly in the face of common sense (as we have seen), surely this family was self-evidently wholly unsuitable to have the care of Maria? Were not the Kepples a lifelong 'problem family', of precisely the sort that so troubled Sir Keith Joseph? The judgement that might be made on the clear intentions of the social workers to return Maria to the care of her mother and to seek to support her placement at Maresfield Road would depend significantly on the answer to these questions.

From the outset therefore, and throughout its 41 days of oral hearings, the Inquiry pursued the issue of whether or not the Kepples could best be understood as a 'problem family', and it was to prove a frustrating line of investigation. At times, the exasperation of the Inquiry's counsel, Mr Mildon, showed through. Failing to persuade the family's GP, Dr Barley, that the Kepples were a 'problem family', he concluded that [Day Twenty-Six: 30]:

From what we know of the family, it is incredible that
anybody could say it was not a problem family.

And yet they did.

Macnicol (1999, p 86) discusses the characteristics that the postwar
Eugenic Society 'Problem Families Committee' had set out as 'at the
heart of a problem family's condition'. These were said to include
'mental backwardness' and 'temperamental instability' of the parents,
compounded by three other features. The first of these was 'intractable
ineducability'. The second characteristic was 'a squalid home wherein
dirt and chaos reign. The third was the birth of numerous "unwanted
children" as well as "high wastage rates" (miscarriages and still-births)'.
It was not difficult to marshal striking evidence, in all these categories,
in Mrs Kepple's past.

In the immediate aftermath of Raymond Colwell's death, in 1965,
Mr Bampflyte, a childcare social worker to whom she was already
well known, monitored Mrs Colwell's circumstances. By this time,
three of Mrs Colwell's six children were already in different forms
of substitute care. Maria, and two others, remained with her. His case
notes summarised what he found [Day Twenty-Six: 6]:

> Rumours were rife about Mrs Colwell's behaviour and there
> were visible signs of neglect in the house and of the children.
> Windows were often broken and the front door was not
> secure. Furniture was broken up for firewood and there were
> no bulbs in the light sockets. At times the children appeared
> inadequately dressed and were always dirty. The electricity
> meter was broken into and no attempt was made to pay
> the rent. The children stopped going to school altogether.
> Mrs Colwell made no effort to help herself and did not
> use any of the constructive help offered by myself or other
> social workers.

If by 'intractable ineducability' problem family discourse suggested an
unwillingness, or inability, to learn from experience, then Mrs Colwell
soon provided further evidence that appeared to corroborate such
analysis.

In 1968, with all of Pauline's children now in care, a weary social
worker had summed up the position in this way [Day Twenty-Six: 7]:

> Since the time that Mrs Colwell's five oldest children have
> been in care, she herself has been leading a somewhat

nomadic life, with about 15 or 20 addresses over a period of two years. She has been to the office intermittently, but seldom at the time that appointments have been arranged. She has often expressed concern for the children but her behaviour has never substantiated this, for instance, she seldom remembers their birthdays.... For nearly two years she has been associated with Mr Kepple (alias Murphy, alias a few other names) who is an Irishman with quite a wild reputation. At times they have been living together and have been thrown out of a number of flats and rooms. At other times, Mr Kepple has been working in Manchester or other distant parts and has only visited on occasions.

A nomadic existence, heavy and recurrent debt, complaints of children being left outside public houses while their parents went drinking for long hours, a deepening feud between Mrs Colwell and the Coopers, and a further pregnancy were among the recurring themes of social work records over the following year. Mr Bampflyte made a home visit in July 1969. He recorded what he found in this way [Day Twenty-Six: 8]:

Called with Mrs Colwell and found her living in atrociously sub-standard accommodation. The basement of the house is condemned as being unfit for human habitation, and the smell from it permeates the house. Half of Mrs Colwell's kitchen ceiling has no plaster on it and water drips through from the bathroom above.

Only a fraction of this information was to find its way into the Inquiry report. Without it, the emphasis that social workers were to place on the improvement in Mrs Kepple's material and emotional circumstances is far more difficult to understand. It was reflected, however, in much of what was said by other workers with whom the family came into contact during their time at Maresfield Road.

For example, George Smith, Area Housing Officer in charge of Whitehawk Area Office between May 1970 and May 1973, the whole period in which the Kepples lived at Maresfield Road, was questioned closely on this point. 'You were not aware of any problems regarding the family at that time?' he was asked, to which he replied emphatically: 'no not at all' [Day Eleven: 2]. The point was then put to him again in this exchange [Day Eleven: 14]:

Q: Were the Kepples regarded as a 'problem family' when they first came as tenants?

A: No, they were not....

Q: Did there come a time when they were so regarded?

A: No. The situation had not developed where we could regard them as such....

Q: If anybody had contacted you at any stage up to the date of this tragedy and asked you about the Kepples, you would not have said that it was a 'problem family'?

A: No Sir.

Nor were housing officers alone in this conclusion. Dr Barley, the family GP with more than 3,000 patients on his books, about a quarter of them children, replied in the same way, emphasising that he 'would not have thought this was a problem family' [Day Fourteen: 57].

Mrs Kirby, of the NSPCC, questioned by Treasury counsel, took the same line [Day Twelve: 38]:

Q: When you were called to the scene, in April 1972, you knew that this was a problem family, did you not?

A: I do not think at that time I would have called it a problem family.

In addition to the evidence of much improved physical conditions, Mrs Kirby pointed to Mrs Kepple's record in relation to her more recent children. Led by Mr Mildon, she put it this way [Day Twelve: 40]:

A: As far as I know it had not been a problem family with the three Kepple children.

Q: That may be a very important point. Mrs Kepple's children by Mr Kepple had never at any time before the tragic events of the 6th January been in care...?

A: No.

Q: They had never been subject to a Supervision Order before that?

A. No.

Q: Nobody had ever pointed an accusing finger at Mrs Kepple to the effect that she was an inadequate mother to those children?

A. No.

Yet, these conclusions were not unanimous, even among social workers, including Pauline Edwards, social worker to Maria's eldest brothers. As described in Chapter Two, she was one of the last workers to have visited Maresfield Road, when accompanying the two boys on a Christmas visit to their mother on 21 December 1972. This was the point at which other workers, used to visiting over a longer period, were most impressed by the improvement in living conditions and family relationships. Miss Edwards' visit was brief, but left a clear impression on her [Day Ten: 8]:

> I would say it was a very poor house. It sounds rather trite, but it was what we would call a family with problems, and there was a family-with-problems-type smell, the look of the furniture and the general décor.

In a very clear echo of Eugenic Society thinking – in which 'problem families' were always easier to spot than to define – she told the Inquiry [Day Ten: 8]:

> It is difficult to describe it; one recognises it when one goes into a house; even just putting your head round the door you know.

A clear consensus on the demonstrable incorrigibility of the Kepples and their formal classification as a 'problem family' would certainly have made a harsh judgement on the part of Miss Lees' and Mrs Kirby's professional practice much easier to make. However, and somewhat ruefully, the chair was forced to conclude that, '"problem family" is not a term of art' [Day Twelve: 40].

Exercise of judgement

As well as being tied to questionable assumptions, social workers were also portrayed in the Inquiry as weak in the exercise of their professional judgement. Two brief examples are used here to illustrate the point.

Moral relativism

As well as being predicated on the basis of some highly dubious 'fundamental assumptions', the approach taken by social workers to the practical application of those assumptions was also a key issue for the Inquiry. In essence, the majority report creates an account of social workers trapped in a form of moral relativism, or non-judgementalism. This cut them off from the grounded reality of the world in which they worked, and fatally undermined the decisions that they made, or, more often, failed to make.

The Committee heard evidence that, for two of its members at least, demonstrated how far social work had proceeded in this direction. Early evidence from the NSPCC's Inspector Curran, and the extensive documentary evidence from the pre-Seebohm Children's Department, revealed a world of moral certainty. During his involvement with Pauline around the time of Raymond Colwell's death, Inspector Curran used the tests of 'physical and moral danger' [Day Seven: 40] without any sense of struggle as to their meaning or as to how they might be operationalised. He represented a straightforward 'inspectoral' service, willing without qualms to keep watch on houses and to gather evidence of morally dubious conduct. Second, and even more importantly, the evidence demonstrated a willingness to act, and to act decisively, when those in authority were able to protect children from harm. This evidence of earlier social work intervention set a tone which, to some members of the Inquiry, provided a sympathetic touchstone of certainty: social workers of the time knew what was right, and they acted on it. They knew that Pauline Colwell (as she then was) was unfit to look after her children and that the Coopers were; they intervened to make sure that this arrangement was put in place, and kept in place, despite repeated attempts by Mrs Colwell to reverse it.

Less than 10 years later, the Inquiry appeared to have entered a world where these old certainties had been abandoned, where even rudimentary standards of behaviour were no longer to be expected and where their absence was not regarded as problematic by a series of state-sponsored services. It was also a world where even direct evidence of physical injury was to be hedged about and explained away so as to *avoid* the need to take action, rather than evidence for its necessity. A single exchange between Miss Lees and Alderman Davey must suffice to illustrate the extent to which a social work view of the world had moved ahead of that shared by others.

Questioned about her assessment of the Kepples' fitness to resume care of Maria in April 1971, Miss Lees emphasised Mrs Colwell's changed circumstances and the way in which such a narrative would be likely to underscore any application made to the court for revocation of the Care Order in respect of Maria [Day Twenty: 29]:

> We looked at Mrs Kepple's situation as it was at that time, a very great improvement on what it had been at the time the Care Order was made. She appeared to have a stable relationship with Mr Kepple, mothering her own children of that union very adequately, and the conditions existing at the time the Care Order was made no longer seemed to exist.

At this point, Mrs Davey, the least active member of the Inquiry team, intervened. To cries of 'Hear! Hear!' from the public gallery, she suggested that 'most people' would have described the 'stable relationship' which Miss Lees had outlined as 'Mrs Colwell was cohabiting with an Irishman of unknown origins' [Day Twenty: 30], to which Miss Lees replied, 'I would say that there is such a thing as a stable cohabitation.'

Headlines in newspaper accounts screamed their incredulity. 'I saw no risk to Maria', reported the *Daily Express* (6 November 1973), quoting Miss Lees' belief that Mr Kepple was 'not a violent person'. The *Daily Mail* (8 November 1973) summed up her evidence as focused on 'Maria's "happy family" life' with the Kepples in which, despite the evidence since provided by forensic pathologist Professor Cameron, she had 'never felt she was ill-treated or hungry'. '"Maria not exploited", says social worker', reported the *Daily Telegraph* (8 November 1973), recalling the evidence of shopkeepers, teachers and neighbours to the contrary. It all suggested an unwillingness, as well as an inability, to draw conclusions from evidence which appeared obvious to others.

Rule of optimism

Moral relativism was not the only way in which social work decision making was constructed by the Inquiry. An allied allegation emerged as evidence accumulated that suggested that social workers were prey to a 'rule of optimism' (a term first used by Dingwall et al, 1983), in which good news was always sought out and over-valued, while bad news was avoided and overlooked.

The Inquiry report, for example, quotes Miss Lees' assessment of the Kepples, on 8 October 1971, two weeks before Maria was to be moved to live with them. It read: 'this family is at long last on, I hope, a steady upward trend. The improvement over the year since they had been in this house is considerable in all spheres of family life' (DHSS, 1974a, p 305). For the authors of the majority report this was 'putting a gloss' on the situation, a charge which Olive Stevenson rejects as seeming 'to suggest a degree of deliberate distortion' (DHSS, 1974a, p 308).

For the critics of social work, the rule of optimism was at its most pernicious at crucial points, such as the 'April incident' and, even more so in the final weeks of Maria's life. Thus, despite the shared, and independent, conclusion among social workers, the health visitor and the family GP that there was nothing alarming in Maria's condition in December 1972, the report (using evidence which was available to it, but not necessarily to those working directly with Maria on the ground) concludes that, 'there was abundant evidence of a steady deterioration in Maria's appearance, both physical and otherwise' (DHSS, 1974a, p 111). Instead, Miss Lees, investigating the situation on 5 December, was 'completely reassured' by what she found (DHSS, 1974a, p 132), despite not having been 'prudent' enough to have checked Mrs Kepple's story of medical treatment by telephoning Dr Barley (DHSS, 1974a, p 133).

Boundaries of social work

The fourth main charge against social work was that it had failed to manage its boundaries with other professionals properly. However, this was not the limit of its failure to manage its boundaries. The social workers directly involved in the supervision of the Kepples had to operate against some tensions in their own, organisational relationships. Indeed, the relationship between the voluntary and statutory sector providers of social work in this case lies just below the surface of the account of social work that the Inquiry developed, and yet it would be critical to the future that was to flow from it.

The NSPCC and social services departments

The creation of the new unified social services departments involved a considerable amount of publicity and led, as noted already, to a substantial acceleration in referral rates across the UK, including to the social services departments of Brighton and East Sussex. We have indicated how social services departments had grown in size and reach, even to the point where they dominated the employment opportunities for social workers available in the back pages of *Social Work Today* (see Chapter One). For the voluntary sector, the departments were a possible threat to their very existence or at least threatening to reduce their role and push them to the margins. At the level of social services department directors and headquarters staff of the NSPCC, the discourse deployed at the Inquiry was very different – cooperation, shared understandings and complementary services was the order of the day but, nevertheless, with a wariness on both sides that 'give' on one side would be met only with 'take' on the other.

On the ground, the relationship between the two sectors reflected some of these tensions. Inspector Curran, of the NSPCC, who gave oral evidence, suggested that while NSPCC staff were under a well-observed and willingly undertaken obligation to inform social services departments when they became involved with a family, this was not reciprocated by the statutory bodies. He criticised the failure of local social workers to involve the NSPCC in discussions about Mrs Colwell's application to revoke Maria's Care Order in November 1971, despite the NSPCC's close involvement in obtaining the Care Order in the first instance. Asked about this during the first of her four days of oral evidence, Diana Lees dismissed the accusation: 'I did not think there was anything they could usefully add to a discussion' [Day Twenty: 26]. Mr McBurney, Miss Lees' counterpart at Brighton and a former police officer, told the Inquiry that while 'The areas I have been to have always been appreciative of the NSPCC.... One could say that the NSPCC perhaps does have an image of people in uniform and people in uniform are perhaps abhorrent to many families – that image exists' [Day Eighteen: 17]. Where the social services department represented the future, the NSPCC clearly represented the past, as far as Mr McBurney was concerned.

On the social services side the perennial subtext can be detected that statutory services have to deal with all the intractable, insoluble and chronic cases on which all other services had turned their back, and to do so in an unrewarded and unrecognised way. Voluntary bodies, by contrast, were able to pick and choose, passing on work that was unpalatable or overly problematic, while retaining those elements that attracted public sympathy or satisfaction. Mrs Kirby, for example, while strongly supportive of Miss Lees in most ways, always firmly agreed with any propositions that she was the second string as far as case responsibility was concerned. Difficult questions were quite regularly answered by her, with the observation that 'it would have been Miss

Lees' place not mine' (see, for example, Day Eleven: 48) to have taken any action.

The clearest impression that the Inquiry took of relationships on the ground was an absence of rancour or competitiveness, but not a great deal which could be described as active cooperation. The two social workers did not seem to have worked as a team, in any credible sense: they pursued (or in Miss Lees' case, failed to pursue) their own courses of action, coming into contact with one another rarely, and then only when specific reasons caused that to take place.

Yet, one of the most striking features of the whole Inquiry was to be the way in which this apparent creation of an enhanced public profile for statutory social work appeared to have almost no impact when it came to cases of child cruelty or neglect. Without exception, any member of the public who wished to bring Maria's situation to the attention of the authorities reached unerringly for the NSPCC, rather than the social services department. Almost every professional worker with whom Maria was in contact was of the same mind. Professor Cameron, the forensic pathologist, agreed that the man in the street 'immediately thinks of the NSPCC' in cases of child cruelty [Day Eight: 46], but the association of child cruelty with the NSPCC, rather than social services, was not confined to the 'man in the street'. When, very late in the story, Miss Bodger, the health visitor, decided to make contact with other agencies, it was to Mrs Kirby of the NSPCC that she made her first approach, learning only from her that 'the Hove Children's Officer [sic] had a Supervision Order on Maria' [Day Fourteen: 15]. Later on the same Inquiry day, Dr Barley, asked whom he would contact in cases of suspected child abuse, replied, 'I contact the NSPCC normally' [Day Fourteen: 43]. There is even the 'extraordinary statement' (DHSS, 1974a, p 126) of Mrs Hodgson, the social services duty officer with whom Mrs Dickenson discussed her concerns on 1 December 1972, whose own notes read, 'I stressed that it was definitely Mrs Kirby's territory if there was a suspicion of ill-treatment' [Day Eighteen: 9].

Nor was this an unwelcome situation, at least to Mrs Kirby, as the following exchange between her and the NSPCC's counsel at the Inquiry demonstrates [Day Eleven: 29]:

> Q: Mr Mildon [the Inquiry's own counsel] has put it that persons tend in cases of child cruelty to think first of the NSPCC. In your experience is that correct or not?
>
> A: I think it is correct. I would like to think it is.

When the Inquiry itself came to consider this matter, the chair drew on his own attempt to locate the department in the local telephone directory where, for example, there was nothing to be found listed under 'welfare'. He summarised his conclusion in this way [Day Eighteen: 26]:

> One of the difficulties, if I may be permitted the general observation, about this sort of thing is that a member of the public faces the expression "Social Services" which is wholly insignificant – it does not ring a bell with anybody when they want to raise a question of ill-treatment, for instance, of a child, whereas the NSPCC, of course, has the advantage of a very long connection in that field and that does ring a bell. Just the expression "Social Services" does not register with most people who want to do something in an emergency.

Relationships between social work and other professions

At the heart of the charge of 'over-confidence' was the apparent willingness of social workers to take on themselves matters that ought to have been informed by the professional judgement of others. Abrogating to itself matters which properly belonged to other professionals, especially medical professionals, meant that, as an occupation, social work in its post-Seebohm incarnation had trespassed into territories that were outside of its ambit. Social work was thus a discipline that did not have a proper sense of its own boundaries. In particular, it claimed, and acted on, a field of knowledge in which it was not expert. For the majority report writers this emerged most closely in relation to the boundary between social work and 'medicine'.

Here the majority report argues, insistently, that Miss Lees ought to have sought a psychiatric opinion as part of her assessment of Maria's reaction to the prospects of returning home. Miss Lees' refusal, in her evidence, to give any ground in this area left the majority of the Inquiry baffled, and then aggrieved. Pressed as to why she had not sought the advice of 'an independent medical man' ([sic] – and we can be sure that the Inquiry meant a man), her exchange with Mr Mildon QC went as follows [Day Twenty-One: 8]:

> Q: It is quite obvious, is it not, that the one person who can really give us excellent information about any battered child is the doctor?

A: Medical information, yes.

Q: But of course, he could not assist us upon other matters such as deprivation of affection?

A: I doubt it.

Mr Field-Fisher and Alderman Davey were unconvinced. They provided a paragraph in their report which contrasted with Miss Lees' willingness to rely on an 'intelligent guess' as to Maria's feelings – 'we do not consider an intelligent guess to be sufficient in this case' (DHSS, 1974a, p 59) – with the willingness of more mature disciplines (such as medicine and the law) to call on second opinions in cases of difficulty or doubt. Their conclusion was blunt. Social work's claim to disciplinary territory was ill founded and dangerous (DHSS, 1974a, p 61):

> ... there are overlap areas between the medical and social work professions. If there is a reluctance to seek a second opinion, from another discipline, and too much emphasis is placed on independent judgement, then clients will suffer, as Maria did.

The result was that 'insufficient efforts' were made by social workers (DHSS, 1974a, p 63) to understand and to represent the scale and nature of Maria's trauma. The insufficiency of those efforts was not because of lack of time or resources, but because social workers had made 'assumptions' which 'they were not qualified to make' (DHSS, 1974a, p 67).

Olive Stevenson, in her minority report, noted, pointedly, that neither of two other 'medical men' with whom Maria was in touch during the her last months with Mrs Cooper – Dr Robinson and Dr Coe – made any suggestion about a referral for a psychiatric opinion (DHSS, 1974a, p 291). She took, head on, the argument made by her colleagues about the 'competence' of 'qualified social workers' to make assessments of this sort (DHSS, 1974a, p 318). It was, she said, 'an integral part of their job' (DHSS, 1974a, p 318):

> In my view, Miss Lees had a right, indeed a duty, to consider and interpret Maria's feelings at this time. To deny her that would be to deny her a basic tool of her trade. This is not an attempt to argue for professional omniscience, simply to point out that social workers in childcare see more than any

other professional or lay group of people, children under stress. To deny them the right, therefore, and indeed the necessity, to interpret such behaviour, and to make decisions in the light of the interpretation, is a contradiction of one of the very functions they are set up to perform.

The insistence that social workers had acted beyond their competence, and ought to have taken the initiative in engaging with others, did not extend to those other professional groups. These differential standards are most evident in relation to medicine. While Miss Lees was regularly criticised for not having sought medical advice, there is no suggestion, at all, that Dr Barley, the family GP, might have contacted the social services department, despite having been alerted, by Mrs Dickenson, to anxieties about Maria's welfare. Indeed, despite just one note of exasperation at his failure to consult such notes as were available to him about Maria – 'one is at a loss to know the purpose of such medical histories if they are put out for a doctor and not used by him when he is seeing a patient either for the first time or after a long interval' (DHSS, 1974a, p 136) – the majority report's conclusions about Dr Barley are remarkably understanding: 'we cannot fault Dr Barley'; 'Dr Barley's reactions were not unreasonable'; he was 'not to be criticised in all the circumstances' (DHSS, 1974a, p 137).

Conclusion

In the analysis of social work both as a form of practice and as an emergent profession that the Committee of Inquiry into the case of Maria Colwell provides, we can detect a number of tensions that had exercised Seebohm and his predecessors some years prior to Maria's death and which would occupy the New Right architects of the welfare state subsequently. Social work seemed to exemplify and to embody some of these tensions; was it intended as a community-based, universal service helping families with their problems, or was it to be constructed as a residual service, rescuing children from the fecklessness and incompetence of their 'problem' families? Was it to be a progressive, liberal and morally unaligned practice that might be reluctant to act decisively in a crisis, or a traditional, inspectoral service, founded on common sense and practical action, even at the expense of the natural rights of parents and the needs of children? Was it to rest on the interpretive sciences of sociology and psychology, or to follow the example and show respect to the 'harder' science of more established professions?

Olive Stevenson's minority report offers some defences to the specific charges that were laid against the practice of social work in this case. Confining herself largely to the period preceding the decision to return Maria to the care of her mother, Olive Stevenson introduces much of the contextual information on which social workers based that critical decision. This has the effect of reintroducing much of the ambiguity and uncertainty that surrounds direct practice itself. In doing so, Olive Stevenson far from exonerates the social workers involved. Indeed, she makes it clear that she agrees with 'some of [her] colleagues' final list of criticisms' (DHSS, 1974a, p 334). However, she makes it clear that she does not believe that all of the fault can be laid at the social workers' door and specifically disassociates herself from the 'hierarchy of censure' with which the majority report concludes. Her reasons for doing so are clear (DHSS, 1974a, p 334):

> For one thing, it leaves a predominant impression of weakness rather than strength in the East Sussex social workers which is misleading. There was much that was excellent in their work, as I hope my report illustrates. As to the others involved, all played a part in the tragedy....

Referring directly to the social workers involved, Olive Stevenson also makes a specific request that a society (DHSS, 1974a, p 333):

> ... that is compassionate to Maria, Mr and Mrs Cooper and, hopefully, also to Mr and Mrs Kepple, should extend similar sympathy to those whom it employs to perform tasks of the utmost difficulty and complexity, under conditions of great strain.

In particular, as we have already indicated, Olive Stevenson was at pains to indicate her own sympathy for Diana Lees. In Olive Stevenson's opinion, '... most social workers in the local authority service would say, if they were ever asked, "there but for the Grace of God went I"' (DHSS, 1974a, p 8). She continued:

> It is to be hoped that Maria's death and the grievous distress that it has caused, not least to the social workers involved, notably Miss Lees, will prompt urgent consideration of the stresses upon the profession and the ever increasing expectations of it.

In the chapter that follows, we turn to consider the wider reaction that followed publication of the report, and the extent to which Olive Stevenson's plea for compassion was to be borne out in the wider world.

SIX

Afterwards ...

If social work had been on trial during the Colwell Inquiry, the final verdict on the profession was to be delivered elsewhere and much later. In this chapter, we describe the immediate and medium-term consequences of the Maria Colwell Inquiry and begin to consider the influence it had, ephemeral and lasting, on social work in particular and the welfare state more generally. We begin with the production of the Inquiry report itself, and its immediate reception in Whitehall, focusing on the struggle that went on inside government to craft a response to the recommendations made by the Inquiry team. We then turn to the micro-processes of government as it drew together a series of administrative and procedural reforms that Colwell implied and that did so much to shape the future of social work both organisationally and professionally. Finally, we deal with the major legislative consequence of the Colwell case, the Children Act 1975, exploring the ways in which the major preoccupations of the last three chapters were pursued and resolved in the complexities of law making.

The Colwell Inquiry report

The most immediate outcome of any inquiry is, of course, the report that it produces. But in the same way as the proceedings of the Maria Colwell Inquiry were an emotional, intensely human activity, so too was the writing of its report. The only direct source that we have for its production comes from Olive Stevenson and we should recognise that, as author of the minority view, hers is, inevitably, a partial account.

Although dissenting from the interpretation advanced by her colleagues at critical points, Olive Stevenson was clear that a 'really good chronology' was a fundamental necessity 'if you are going to be fair to the parties', and that provided in the report was one with which Miss Stevenson was generally content. She herself wrote the agreed and uncontested section on interagency and interprofessional work (see DHSS, 1974a, chapter three), the element of the report, which, in her view, 'in the longer run has been the most important'. In the remainder of the agreed text, her struggle with the chair was, she said, 'to curb the excesses of his purple prose'; to avoid phrases included, as she thought, simply to provide headlines in newspaper reports. As an example, she cited the portrayal, in the agreed part of the report, of Mrs Kepple as a woman worn down by childbearing and poor health. In fact, Miss Stevenson said, Mrs Kepple was 'a fearsome woman' whom, left to himself, Mr Field-Fisher had wished to describe as 'a perfectly awful woman who ought to have been sterilised', perhaps suggesting once more just how close to the surface eugenicist sentiment sat at the time.

It can be seen, therefore, that on critical matters of interpretation, there were some obvious differences between Miss Stevenson and her fellow Committee members. As we have described, two more immediate strands of disagreement, in her recollection, lay behind the 'enormous' decision that she took to write a dissenting chapter. 'One, which one could have lived with, was a sort of judicial arrogance ... and certainly buckets of male chauvinism. And a dislike of someone like me, a professional woman, with a mind of my own.' The second strand, 'which was more serious', was 'an *absolute* lack of sympathy for the people concerned. If I tell you he referred to Maria's mother's children as her "droppings" you will perhaps understand why it wasn't easy to relate. He had no children of his own. He had no experience in family law. His view was "they all ought to be sterilised anyway".'

It was against that background, then, that Miss Stevenson came to the view that, while she was prepared to agree the core narrative that was drafted in the first weeks of report writing, she was not able to reach a consensus on its interpretation. As that became apparent, so it also 'became apparent that he [Field-Fisher] wouldn't tolerate me'. The 'meeting mode' in which the report writing had begun was abandoned, and 'we didn't have those meetings anymore. So I would get letters from the Inquiry secretary saying, Mr Field-Fisher has asked me to write and tell you the following. And I would write back and say, "please would you tell Mr Field-Fisher ... blah, blah, blah."'

Once the report was completed, as far as Olive Stevenson was concerned, there was no further involvement of any official sort: 'Nothing! It was a total damp squib. No discussion with the Department at all. We just waited and waited for it to be published.' For her, personally, 'the intensity of the experience is very difficult to describe'. What had been put to her as three weeks of professional inquiry had turned into months of concentrated, ill-tempered work, under the intense spotlight of legal and media attention.

Within Whitehall and Westminster, however, there was no such hiatus. Government responses to such scandals as that occasioned by the death of Maria Colwell follow a somewhat predictable pattern, as we shall see. However, in this instance, an additional layer of complexity was added by the fact of two general elections being called during the course of the year. The first of these, on 28 February 1974, saw Harold Wilson's Labour Party replace Edward Heath's Conservative government but without an overall majority. The second, on 10 October, marginally strengthened the Wilson government's parliamentary position, leaving Labour with a majority of three seats over all other parties, a majority which was soon eroded, and then eliminated, in a series of by-elections.

Struggles inside government

At the start of May 1974, five months after the last evidence-taking session, the report of the Inquiry was received at the DHSS. Two weeks later, with the agreement of the Secretary of State, Barbara Castle (Sir Keith Joseph's successor following the 28 February general election), it was sent to the printers. The *Argus* (23 May 1974) reported that, 'July seems the most likely date for the publication of the official report.' In the meantime, as discussed more fully later, in April, the DHSS had already issued a circular to all area health authorities and social services departments on the subject of 'Non-accidental injury to children', prompted by 'recent events' and the 'unusual amount of movement between posts' brought on by local government reorganisation (DHSS, 1974b).[1]

On first receipt of the report, civil servants across Whitehall began to mobilise a governmental response. Those outside the DHSS were motivated, as much as anything else, by the need which Mrs White of the Home Office identified as, 'to prevent premature decisions on this all from being taken from the natural wish of the DHSS to demonstrate active concern' [NA: BN 29/1412]. An early draft submission to ministers noted that, despite the Inquiry's own conclusion that it was both impossible and unfair to 'lay direct blame' on any one individual, or small group of individuals, 'they have in fact allowed criticisms of the actions taken by people responsible for Maria's welfare to enter into their narrative and of these Miss Diana Lees the social worker employed by East Sussex Council, is the main target'. The focus on the state of social work was thus built into the government's response.

---

[1] Papers from four different ministries are now available for public inspection at the National Archive in Kew – the Home Office, the Department for Education and Science, the Welsh Office and the DHSS. Frustratingly, the ministry least well represented in the documents that have survived is the one by which the report had been commissioned and to which the bulk of its observations were directed, the DHSS. Most of what we can discern about the DHSS has to be derived from what survives in the files of other ministries.

Even at this stage, however, the submission pointed to potential problems that might have the effect of delaying publication; these included industrial unrest at Her Majesty's Stationery Office (HMSO) (the government's printers) and the possibility, soon to be realised, of an autumn general election. In the event of delay, ministers were advised to 'carry out an urgent study with other departments to see how many of the Committee's suggestions could be given immediate effect' [NA: BN 29/1412]. As it became clearer that the prospect of delay was increasing, this was the course of action adopted. A paragraph-by-paragraph analysis of the report now followed. Analysts of social policy will recognise, immediately, the defensive spirit in which this was undertaken. At the Home Office, admittedly the most conservative of all the relevant government departments, officials concluded, with relief, that most of the report's concerns lay with services outside its remit. The probation service 'had not been involved with Maria'. The Sussex Constabulary could be 'criticised to only a very limited extent'. Miss Stevenson's criticisms of the legal system, and in particular the operation of the Juvenile Court, showed 'considerable confusion of mind'. As to reform of the Supervision Order – 'the point on which we are likely to become most involved' – officials advised ministers that they were 'doubtful of the value of regulations in improving the standard of supervision', and that change would produce 'obvious problems' [NA: BN 29/1412].

Together, these exchanges demonstrate a tension which ran through the entire process of developing a response to Colwell within government, and which itself is indicative of a more general contest, across a far wider range of policy areas. On the one hand, ministers, faced with the weight of public opinion, intense media coverage and the partisan pressures of everyday politics, needed to show that 'something was being done'. On the other hand, civil servants generally pursued a series of arguments which suggested that (a) nothing needed to be done (as in the case of reforming Supervision Orders), or (b) that something had already been done (as in the case of interagency cooperation), or (c) that what might be done would only make matters worse (Miss Law of the Home Office dismissed the report's recommendation that police forces should be required to report breaches of the peace involving children to local social services departments on the grounds that this would 'require a trebling of the police manpower while being ineffective in practice' [NA: BN 29/1412].

One example will have to stand for a wider series of such contests that now followed – that of Dr David Owen's determination to move ahead with a commitment to independent representation for children in court proceedings. The *amicus curiae* ('friend at court') proposal, as it was then known, was strongly resisted by Home Office officials, while noting that 'an obvious point of difficulty' existed 'as Dr Owen is adamant that he wishes a reference to the *amicus curiae* to be included'. The political imperative in favour of the *amicus curiae* had been much sharpened by the focus of the Inquiry report on the decision made at Hove Juvenile Court not to oppose Mrs Kepple's application for the revocation of Maria's Care Order. Consistent with the general way in which the court system appeared to place the interests of parents over those of children (or not to recognise the distinction to be drawn between them), the Juvenile Court had not heard from anyone with a separate and primary responsibility to advance the views and best interests of Maria. The Inquiry report concluded that social workers in such court proceedings were obliged to occupy an unsustainable 'plurality of roles' (DHSS, 1974a, p 227). The Inquiry's solution was to make an 'independent social worker' available to the court, in order to provide 'a second opinion which might or might not have endorsed the conclusions and recommendations contained in Miss Lees' report'. In Dr Owen's formulation, this 'independent social worker' was to be achieved by the introduction of an *amicus curiae*. Home Office officials rejected that interpretation of events. The problem at Hove, they suggested, was not only that Mrs Kepple had been represented, but that magistrates had been 'greatly influenced by the social enquiry report with its unequivocal support of the mother's application' [NA: BN 29/1412].

Through the early summer of 1974 efforts continued to be made to reach an agreement, at official level, over the *amicus curiae* question. By 3 July a further draft of the proposed Secretary of State's statement had been submitted to Dr Owen, and was returned with a series of his handwritten amendments. Without official resolution, the issue was passed to the Minister of State at the Home Office, Alex Lyon. One of the most progressive and liberal ministers of his generation, he replied, in a handwritten note, setting out his agreement both to the principle of a separate children's advocate and to the availability of legal aid to represent children in court. More generally, he concluded that 'I do not see that any more regulation would help in Maria Colwell's case. What is needed is a change of attitude by social workers, and the case has probably achieved that.'

Despite this helpful resolution, the official process now found itself overtaken by events that would indeed confirm further delays in publication. First, for the first time in their history, the printers of HMSO did indeed go on strike. The prospects of an 11 July statement receded to the point where it was decided to remit the government's response for consideration at the Cabinet's Social Services Committee on 15 July. There, a memorandum submitted in the name of Mrs Castle was approved. A consultation paper was agreed for the autumn, in which the government would advance the idea of an independent advocate for children in court proceedings. A planned Children's Bill, already announced in the post-March 1974 general election, was to be enlarged to include powers to make regulations governing the supervision of children who had been made the subject of Supervision Orders (thus overriding the concerns of the Home Office), and providing for separate legal aid for parents, as well as children, in care proceedings where the interests of parents and children differed.

Industrial action at HMSO dragged on throughout the month of July. At the start of August, Mr Linge wrote to his counterpart in the Home Office to report that 'the position about publication is that the report has been set up at the printers but no copies have been run off because of a total stoppage of work due to industrial action of which no solution is in sight. I am advised that the report is "locked in" at the printers which I take to mean that it cannot be removed for printing elsewhere.' With ministers about to embark on their August holidays, he concluded that 'it is unlikely that the Report will be published until September, even if the strike were to be over before then'.

The second cause for delay was to be found in the immediate political context. Mrs Castle returned from her holiday in Mauritius at the end of August to hear reports of plans by the Maria Colwell Memorial Fund to disrupt the appearance of Prime Minister Harold Wilson at the TUC's Annual Conference, due to take place in the first week of September, in Brighton. The Fund's notorious Secretary, Robert Beaumont (see Chapter Four), was quoted in the press as intending to use the occasion to 'shame' the government into publication of the Inquiry report. 'Thousands of people', he said, were 'sick of waiting' for its appearance. 'We have been battering our heads against a brick wall for months trying to get some action. We now intend to take our campaign to the top' (reported in *Argus*, 28 August 1974).

The particular significance for the government of the TUC's Annual Conference lay in the fact that, from February onwards, those involved in the minority Labour government, as well as the whole of the commentariat, had been preoccupied primarily with the timing of a second general election, which was regarded as inevitable. Almost immediately after he became Prime Minister for the third time, Harold Wilson had told those closest to him that he favoured an election in October when he hoped (and was again, widely expected) to repeat his success of a decade earlier, when a Labour majority of three, in 1964, had been turned into one of 97 in the general election of 1966. While there were persuasive voices that argued for a June 1974 poll, the government had survived until the July summer recess without much difficulty. The result was that, as politicians returned from their August break, the prospects of an autumn election were now seen as inevitable.

Mr Wilson himself had spent August at his bungalow on the Scilly Isles. He returned to Downing Street on Tuesday 3 September. His first evening was taken up with a disputatious discussion of his speech for the TUC Congress, due to be delivered two days later (Donoughue, 2005, p 175). The speech was the subject of argument because it was now to be the launching pad for an October election, and getting its tone and content right were of real importance to the campaign that lay ahead. Quite certainly, anything that distracted attention from its main theme was highly unwelcome. The need to avoid any demonstration arising from Colwell, a case that had already proved its capacity to command national headlines, was therefore critical.[2]

Mrs Castle immediately went onto the attack. In an 'exclusive interview' with the *Argus* (29 August 1974), and reported with banner headlines on its front page, she rejected any allegations that she had 'sat on' the report, explaining the problems with printing, and emphasising her belief that the document had to be published in full because of the need to ensure 'justice for those people criticised in it'. She signalled her intention to make a limited number of copies of the report available, and was rewarded with sympathetic media coverage in which the minister appeared determined to do 'everything within my power' to make the report public and respond to its recommendations. Nationally, the *Daily Mirror* (2 September 1974) was briefed to expect imminent publication of a 'do-it-yourself' version of the report. The minister was rewarded with a prominent story, headlined 'THE LIFESAVER: Barbara speeds up report to help the battered babies', in which readers were informed

---

[2] Nevertheless, one of those most closely associated with the Colwell case did make the headlines on the same day as the TUC speech. Sir Keith Joseph, whose recantation of his high-spending days at the DHSS was now already complete, delivered a speech at Preston on the same day in which he set out the new monetarist creed – that the only cure for inflation was strict control of the money supply, even if that led to high levels of unemployment. News coverage contrasted the warm reception which the Prime Minister's speech received at the TUC with stories of 'Tory splits', as Sir Keith's speech was reported as a thinly veiled attack on the record of the former Prime Minister, but still Conservative leader, Edward Heath.

that 'a document which could save hundreds of child-battered victims every year is being rushed out by the Government this week'. Two days later, on 4 September, with strike action still proceeding, Mrs Castle issued a 'limited number of typed copies of the report of the Committee set up by my predecessor'. Locally, it had the effect of calling off the demonstration at the TUC Annual Conference, planned for that day.

In an accompanying press statement, Mrs Castle again made it clear that:

> The report was sent for printing within a fortnight of our receiving it from the Committee last May. I am releasing it in this way now because printing is held up by industrial action at HMSO and because I feel that the deep public concern about the case, and the anxiety of those concerned to know of the Committee's findings without further delay, outweigh the obvious disadvantages.

Acknowledging that the report pointed to 'shortcoming and errors of judgement on the part of authorities and agencies responsible for Maria's care', the statement concluded that its 'essential message' concerned failures in communication between agencies in passing 'highly relevant information' between one another. This was a message, Mrs Castle said, which 'goes wider' than the particular agencies and professions involved in the Colwell case to 'all the professions concerned with the welfare of children'. In order to reinforce that point, and to demonstrate the coordinated nature of the government's response, Reg Prentice, then Secretary of State for Education, used the same day to issue a circular to all schools, asking them to review their arrangements so that teachers knew what action to take when faced with a possible case of child abuse. The circular had been consciously prepared with a view to being 'explicitly' linked to the Colwell report, and to form 'part of the Government's response' [NA: BN 29/022].

Nevertheless the statement focused squarely on social work. Each of the three points which Mrs Castle said she 'particularly wanted to stress' drew on implied criticisms of the way in which social work services had responded to Maria's needs and circumstances. Each reflected a strand in the criticism of social work services discussed in Chapter Five. First, Mrs Castle focused on the impact of local government reorganisation and the formation of generic social services departments. These had, she concluded, drawn social workers with 'less experience of child care than their predecessors in children's departments, into direct work with children'. Additional training was needed for such individuals 'to acquire and develop skill in communicating with children and interpreting their reactions'. In the meantime, 'I shall be reminding social services departments of the need to ensure that the best possible use is made of experienced social workers with specialist skills in child care.' Second, the statement dealt with the need for courts hearing care proceedings to be provided with 'full and detailed exploration and assessment of the people with whom [a child] is to live, and of their background and circumstances'. 'I do not think I can over-emphasise,' said Mrs Castle, 'the importance of this procedure where there is a stepfather who will be a new person in the child's life.' It was this latter issue in particular that was to assume major significance in the legislative, rather than the procedural response, that was to follow publication of the report.

Third, the statement turned to the most contentious of all the Inquiry's debates. The report provided 'a much-needed reminder that the significance of the blood-tie is not absolute', a conclusion which was to be reinforced prominently in any future training programmes.

The publication of the report inevitably provoked a widespread reaction. Publication made the front pages of every national newspaper, with extensive reporting of the majority and minority conclusions, as well as comments from Mrs Castle, Diana Lees and extensive interviews with Mrs Kepple. Comment columns in the *Daily Mirror* and *The Sun* were matched by leading articles in *The Times*, *The Guardian* and *Daily Telegraph*. This national coverage focused heavily on social work, and social workers, rehearsing the arguments over the 'blood tie', caseloads, communication between agencies and the minister's commitment to use the promised Children Bill to include proposals for 'independent advocates' in care proceedings. A panel of social workers, set up to review press coverage of the report, concluded that, 'while the popular papers rivalled each other in their bid to squeeze every last ounce of human drama out of the tragedy, the overall standard of reporting and editorialising in the national press on the Maria Colwell affair was fair and sympathetic' (*Community Care*, 1974).

In Brighton, the *Argus* provided comprehensive coverage over the rest of the week. On the day of publication, it devoted more than two full broadsheet pages to a summary of the report's findings, reflecting its conclusions that, while individuals had made mistakes, it was the system itself that was to blame (*Argus*, 4 September 1974). On the following day it included equally extensive coverage of the reaction to the report of key local organisations and individuals. At a press conference in London, the director of social services for East Sussex, Denis Allen, had rejected any suggestion that East Sussex County Council had been scapegoated. The report should be read, he said, not on the basis of 'who can we blame?', but 'what can we learn?'. Diana Lees repeated the basic stance that had underpinned her evidence to the Inquiry. While she 'felt a certain amount of responsibility', she did not 'have a guilty conscience', having done all that could have been expected of her in the circumstances of the time. More generally, she suggested, 'public expectation of social work is higher than the resources the public is prepared to put into it'.

In a widespread welcome for the report and its publication – from organisations and individuals – only three dissenting voices were recorded. First, Councillor Danny Sheldon, now the Mayor of Brighton, who had played such an important part in bringing the case to a public inquiry, believed the report was flawed by 'one glaring omission', in its failure to provide a forensic analysis of the decision taken by Hove Juvenile Court to revoke Maria's Care Order and, in particular, to deal directly with the failure to investigate the background of Mr Kepple at that hearing.

Second, Mr Beaumont, on behalf of the Maria Colwell Memorial Fund, criticised the report for its lack of 'tough and positive recommendations', and the minister for not taking immediate action. He rejected the report's suggestion that the emotional and angry reaction of the public might indicate a troubled conscience about ill-treatment of children.

Third, for once making something of a common cause with Mr Beaumont, Andrew Bowden MP also took issue with Mrs Castle's statement in which she had pointed to the social circumstances that, she said, gave rise to the particular case. Echoing the critique developed by Sir Keith Joseph and the cycle of deprivation theory, he argued that this was 'an unjustifiable slur on the people of Maresfield Road and Whitehawk'. Environmental and social conditions had played no part in Maria's death and to suggest otherwise was 'a travesty of the truth' (reported in *Argus*, 5 September 1974). The deep and underlying argument between those who regarded the Colwell case as essentially a product of individual failure and personal viciousness, and those who regarded it as a systemic breakdown at every level, was thus entirely unresolved, at least at a local level.

The twists and turns around the publication of the report, however, were not yet over. On Wednesday 18 September, Prime Minister Harold Wilson called a snap general election for 10 October. Civil service rules precluded publication of the report as a Command Paper during the dissolution of Parliament so that, even though the strike was over, and printing of the report had resumed 'as a high priority', it seemed once again that publication would be further delayed. In the event, it appeared as a non–parliamentary departmental document, on 2 October, priced at £1.00.

In even this brief account, we see clearly how chance (the printers' strike), policy differences and 'turf wars' between departments (the Home Office's innate conservatism and its reluctance to cede ground to the DHSS on almost any matter) as well as political expediency (the possibility of a distraction shifting attention away from a political priority) all played their part in the government's initial handling of the Colwell report. In terms of professional practice, however, much had already been set in train.

Administrative and procedural reforms

More than six months earlier, and less than two weeks after the first of the 1974 general elections and her appointment as Secretary of State at the DHSS, Barbara Castle had received a prompt, and very anxious submission from her civil servants, urging her to approve and publish 'the draft memorandum of professional guidance' which Sir Keith Joseph had already undertaken to issue before he had left office. Early issue of the circular, if agreed, would 'consolidate and supplement earlier departmental guidance. Unhappily in most weeks, cases come to public notice which show only too clearly the need for all concerned to review their measures to deal with cases and to ensure that everything possible is done to help these children and also their parents' [NA: MH 152/198].

The structure of child protection 'registers' and 'area review committees' which the circular established – and which Mrs Castle authorised in essentially unchanged form – changed the face of social work practice irrevocably in so far as social work was to be an extraordinarily closely 'managed' profession from this point on. The essential architecture of the system that would ultimately indirectly govern the profession was established in circulars issued by the DHSS to local authorities and health authorities on 22 April, 2 October and 6 November 1974. These circulars set out guidance on the 'diagnosis, care and management of cases of non-accidental injury to children, and the need for improvements between the agencies concerned with children'.

The 22 April circular (LASSL[74]13; CNO[74]8), clearly bearing the impression of the febrile atmosphere in which it had its origins, expressed the Secretary of State's hopes 'that the growing public interest in and discussion of the problem [non-accidental injury to children] will lead to the emergence of informed, alert but compassionate attitudes and produce an atmosphere in which more preventive work can be done' (DHSS, 1974b, p 1).

The first part of the circular dealt with 'Diagnosis, care, management and rehabilitation'. Notwithstanding that the circular was specifically directed towards cases of 'non-accidental injury', the degree to which the management of the case was to be entrusted to the medical profession was striking: 'When there is reasonable suspicion of non-accidental injury the child should at once be admitted to hospital' (§3). From this point on, 'the paediatrician will normally be responsible for an assessment of the case and for arranging expert attention to any psychiatric aspects'. The circular noted that the paediatrician should contact the director of social services (and others), 'informing them that the child had been admitted and involving them in the assessment of the home and family situation' (§5). On the other hand, the role of the social worker was acknowledged, at least as far as they had a part to play in carrying into effect the 'collective advice of the case conference' (§9) in the event of it being decided that a child should be returned home to the care of the child's parents:

> Such a decision should only be taken when resources are available to protect the child and help the parents with close and continuing direct support, and indirect support such as that provided by home helps and daycare facilities.

One might note, in passing, that the eugenicist arguments of a previous generation remain only just below the surface (§9):

> The case conference should also consider whether there is a need to raise the subject of family planning with the parents.

The case conference itself was to take responsibility for the '*medico-social assessment of the family and its circumstances*' (§14; emphasis added) and their decisions would be considered, in turn (and in aggregate), by the area review committees that the circular wished to see established. Such committees would be strategic bodies, responsible for providing advice 'on the formulation of local practice and procedures to be followed in the detailed management of cases' and approving 'written instructions defining the duties of all personnel concerned with any aspect of the case' (§12).

As far as improving what would later be called interdisciplinary working was concerned, but which at this point was understood simply in terms of improving 'communication', the circular advocated the establishment of 'registers', and, as though reading from the report of the Inquiry itself, identified the 'constraints' that may interfere with effective communication between professionals (§18). These included:

a) Emotional resistance and denial of the problem
b) Plausibility of the parents
c) Reluctance to intervene in the family situation.

The Home Office issued parallel instructions to probation and after-care committees and to chief probation officers on 26 April 1974, 11 October 1974 and 3 January 1975, while the Department of Education and Science issued instructions to local education authorities on 4 September 1974. Further circulars were issued by all three departments on interagency communication, with the DHSS taking the lead on collecting reports on the operation of the new system and considering the outcome of them.

In terms of the trial which social work had undergone, this set of apparently administrative processes and procedures contained within them a more profound set of verdicts on the failings that the Inquiry report had identified. For Mr Field-Fisher and Alderman Davey at least, the problems of interagency communication and cooperation, which Maria's history so vividly illustrated, were more than simply matters of organisational discontinuities between services, bureaucratic complexity and the failures of either systems or individuals. At a series of crucial points, social work itself had demonstrated an over-confident and self-important determination to push its professional boundaries beyond the point warranted by either its knowledge or its expertise. Moreover, having invaded professional territory that properly belonged to others, it betrayed an arrogant determination not to share information or to communicate decisions with other professionals. In the process, a series of 'commonsense' yardsticks against which judgements ought to have been made had been discarded or ignored.

Thus, the Inquiry concluded that the errors of 'commission and omission' (DHSS, 1974a, p 240) in 'communication between Schools and Social Services' were not sufficiently explained simply by 'weaknesses in the chain' between the two departments. Rather the problems were 'not simply administrative'. They were rooted in a 'lack of confidence in, and understanding of, respective roles and responsibilities between the professions' (DHSS, 1974a, p 178). While evidence from Maria's class teachers had left the Inquiry team 'impressed by their sincerity and perceptiveness', they had been prevented from making a full contribution to Maria's welfare because social workers did not 'always explain carefully enough to teachers' what was taking place (DHSS, 1974a, p 179).

It was in relation to the border zone between social work and medicine, however, that the report brought this general issue most fully to the fore. Chapter Five has already set out a series of instances in which the majority report concluded that social workers had been in error in failing to obtain the opinion of a 'medical man'. Miss Lees' scarcely veiled scepticism of the value of psychiatric opinions, or of the need to have her own assessments provided with the seal of medical approval, had provoked a set of disagreements which ran across the four days in which she was cross-examined. It was an attitude that, the final report said, was 'difficult to understand' (DHSS, 1974a, p 60). Giving evidence on Day Twenty-Six, Dr Alfred White Franklin of the Tunbridge Wells Study Group (see Chapter Five) was more explicit:

> It is the stepping out of roles which has caused the tragedy here. People have taken it upon themselves assessments and decisions which really they are not professionally competent to make. [Day Twenty-Six: 37]

From this perspective, the need to invent the new machinery of registers and committees was not simply about better coordination or a strengthening of the safety-net of the welfare state. It was about disciplining the unruly, ambitious and *arriviste* profession that the Seebohm reforms had sanctioned, and putting social work back in its place (not least behind medicine). Multidisciplinary forums required not so much a blurring of professional boundaries, but a clearer recognition of the different contribution that each perspective had to make to a shared decision. And in the case of social work, those boundaries needed to be reined in and confined within a forum where other, more mature, voices could not be sidelined or ignored.

In doing so, the failures of judgement of which social work had also been convicted could now be remedied, or at least redressed, in part at least through the 'written instructions' of the area committee. The 'rule of optimism', for example, would now be tested in an environment where police officers and others could bring their more hard-headed assessment to bear. Chapter Five traced the persistence with which the Inquiry pressed its view that the Kepples were a 'problem family', and the equal doggedness with which that definition was denied by successive witnesses. The administrative reforms of April 1974 came down heavily in favour of the Inquiry's own view. The 'registers' that were introduced at this point were the start of a process, to be traced in Chapter Seven, in which families were to be singled out, identified, labelled and recorded precisely on the basis of their problematic (actual or potential) nature. The notion that social services might be provided on the sort of universal, accessible, non-stigmatising and preventive basis rehearsed by Seebohm had been tested and found severely wanting. Not only was the practice of social work to be restrained and restricted, but those with whom it would be carried out had also been significantly and much more narrowly redefined.

The Children Act 1975

This chapter now turns to the third and final area in which a verdict on social work was delivered in the period immediately surrounding publication of the Inquiry report. The Children Act 1975, as it was to become, was very much a product of the Colwell Inquiry, but also owed much to the Houghton Report of 1972 (see Chapter Five). The Houghton Committee's membership had been made up of politicians with a known interest in social policy and children's issues, such as Labour MP, Leo Abse, and the Conservative, Dame Joan Vickers. They were joined by acknowledged experts in the field, such as Jane Rowe, then director of the Association of British Adoption Agencies, and representatives from fieldwork services. Joan Cooper, principal social services officer at the DHSS, acted as the Committee's adviser. When the Houghton Committee came to report, however, it had lost both its chair and its sponsoring department. Sir William Houghton had died before the Committee's work was concluded, and had been replaced by Judge Stockton. The Home Office had, following a considerable fight, lost most of its remaining responsibilities in child welfare, seeing them transferred to the DHSS during the Heath administration of 1970-74.

Receipt of the Houghton Report coincided with the onset of the Colwell Inquiry. Advice to ministers, from civil servants, emphasised the complexity of the Houghton recommendations and the overlapping nature of the territory covered by both inquiries. The preoccupations of the Heath administration had been increasingly focused on industrial relations but, with a secure majority and nearly half the course of a normal parliament still to run, Sir Keith agreed that government activity in the 1973/74 parliamentary session should concentrate on securing the necessary cross-departmental policy clearances – both the Home Office and the Lord Chancellor's office had direct interests in the Houghton Report's proposals – and that any Bill could be postponed to the parliamentary year of 1974-75 [NA: MH 152/198].

These plans were disrupted by two events, one major, and one relatively minor. The more minor event came when the Labour MP Dr David Owen won third place in the ballot for Private Member's legislation in the 1973-74 Session of Parliament. He announced his intention of bringing forward proposals to put the Houghton recommendations onto the statute book. The House of Commons debated the report itself on a 'take note' motion in November 1973, when its contents were widely welcomed by politicians of all parties, with opposition politicians exerting strong pressure for early legislation. Negotiations were attempted between Sir Keith and Dr Owen (who, in the spring of the following year would become a junior minister under Barbara Castle in what had been Sir Keith's own department), to see if government assistance could be offered to any legislation. These negotiations came to nothing because Dr Owen declined to accept government advice to restrict the scope of his proposals to what he later described as 'a very short piece of legislation which would deal with the problem of child abuse and the specific issue of the Maria Colwell case fostering only' (Owen, 1986, p 2). Behind the scenes, civil servants briefed Sir Keith, very strongly, to resist the mounting pressure to legislate early. Sir Keith attended a meeting of the ministerial Home and Social Affairs Committee on 19 December 1973. His written advice explained to fellow ministers that Dr Owen's tactics were such that, 'he may introduce a botched Bill hoping to attract so much sympathy that we are forced to take it over'. In itself, this was 'out of the question', but such was 'the background of the Maria Colwell case, the considerable public interest in child abuse, and the powerful lobbies interested in various aspects of the Houghton/Stockdale report, there would be advantage in offering limited help on a bill of say a dozen clauses on which we are in agreement with him and that are suitable for inclusion in a Private Member's Bill' [NA: MH 152/198].

By this stage, Dr Owen had published his Bill. Its short title was:

> ... to amend the law relating to the adoption, guardianship and fostering of children: to make further provision for the protection and care of children: and for purposes connected with these matters.

A second reading date had been scheduled for 8 February, and there was 'some urgency' for ministers to agree a course of action at their meeting of 19 December. In the event, they endorsed officials' advice that one more attempt should be made, through a meeting scheduled between the Lord Chancellor and Dr Owen for later that same day, to put forward, once again, the advantages of a Private Member's Bill dealing only with Colwell-related matters. While these points continued to be debated, however, the second, and major disruption to Sir Keith's plan for limited legislation was overtaken by events, namely, the calling of the first general election of 1974 that would take place on 28 February. It ended both the progress of Dr Owen's Private Member's Bill and Sir Keith's tenure as Secretary of State at the DHSS.

A new Labour government

Hence, through Dr Owen's appointment as a junior minister to Barbara Castle at the DHSS by the incoming Labour government, the prospect of legislation once again came to the fore. The new administration's first Queen's Speech was given on 12 March. It contained the following commitment to a Children Bill:

> Comprehensive proposals will be brought forward to reform the law relating to the adoption, guardianship and fostering of children on the basis of the recommendations of the Interdepartmental Committee on the Adoption of Children.

Unusually, the fourth day of the Queen's Speech debate continued on Friday 15 March. The Children's Department of the DHSS had already provided a brief for Mrs Castle, dated 13 March 1974, dealing with the potential content of the Bill. Her own attitude was shaped mostly by scepticism about the legacy of her predecessor as Secretary of State. Less than a month after taking office, on Friday 29 March 1974, Mrs Castle spoke to a conference organised by BASW. Her diaries record the event in the following way (Castle, 1980, p 58):

> Rejigged most of the BASW speech – to the consternation of Private Office, who don't like the cavalier way I am dismissing Keith Joseph's studies on "Preparation for Parenthood" and other academic irrelevancies about the "cycle of deprivation".

The Bill itself, however, was primarily the responsibility of Dr Owen. He was quickly into the fray, keeping alive his proposal for provision of separate legal representation for children involved in court proceedings – an idea *against* which Home Office officials had also already briefed their minister, on the grounds of 'misgivings as to the practicability of the proposals which existed in the Department' [NA: MH 152/198].

Labour's victory at the polls had been unexpected, and the lack of an overall majority meant that, from the outset, a second election was expected either in the summer or early autumn. All this placed a premium on legislation that could be made ready relatively easily and which, in principle, if not in detail, commanded support across the political spectrum. The Children Bill was thought to fit both criteria and, as soon as the Easter recess of 1974 was over, efforts were made to bring it forward. Mrs Castle's principal private secretary, Graham Hart, was commissioned to write, on 10 May, to the Lord Chancellor's office, asking for agreement to proceed and noting that preliminary drafting was already available because 'First Parliamentary Counsel was consulted by the former Secretary of State Sir Keith Joseph in February of this year about Dr Owen's Private Member's Bill'.

This letter was a precursor to a meeting of the Cabinet's Social Services Committee on 17 May. Public Record Office files retain a note circulated in advance to Committee members which reminded them of the 'public pressure for legislation which has been stimulated by the Maria Colwell case', and which noted that:

> ... at a time when public confidence in the blood tie is weakening ... amendments to the law which would tilt the balance in favour of the long-term welfare of the child where parents have shown themselves unable or unwilling to look after their children are likely to win general support.

On 22 May Barbara Castle wrote to Ted Short, Lord President of the Council and the minister in charge of the new administration's legislative programme. The Social Services Committee had agreed the urgent policy clearance needed to provide instructions to parliamentary counsel and, as a result, the letter confirmed that 'our target will be to get the [Children] Bill ready for when the House reassembles in the Autumn'. In fact, work on the Bill continued right until the end of the year. The Colwell critique of social work was, consistently, to prove more difficult to translate into practice than assumed in the original and uncontroversial proposition that the law in relation to children needed to be improved.

Thus, one of the key reasons why the Bill proved difficult to deliver was an ongoing concern, reflected in official advice and ministerial discussion, to find a proper balance between planning for children's futures in a way which 'did not weaken parents' confidence in the whole fostering system and reinforced, not undermined, social workers' proper efforts to keep families intact' [NA: MH 152/198]. The importance of the 'blood tie', which had formed such a central charge in the trial of social work in the Maria Colwell case, had by no means disappeared from the minds of policy makers. Indeed, while the Act of 1975 did redraw the balance between the rights of birth and substitute families, those responsible for framing it were anxious to avoid the dangers of doing so in a knee-jerk or paradigm-shifting fashion. Rather, its intention was a careful recalibration of what its authors recognised as competing demands, which needed to be kept in balance.

There were innumerable, immensely detailed discussions between policy officials, parliamentary drafters and ministers as the Bill moved through 11 different internal drafts during the rest of 1974. The struggles were as much over finance and language as over content. Dr Owen, as the minister with day-to-day responsibility for the Bill, was anxious to secure an early timetable for implementation, demonstrating to local authorities and others that the financial consequences of the legislation would be absorbed gradually, and over time [NA: MH 152/181]. In terms of language, as the final internal versions of the Bill came to be produced, the leading parliamentary counsel, Francis Bennion, suggested to his policy colleagues that the primary principle around which the legislation had been framed was one in which [NA: MH 152/181]:

> We are not inventing any new doctrine here about what these basic [parental] rights and duties are, but are simply laying down the ways in which these might be parcelled out.

In the 'parcelling out' process, it was Mr Bennion who (successfully) proposed that the language used in the Houghton Report (relinquishment of parental rights) should be replaced by a language of 'freeing for adoption'. In a letter to his DHSS counterparts, dated 30 October 1974, he explained that 'I have chosen the concept of freeing the child for adoption, rather than relinquishment, because it is a positive concept and I see no need to accentuate the painful aspect of this procedure.' He had less success with the search for an alternative term to 'guardian' (as used by Houghton) to define the status of foster carers who had been looking after a child for an extended period of time. Having discarded the suggestion of 'sub-parent' and 'sub-parentage' – 'the social workers took up arms against this' – the draft Bill settled (despite 'protracted efforts by everyone to improve on it') for 'custodian' and 'custodianship'. Unsurprisingly, perhaps, Home

Office ministers were reported as being 'happy' with that term, but 'Dr Owen is not' [NA: MH 152/181]. Nothing better was forthcoming, however, and the terms 'custodian' and 'custodianship' remained in place.

All of this, and other policy dilemmas – such as the Home Office reluctance to agree to the *guardian at litem* proposals (successor to the *amicus curiae* as a form of independent representation of the child's views) – meant that not only the spring, but the autumn deadline too was missed. It was not until 10 December 1974 that Dr Owen was in a position to return to the administration's Legislation Committee, looking for agreement to proceed.

This meeting represented the culmination of the detailed process that underpins any piece of serious government legislation. True to form, civil service advice only unwillingly agreed that the Bill was ready for introduction. The Bill 'would benefit if more time were available', they argued, before concluding that 'the amendments that still need to be made are not so substantial as to justify postponing introduction'. With that concession out of the way, ministers were provided with the detailed advice needed to clear this final, internal hurdle. The case for legislation repeated the arguments that had now been in circulation for more than a year. The covering memorandum, supplied to Legislation Committee members, is worth reproducing in some detail, because of the repeated attention it drew to the significance of the Colwell Inquiry in shaping, and gathering support for, the Bill's proposals:

> The attached Bill carries out the Government's intention, as announced in the Queen's Speech, to introduce legislation to reform the law relating to the adoption, guardianship and fostering of children. The main purpose of the Bill is to give effect to the recommendations of the Departmental Committee on the Adoption of Children (the Houghton Committee) and certain related matters arising from the report of the Maria Colwell Enquiry....

> There has been strong support for the legislation on both sides of the House ... and the extensive consultations which have taken place with local authority associations and other interested bodies show that most of the proposals would be welcomed in principle provided sufficient time is allowed for them to be brought into force. Public pressure for legislation particularly on the protection of children in care proceedings has been stimulated by the Maria Colwell case and concern about the general problem of child abuse.

In policy terms, ministers were advised that aspects of the Bill remained controversial. Proposals likely to attract dissent included:

- the right of adopted children to be given the information required to obtain a copy of their birth certificate;
- a ban on independent placements for adoption where the adopter is not a relative of the child;
- enabling persons who have looked after a child for five years or more to apply for adoption without fear that the parents will remove the child before the court hearing;
- extending the powers of local authorities to provide greater security for children who have been in their care for 12 months or more.

The final two items had a direct policy line to the circumstances of the Colwell case. As advice to ministers made clear, these aspects 'introduce the passage of time as a factor in balancing the claims of natural parents, foster parents or other caring agencies in matters affecting the long term welfare of children' [NA: BN 29/1412] and, as such, divided opinion, across the professional and political spectrum.

The negotiations which were played out in the months that followed Labour's resuming office in February/March 1974 reflected, in very large part, the precarious financial position which the new administration faced. For every new item of expenditure that the Bill contained, compensatory savings had to be identified, or some other device proposed, in order to secure Treasury approval. In this context, the 1973 publication, by academic researchers Jane Rowe and Lydia Lambert, *Children who wait* (1973), proved especially influential. They estimated that approximately 7,000 children were caught up in the care system, waiting for permanent family placements. A series of barriers to planning for permanency were identified, together with an argument that the longer such arrangements were delayed, the worse the long-term prospects for individual children. Inside government, the significance of this conclusion was financial as well as social. If children could be released more rapidly for permanent fostering or adoption, then the substantial costs associated with residential care could also be reduced. Although the National Archive papers do not include anything more than indicative costings, DHSS civil servants, in their discussions with the Treasury, point to a potential 20,000 children who might be released for long-term substitute care, in order to create a sufficiently authoritative impression of potential savings. For some later analysts, this figure was part of a general inflation, derived from the figures produced by Rowe and Lambert, in which the number of children who needed adoption was exaggerated, in order to support the cutting of ties between children and their family of origin (see, for example, Holman, 1988). The National Archive files suggest a rather different emphasis. The figures used of children who might be released for adoption were deployed, not in relation to the virtues of 'permanency' *per se*, but in arguments which had to be won with the Treasury, that the extra expenditure required by the Act would be balanced by savings through reductions in the number of children requiring expensive long-term public care.

The Legislation Committee of 10 December agreed that the Bill should be introduced before Christmas 1974, with a second reading delayed until the New Year. For reasons of parliamentary management, the Bill began its parliamentary progress in the House of Lords [NA: MH 152/209], where its publication was immediately welcomed by, among others, the *Argus* (1 February 1975) as a 'memorial to Maria'. There, a series of lengthy debates displayed a highly detailed knowledge of the Colwell report, the history unfolded in it and the analysis it offered. In the first debate, for example, held on 20 February 1975, opposition peers moved a set of 'probing amendments', designed to strengthen the obligation on statutory authorities to share information, with one another. Lord Elton, speaking for the Conservative Party, put the case for the amendments in dramatic and emotional terms (*Hansard*, 1975, vol 357, cc 460-532):

> They are intended to remedy a situation the arising of which was largely responsible for the drafting of this Bill in the first place. I refer to the Maria Colwell case, which must be written upon the hearts of all those who have read the Report upon it. Those who have so read will be aware that this tragedy could have been easily averted, were the various branches of the Social Service and the local authority aware of each other's actions, commitments and knowledge.

> Had the policeman who was called to the fracas at 119, Maresfield Road, known that the child was subject to a supervision order, he would, perhaps, have voiced his opinion in stronger terms.... Had the schoolteacher known the situation of the child, I cannot believe that she would not have visited in person, or ensured that the health visitor had visited, or at least made certain that the education welfare officer received a satisfactory answer to her visits

to the house. But the detective constable did not know the circumstances, the schoolteacher was not aware of the supervision order, the doctor had not been informed of the circumstances; thus the small pieces of this great tragedy never fell into place until the whole puzzle had been upset on the floor…. If we do not protect the Maria Colwells, the 7 year-old children, from the appalling horror story which their lives can become at an early age, then we have no business in politics or government at all.

Replying for the government, Lord Winterbottom agreed that, 'no one who has read the Report on the Colwell case can have closed its covers without her name being engraved upon his heart', but resisted the amendments on the grounds that the proliferation of copies of orders would result in them coming to 'be regarded as routine notifications, and would merely be filed away for possible future reference'. The actions already taken by the government, together with the Bill's proposals, were sufficient to ensure that, in future, 'the left hand shall now be informed of what the right hand is doing' (*Hansard, 1975, vol 357, cc 460-532*).

Later in the same debate the government proved more amenable to amendments designed to make *guardian ad litem* reports mandatory where, in the court's view, a conflict of interest existed between the child and the parent. Lord Wigoder, making the case for amendment, dealt with those who argued that discretionary powers were sufficient in this way (*Hansard*, 1975, vol 357, cc 460-532):

> The short answer to that argument lies in the name Maria Colwell, because in that case the application by the mother for the return of the child by the discharge of the care order, was not opposed, and it is to avoid any possible repetition of that situation that I beg to move the Amendment.

A detailed and nuanced debate followed on 6 March 1975, dealing with the issue of 'paramountcy'. An amendment was moved by Lord Wigoder, seeking to make it a duty that (*Hansard*, March 1975, vol 357, cc 1360-443):

> … where local authorities are making decisions about a child in their care, they shall again make the welfare of the child the first and paramount consideration and not merely,

as the Bill says, take full account of the need to safeguard
and promote the welfare of the child.

In doing so, he said (*Hansard*, March 1975, vol 357, cc 1360-443):

> We are all, in this Part of the Bill, acting, to some extent, in
> the shadow of the Maria Colwell case, but it is necessary
> to repeat to your Lordships what your Lordships know
> already; that is, that that case was, perhaps, notorious but in
> no way unique, since there have been many other cases in
> which children have been too readily handed back by local
> authorities into the care of their parents, with disastrous
> results.

The amendment was agreed, together with a future government
amendment designed to deal with another Colwell report
recommendation, that foster parents should be provided with notice
of court proceedings in relation to any child in their care, and given
an opportunity to make their views known to whoever had been
appointed to represent the child.

In an early legal commentary on the Act, Mumford and Selwood
(1976, p 11) pinpointed both the important departure embodied in
the 'paramountcy' clause, and the balancing act which lay behind it.
Making the welfare of the child the 'first consideration' in all decision
making was a new principle 'of the greatest importance'. Yet, 'the Act
does not go as far as some people wished'. While the child's welfare was
now the first consideration it was not the *sole* consideration. Mumford
and Selwood (1976, p 12) summarised the debate in this way:

> Critics of the Act say that this does not go far enough, that
> consideration for the natural relationship should never
> be allowed to put a child's future at risk. The courts have
> recognised however that it is one thing to put the child's
> welfare first but quite another to say wherein it lies. Future
> happiness cannot be gauged in terms of material standards
> or even security alone. The poor home, the temporarily
> unstable parent, may in the end provide the most caring
> environment for the child. That is the possibility which the
> Act preserves.

The Bill received its third reading on 17 April 1975, at which point
it transferred to the Commons. On 5 August it completed its detailed

its importance as the first inquiry into a child death to be ordered in the post–Colwell period [NA: BN91/21].

Finally, the attempts to draw up terms of reference, including a wide range of relevant authorities, also came to nothing. The Home Office mounted its usual and familiar rearguard action against any investigation into the police or probation service – it was not a 'relevant service', nor were there 'genuine grounds for concern about competence, in managerial or professional terms' [NA: MH 152/232]. Those questions had been raised, properly, only against social work. Officials responsible for social security matters protested that they did not provide a 'service', at all, being involved simply in the disbursement of money.

In vain did directors of social services departments contact Miss Cooper, complaining that what was proposed now amounted to a 'sensation-mongering public inquiry' modelled on the 'Maria Colwell case'. In vain did she attempt, once again, to persuade others that 'public enquiries are not trials for criminal negligence with all the safeguards attached and references to Kangaroo courts are indicative of real concern and unrest and a danger signal' [NA: BN 29/1412].

It was not that senior officials, or even ministers, did not agree. It was much more that the trial which social work had undergone in Colwell had already delivered a set of verdicts that could not be resisted. When a child died in such circumstances, it would be social work, and no other service, which would appear in the dock. The charges would be sufficiently serious to require a national tribunal, and their prosecution would have to take place in public.

Rescue and repair

In the event, the Auckland case ran in parallel with the parliamentary consideration of the Children Bill, which concluded in November 1975. The issues which the report highlighted contributed one small, but direct, change to the Act, in amending the law in relation to the care of children by people discharged from prison. Yet, even before the ink was dry on the Act, opinions were sharply divided on the more general balance it struck between the rights of children and the rights of parents – a debate directly rooted in the 'blood tie' argument, and vividly brought alive in the decision made by social workers to return Maria to the care of her mother, in October 1972, despite her own very clear wishes to the contrary. On the one hand, BASW, while welcoming some aspects of the new Act, was a determined opponent of its redrawing of the balance of rights and responsibilities between birth and substitute parents, the children and the state. The Association's reservations were most fully set out in an article by Chris Andrews (Andrews, 1975), the general secretary of BASW, in an article published in the trade journal, *Social Work Today*, on 20 March. It recorded the progress of the Bill through its House of Lords stages, and set out matters which needed, he thought, to be resolved in the Commons.

The article begins with the usual disclaimers that 'there are many provisions of the Bill which the Association welcomed', before going on to dwell, at much greater length on the issues over which it 'remained deeply concerned ... particularly those which relate to children in care'. Left as drafted, Andrews argued, the Bill would result in parents being reluctant to allow their children to come into care; parent/social worker relationships being made more difficult; children waiting even longer in care because 'parents are going to be very reluctant to allow their children to be placed in foster homes when they know that such placements may lead to the loss of their children'; more, not fewer, 'tug of love' conflicts. 'At one level', he concluded, the Bill could be described as 'an anti-family measure'. It broke a fundamental social work tenet that the 'principal direction of policy concerning the care of children is to enable the family to function adequately and stay together'. While 'the blood-tie does not give rights of possession', Andrews argued, 'it cannot be ignored'. The Bill did not simply shift the balance away from parents in general, it represented a direct attack on 'the rights of a certain group of parents – the poor, the homeless, those living in drab environments with poor facilities, the single-parent family, the oppressed'.

On the other side were those who felt the Act did not go far enough. Sonia Jackson, writing in 1977, conceded that it 'goes further than any previous legislation to redistribute rights between parents and children' (Jackson, 1977, p 85), but still concluded that it stood 'firmly within the British tradition of gradualism'. The parmountcy principle had been one of only a small number of major aspects of the Act to receive early implementation, when Section Three of the Act came into force on 1 January 1976. Yet Sonia Jackson (1977, p 89) contended that the principle 'is given only mild expression in the Children Act, where every diminution of parents' rights is hedged about with restrictions and exceptions'. In continuing to be concerned about the effect of the Act on parents, critics were, she said, allowing 'social work dogma to fly in the face of commonsense, research evidence and the experience of field workers'. The 'deserts of parents', she argued, were 'irrelevant when set against a child's welfare, a point that most critics of the Act do not seem to have grasped' (Jackson, 1977, pp 85-6). The problem with the Act was not that it tipped the balance unfairly away from 'biological parenthood [which] should carry much less legal weight', but that it did not go far enough in doing so.

If debates about the nature of the Act were highly charged at the time, academic analysis and assessment of it, while relatively rare, settled very quickly on one side of the argument. With almost one voice, authors have echoed the verdict of David Bradley (1976, p 452), who concluded that it was the 'shift away from the rights of natural parents' which was 'the most important feature of the Children Act 1975'. The law had, he suggested, 'moved as far as possible towards abolishing the requirement of parental agreement to adoption without actually doing so' (Bradley, 1976, p 454). The rights of foster parents, in particular, had been strengthened in non-contentious and contentious cases alike, with the passage of time tilting the playing field in the direction of those adults with whom a child had established a sense of 'permanency'.

It is one of the major distinguishing features of the Act that financial considerations resulted in a timetable for implementation which stretched out over many years. The first set of enactment dates were set out in a government circular published as the Act completed its parliamentary process. It makes clear that no such dates had been set for many of the Act's provisions. 'Discussions will continue', it said, 'on the detailed timetable and future decisions will depend on the resources outlook in the summer of 1976 for the financial year 1977-78' (quoted in Freedman, 1976, p viii). Yet, Jennifer Terry (1979, p 7), writing in the second edition of her *Guide to the Children Act 1975*, noted that, 'at the time of writing approximately half of the sections of the Act remain unimplemented'. Marking the 10th anniversary of the Act, Holden (1986, p 1) was still lamenting that 'major parts of the Act are still not in force'. It was against this background that, in 1984, the House of Commons Social Services Committee, chaired by Labour MP Renee Short, produced a report into services for children in care (Short, 1984). It explicitly focused on the way in which, it believed, the Act of 1975, formulated under the pressure of 'tragedies involving the death of children' (Short, 1984, p 3, had 'focussed attention on the removal and "rescue" of children' (Short, 1984, p 157). Despite the views expressed in popular newspapers, the Committee had not received 'any serious evidence to suggest that local authorities have abused their powers'. Indeed, they had been used 'just as Parliament intended' (Short, 1984, p 135). The problem was that, 'in the prevailing atmosphere of "planning for permanency"', social workers had been discouraged from making 'whole-hearted and persistent efforts to rehabilitate a child with his natural parents' (Short, 1984, p 192). In other words, the pressure to 'rescue' children from abusive homes had led to a turning away from the hard work of 'repairing' families, where things were going wrong. The Committee concluded that, 'if half the funds and the intellectual effort which had gone towards developing strategies for finding alternative families had been put into what we can only lamely call preventative work, there would be unquestionable advantage to all concerned.'

The Short Report, as it became known, called for a formal review of childcare law. When this was published in 1984 (Short, 1984) it demonstrated a clear shift away from the 1975 Act settlement. 'The interests of children', it concluded, 'are best served by their remaining with their families and the interests of their parents are best serviced by allowing them to undertake their natural and legal responsibilities to care for their own children' (Short, 1984, para 2.8). In order to bring all this about, 'fairer protection must be given to the interests of parents, fairer protection than is given at present' (Short, 1984, para 2.9).

The way in which these debates remained rooted in the Colwell experience was repeatedly emphasised at a special conference, called to review the first decade of the Act of 1975's impact on foster care policy and practice (Holden, 1986). The opening speaker was Dr Owen. He reminded his audience that the 'Maria Colwell case had an absolutely decisive influence in putting the weight of public opinion behind the need to legislate' (Owen, 1986, p 2). The extension of what had begun as, essentially, an Adoption Act to a Children Act ('almost certainly a mistake', Jane Rowe told the same conference; see Rowe, 1986, p 39), had been driven along by 'increased public concern about non-accidental injury following tragedies like Maria Colwell' (Triseliotis, 1986, p 29). The fundamental question, however, remained. 'Were we right', asked Dr Owen (1986, p 4) 'on the fundamental question of there being too much respect in the 1960s for biological ties, and too little respect for psychological links?' The answer, the Conference heard, was a qualified 'no'. Jane Tunstill had reported (1986, p 9), 'a major increase in *compulsion*', by social workers, in removing children from natural parents, and into local authority care. Once that had happened, such parents received 'a very poor deal from social services departments' (Tunstill, 1986, p 15). For children in 'voluntary' care, the Act had produced a substantial increase in local authority use of parental rights resolutions, in which councils turned voluntary arrangements into ones based on compulsion. In 1975, 26 per cent of children in voluntary care had been subject to such resolutions. In 1981, the figure had increased to 41 per cent (White, 1986, p 27). Jane Rowe, whose earlier work had been so influential in shaping the Act of 1975, remained convinced, in 1986, that 'fears that foster parents would rush to adopt their foster children against the wishes of both natural parents and social workers have proved unfounded' (Rowe, 1986, p 41). Yet, she too concluded that 'children's needs may have been met but this has been achieved by methods which at least appeared to be unjust to birth parents, and may actually be so' (Rowe, 1986, p 43).

The equivocal note struck by Rowe and others, however, was in the process of hardening against the Act of 1975. A further decade on from the 1986 special conference and academic opinion had settled, with an unusual degree of unanimity, for a hostile verdict. Hendrick (1994, p 241) described it as 'a signpost marking the end of the rehabilitative ideal'. Fox-Harding (1997, p 67), while rejecting charges that the Act was 'anti-mother' and 'anti-family' as 'too extreme', nonetheless concluded that it embodied 'a significant extension of the power of foster parents and local authorities'. Ball (1998, p 166) referred to the Act as a 'statutory "rag-bag"'. Ann James, writing in 1998, suggested that the Colwell Inquiry created a political climate which was hostile to the prevailing 'professional consensus about prevention' (James, 1998, p 175). The 1975 Act, she argued, 'promoted a view of inadequate parents unable to care effectively for their children'. The result was 'a swing towards child protection and child rescue, most evident in the increased use of compulsory measures'. In her account, the research of Rowe and Lambert (1973) had been 'seized upon to support a radical policy of permanent substitute family placement for children separated from their parents' (James, 1998, p 176). This 'radical policy', James (1998, p 177) argues, 'was embodied in a series of draconian measures supported by the Children Act 1975'.

Horner (2003, p 9) perhaps best captures the link between the specifics of the Colwell Inquiry, the content of the Children Act 1975 and the wider policy tides which shaped child welfare services. Colwell, he concluded, had 'proved to be a watershed in the self-confidence of the new Social Services Departments in their formative years'. The 'permanency policy' of the Children Act 1975 'meant the more rapid removal from their birth families of those children seen to be at risk, the severing of parental links while in residential or foster care with the explicit goal of establishing permanent placements, and ultimately the adoption of the child'. The connecting thread in all of this was a policy transition from 'childcare to child protection', in which the universalist ambitions of the Seebohm reforms had been displaced by far narrower preoccupations with what Farmer (1997, p 146) calls the 'Colwell blueprint' of ensuring that any suspicion of child abuse should be detected, investigated and bureaucratically processed, within a social work service reconstructed around the axis of child protection.

Conclusion

In this chapter we have attempted to draw out some of the direct policy and legislative consequences that flowed from central government in response to the Colwell Inquiry. We have shown how later commentaries, for example, detect the direct influence of Colwell, alongside the more formal and routine influences of Houghton and the parliamentary process on the development of the Children Act 1975. Certainly, at the time, the shadow of Maria Colwell, and the continuing hold it exercised over public opinion, fell heavily over events. One final example must stand for the way in which it provided the driving force, not necessarily for the detail of the Act, but for its central purposes.

As Secretary of State at the DHSS, Barbara Castle had little to do with the day-to-day detail of post-Colwell policy making. Her hands were full with pressing issues of pay-beds in NHS hospitals, reforming the pension system, introducing Child Benefit and pressing ahead with the aftermath of the Ely Hospital scandal of 1969 in reforming services for the mentally ill and the mentally handicapped. Nevertheless, when, on 2 May 1975, she addressed a meeting of all the staff of the DHSS, gathered together at the Metropolitan Tabernacle, it was to the Colwell Inquiry that she made direct reference.

A note from her Principal Private Secretary Graham Hart to senior staff suggested that, 'The general purpose of the exercise is to enable staff to hear from the Secretary of State in person a round up of important activities in hand and to enable them to put to her questions of interest to them.' Among these important activities was the Children Bill, referred to in Mrs Castle's notes as a 'charter of new provisions for children who have no family of their own or who for a variety of reasons can't stay with their own parents'. In explaining why the government was determined to find time for this measure, despite the other pressing legislative demands it faced, Mrs Castle reached for a justification which echoes down the years, both before and after, whenever a landmark scandal struck in social welfare. The Bill was necessary and important, she explained, because its provisions would go 'a long way to preventing the recurrence of such tragedies as the death of Maria Colwell' [NA: MH 152/209]. It is to the testing of that contention over time that the next chapter now turns.

SEVEN

The trial continues ...

Mrs Castle was, of course, to be profoundly disappointed in her hope that such tragedies as Colwell could be prevented in the future. It is beyond the scope of this book to describe each and every one of the notorious child deaths that have occurred since (but see Reder et al, 1993; Munro, 2004). Nor is it our intention to provide a comprehensive account of developments in social work practice or welfare policy since the 1970s that have taken place by way of response to such deaths (but see Hendrick, 1994, 2003; Butler and Drakeford, 2005). What we intend to show, however, is that there is a clear line of sight between the key elements that comprise the Colwell case and contemporary debates about social work, 'problem families' and how the state orders the relationship between the two. In our view, the trial of social work occasioned by the death of Maria Colwell continues.

Ghosts

We have argued in this book and elsewhere that the press (and latterly the media more generally) has a critical role to play in the creation of a scandal, not least in developing an attentive audience for the underlying sequence of events. Colwell did not provide the first instance of the public being made aware through the pages of the public press of the part played by the 'authorities' in the death of children (see, for example, Pinchbeck and Hewitt, 1973, for a detailed account of 'baby farming' almost exactly a century earlier). What Colwell did do for the first time, however, was to link the emergent profession of social work with the arguably preventable death of a child. Thus, from the very point at which the 'fifth social service' began to establish itself and forever afterwards it would seem, social work was associated in the minds of the general public with its worst and most culpable failures. We shall examine shortly how contemporary reporting of social work has maintained this association but with extraordinary and increasing venom.

More immediately, what the Colwell case also provided was a ready point of reference for the future reporting of child abuse. It provided the first entry in the cuttings file for any journalist faced with an apparently similar case. Thus, whenever a child dies, the name of a previous child to die is invoked: Peter Connelly invokes Victoria

Climbié, who invokes Tyra Henry, who invokes Jasmine Beckford, who invokes Maria Colwell. Even when no obvious similarities exist, irrelevant, ahistorical but also potentially misleading comparisons may be made and dwelt on, not least in the pages of newspapers, especially if they are in campaigning mode. The ghost of each successive scandal haunts the next.

As one might expect, in Brighton, the Colwell case specifically is an ever-present spectre in the reporting of every child death in which social work is or might be implicated. Even 30 years after the event, in circumstances where the facts of the case have *no* similarity to Colwell (in terms of the age of the child, family structure, placement, cause of death or distribution of culpability), the pattern of history is reported to be repeating itself.

In a 2000 Brighton case in which three children died of neglect at the hands of their parents, Councillor Danny Sheldon's son, John Sheldon was, with the *Argus'* support, organising a petition to have the law changed and to have the matter debated by the council. The paper reported:

> It was Coun. Sheldon's late father, former Brighton Mayor Danny Sheldon, whose petition paved the way for the landmark inquiry into the death of Maria Colwell. Coun. Sheldon said: "Thousands signed that petition. I hope the public will show its support this time by attending the council meeting." (*Argus*, 24 March 2000)

In the meantime:

> *Argus* editor Simon Bradshaw wrote to all 78 Brighton and Hove Councillors asking for their opinions on a public inquiry and change in the law. (*Argus*, 24 March 2000)

In this case, not only were the circumstances of the children's deaths substantively different to those of Maria Colwell, the area of law that the *Argus* wanted to see changed (the law relating to familial homicide) was also a completely different one from the focus of its attention in 1973. Nonetheless, on the same day, the *Argus* devoted almost a full page to an interview with Maria Colwell's brother. He gives a detailed account of his sister's life and death in which he provides a somewhat ambivalent account of the role of social workers. He is, however, clearly aligned with the *Argus'* view on familial homicide, presumably the precise purpose of the article:

> Mr Colwell supports calls for changes to the law, backed
> by Sussex Chief Constable Paul Whitehouse, to make both
> people culpable in similar circumstances, even if only one
> committed the crime. (*Argus*, 24 March 2000)

To make its point as forcefully as it could, a week later, the *Argus* gave
space to its now retired reporter, Adam Trimingham, who, it will be
recalled, had covered the original Colwell Inquiry. He tells, at some
length and in homely detail, the story of his experiences at the Inquiry:

> No one who was at the public inquiry into the death of
> Maria Colwell will ever forget it. Whether they were the
> officials directly involved with the case or Bill Sansom, the
> amiable policeman who kept order when emotions ran
> high, it was an emotive occasion.

He concludes:

> At the end of it all, we said such a dreadful thing should
> never happen again. But of course it did and the latest
> shocking example is the case which the *Argus* revealed last
> month.... (*Argus*, 8 April 2000)

Some 18 months later, after another quite separate and, again, wholly
different, Brighton child death, Maria's brother was interviewed again.
This time, local social services staff had taken protest action after two
of their colleagues had been suspended during the investigation into
the circumstances of the case.

  Under the headline 'Abuse tragedy brother slams protest', the *Argus*
reports Maria's brother:

> I have been reading the letters in the *Argus* and they have
> all brought up Maria and I'm glad they have.

Just in case the point was missed, a week later, the *Argus* sought out
and interviewed Maria's former primary school teacher, Mrs Ann
Turner, who supplied the paper, as she had in 1973, with a headline
and opening paragraph:

> 'Fury at social workers' protest.'

> Social workers have been branded "totally insensitive" for
> staging a protest in the aftermath of the JS tragedy.

And so it continues. On each and every occasion, irrespective of the
relevance, congruence or substance of the comparison, each death is
aligned with every previous one and fitted into an apparently consistent
narrative. Each unique event would seem to be telling the same story,
the story of the practical and moral failure of social work to protect
children.

Invoking the specific case of Maria Colwell is not confined to
Brighton nor the tabloid, local press, of course. In relation to the
more recent iconic case of Peter Connelly ('Baby P'),[1] some elaborate
and extended comparisons could also be found in the national
broadsheets. *The Observer* (16 November 2008), for example, specifically
counterpoises the Connelly and the Colwell cases. Revisiting the
Whitehawk Estate and finding it much materially improved since the
Kepples lived there, the paper reports at length the opinions of Gill
Clough, the former headteacher of Whitehawk's now closed secondary
school.

> The case of estates like these is that the clean front doors
> hide very deprived interiors. There are entire generations
> of families who have never had a job. There is a lot of drug-
> taking, drinking, incest. It's one of these estates where a lot of
> grown men leave and you get middle-aged women hooking

---

[1] Peter Connelly (also known as 'Baby P', 'Child A' and 'Baby Peter') was a
17-month-old boy who died in Haringey, South London, on 3 August 2007.
Haringey had been the local authority in which Victoria Climbié had died
and had been the site of an earlier and significant 'scandal' (see Butler and
Drakeford, 2005, pp 234 ff). Peter Connelly had suffered a catalogue of serious
physical injuries over a period of at least eight months prior to his death.
During this period, he was known to and seen by a number of social workers
and health professionals. Peter's mother, Tracey Connelly, her boyfriend, Steven
Barker and Jason Owen (Barker's brother) were subsequently convicted of
causing or allowing the death of a child. The circumstances of Peter Connelly's
death were made widely known through the pages of the press from August
2009 onwards. At the end of court proceedings, a series of major reviews and
inquiries was launched, including a review of progress in implementing the
changes to law and practice instituted following the Climbié case. (See, in
particular, London Borough of Haringey, 2009, for a factual account of Peter
Connelly's life and the circumstances of his death.)

up with much younger men, which brings its own issues for families. Children would come to school on Monday mornings and weep – they were exposed to violence and abuse. I would say about 70 per cent of the children in my class would have quite serious issues and, of course, that was among those who came to school at all.

As a consequence, the article concluded:

The picture in Whitehawk is far from unique but it is replicated in pockets of social deprivation across the country, where an underclass is untouched by the affluence of modern Britain and distrustful of those trying to help them. Many social workers in these areas are reluctant to place children in care, influenced by a legal system that favours trying to keep children with their families. Rather than risk parents' fury, social workers will often act only if they believe beyond reasonable doubt that the child is being abused.

Plus ça change? Such a commentary might easily have been written, word for word, in 1973.

We will return shortly to consider how the problems of those families living on Whitehawk (and other 'problem' families) are currently represented in the press. However, it is important to note that, as in Brighton in 1973, so today in Britain more generally, social work is portrayed as operating on exactly the same front line between the failing family, the failing community and the failing (welfare) state. Moreover, it continues to be presented as having to exercise the same kind of Solomonic wisdom and to be doing so to much the same effect.

Of course, invoking the ghosts of social work's past may be a useful heuristic device, but the cumulative effect of reporting child abuse refracted through the lens of successive scandals, especially where each scandal inextricably blends with the last one, is to superimpose a spurious coherence on highly differentiated sequences of events that are, in fact, subtle, interpretive, complex, contingent and contested, as this book has shown. Moreover, by constructing a public narrative around child abuse by reference to successive scandals, which by their nature, are episodic, extreme and peculiarly concerned with the demonstrable failures of child welfare professionals, especially social workers, then it becomes only reasonable to identify such failures as the primary means through which any future child death might be prevented. Hence the focus of public inquiries, serious case reviews and the popular press returns each time to the 'lessons to be learned'. In doing so, attention is directed to the mechanisms of the regulation of social work and social workers rather than to the mechanisms or causation of child harm. Indeed, the very seeds of such a managerialist and bureaucratised social work practice were sown directly in the fertile ground of the Colwell Inquiry as suggested earlier. At the very point of its emergence, the Seebohm social work professional was already being prepared for the poor creature of Ofsted that s/he was to become. We return to this point later.

'The peculiarly British sport of social worker baiting'

Reining in the ambitions of 'the fifth social service' has been made easier not only by the content of media reporting of social work but also by its form. In the examples of press coverage provided in this chapter thus far, the tone of the commentary appears somewhat measured. However, we have described elsewhere (Butler and Drakeford, 2005, pp 107 ff) how, in the period following Colwell, the media grew inexorably more strident in its criticism of social work (Golding and Middleton, 1982; Wroe, 1988). According to Greenland, by 1986 (p 164), dragging 'the reputation of social workers through the mire of the gutter press' had become part of a 'peculiarly British sport of social worker baiting'.

In the years following Colwell, successive child death inquires took place, according to the Beckford Report (London Borough of Brent, 1985, p 5) against a 'background of often virulent press hostility ... unbridled media coverage of an unpleasant, harassing nature'. The Beckford Report went on to note that since Colwell:

> ... social workers have become the butt of every unthinking
> journalist's pen whenever a scapegoat was needed to explain
> a fatality or serious injury.... It is the height of absurdity for
> the media, or indeed the public to castigate social workers....
> (London Borough of Brent, 1985, p 13)

Little was to change in the reporting of the inquiries into the deaths of Heidi Koseda (London Borough of Hillingdon Area Review Committee, 1986), Kimberley Carlile (London Borough of Greenwich and Greenwich Health Authority, 1987) and Tyra Henry (London Borough of Lambeth, 1987) that clustered after the Jasmine Beckford case. Martin's meticulous account (1988, p 117) of the press reporting of the Beckford case and the 'trial of social work by the Fourth Estate' is in no doubt that:

> ... the intensity and selectivity of the press response to
> those criticisms [of social work] is not wholly explicable as
> a rational commentary on the conduct of the social workers
> in the case or even of the state of the whole profession.
> (Martin, 1998, p 129)

In the conflation of the contemporary and the remembered, the elision
of opinion and reportage, the blend of description and analysis that
constitutes the press record of over 40 years of child deaths in the UK,
two main news frames for the reporting of social work with children
at risk have emerged (see Franklin and Parton, 1991; Ayre, 2001), to be
used as the occasion demanded. The first is 'over zealous social workers
rip child from loving home' – being 'abusers of authority, hysterical
and malignant' (*Daily Mail*, 1988, quoted in Ayre, 2001, p 890); the
second is 'incompetent social workers leave child to die' – being 'naive,
bungling, easily fobbed off' (*Daily Express*, 1985, quoted in Ayre, 2001,
p 890). At the heart of both frames of reference are direct echoes of the
conclusions that Colwell had reached – of social workers as ineffectual
and bungling, arrogant and over-ambitious, subject to half-baked and
politically correct sets of ideas that anyone with an ounce of common
sense could demolish.

   This general narrative has proved capable of almost infinite extension.
To take one example, Carole Malone, writing in *The Sunday Mirror*
on 17 January, 1999, condemning Cambridgeshire Social Services'
decision not to allow the adoption of a child whose foster carer had
lied about his past, took the view that it was sheer 'arrogance' that lay
behind the decision and this by 'those bozos at Cambridgeshire Social
Services who've learned nothing from their past mistakes'. These were
the 'idiots' who had 'sent the child back home to an abusive mother,
and he died'. The reference is to the case of Rikki Neave, a child whose
family had been known to social workers for almost 20 years, who was
murdered in 1994 and whose mother had been tried for his murder,
acquitted and instead convicted of child cruelty five years previously.
Other than geography and a vivid contempt and loathing for social
work on the part of the journalist, it is difficult to see any rational or
relevant connection between the two Cambridgeshire cases.

   Entirely new levels of irrationality seem to have been reached in the
vilification of individual social workers involved in the management
of Peter Connelly's care. We could easily have devoted the whole of
this chapter to describing how some of the worst excesses of tabloid
reporting woefully and reprehensibly wove a web of meaning around
this child's tragic death, largely for their own political purposes.

We could point out, for example, the predictable misogyny of *The Sun* and the *Daily Star* in their hounding of Sharon Shoesmith, the director of Haringey's Children's Services. Sharon Shoesmith emerged very early, on the first day of the reporting following the completion of criminal proceedings as the personification of all that had gone wrong. Highly paid (her £110,000 salary was repeatedly highlighted), female (she had 'done very well for herself', said the *Daily Mail*, 13 November 2008), Irish (her 'ordinary childhood' in Co Antrim regularly contrasted with the 'spacious flat' which she now occupied in the 'west end of London') and speaking in a jarring jargon marked her as a direct target of the visceral anger which characterised reporting at this point.

Within two days of the 'Baby P' case coming to dominate newspaper headlines in November 2008, a story appeared which was to be repeated, time and again, over the weeks that followed. It first emerged in the *Daily Star* (14 November 2008), but was soon picked up by almost every other newspaper. The story featured a picture of 'the 55 year old who earns £110,000' 'enjoying a lavish day out at the races weeks after his [Baby P's] death'. The 'relaxed snap' was taken at Ascot. It 'showed little concern for the scandal emerging in her department', the *Daily Star* concluded. *The Sun* (14 November 2008) soon deployed the same story of 'Haringey's arrogant head of children's services on a jolly at Ascot racecourse just weeks after helpless Baby P was killed' as part of an emerging campaign to persuade *Sun* readers 'to sign our petition for £110,000 a year Sharon Shoesmith, 55, to be sacked'.

Once a media feeding frenzy of this sort is established then, as others have noted, almost anything becomes grist to its mill. The whole Ascot episode, pre-dating and entirely unassociated with the death of 'Baby P' was deployed very clearly to symbolise the apparent self-satisfaction of a remote, unfeeling, bureaucratically disconnected Brahmin class, complacently and callously indifferent to the fate of those who, ostensibly, they were paid to protect.

We might also describe the implicit racism of the references in the tabloid accounts that lingered over what they portrayed as the sinister and foreign sounding, Saudi Arabian, Dr Sabah Al-Zayyat, the consultant who had failed to diagnose Peter Connelly's severe spinal injuries. Or the 'political correctness gone mad' theme that was perhaps best summed up in *The Sun*'s 14 November 2008 headline 'Incompetent, politically correct and anti white'. This is a quotation from an apparent whistleblower:

> She said political correctness was rampant to the extent of being ANTI WHITE.

Staff have been recruited from the Caribbean at a cost of £6,000 each.

The whistleblower said: 'Black workers outnumber white workers at Haringey. I felt there was racism towards white people on the social work teams. You felt in the minority.'

However, we leave it to Melanie Phillips (Phillips, 2008), that high priestess of the *Daily Mail* saloon bar, to draw together the threads of the tabloid critique of the death of Peter Connelly. She makes explicit the link to Colwell that we implied at the start of this chapter:

> Since the death of Maria Colwell in 1973, inquiry has followed inquiry into social work failings – only to be followed by one shocking case of abuse after another.
>
> Social work is plagued by low-calibre recruits, whose training is more akin to indoctrination in political correctness, working in a culture which intimidates any dissent and turns morality and common sense inside out.
>
> Of course, the book should be thrown at Haringey Council, Ofsted, the Social Care Inspectorate and the assorted professionals who displayed incompetence and worse that led to the death of Baby P.
>
> But the people who really have blood on their hands are the progressive intelligentsia who have simply written orderly, married, normative family life out of the script, enforced the doctrines of multi-culturalism and non-judgmentalism with the zealotry of the fanatic, and caused Britain to descend into an age of barbarism.

'Brutalised psyches and self-inflicted wounds'

We have described earlier and in more detail elsewhere (Drakeford and Butler, 2008) how Pauline Kepple in particular was treated with some sympathy by the popular press during, and indeed after, the facts of Maria Colwell's life and death were known. It is implicit in Melanie Phillips' account that in an 'age of barbarism' the quality of sympathy might be somewhat more strained. Whereas in an immediately post-Seebohm world the objects of social work's attentions might be problem families or even families with problems, certainly in the case of Peter Connelly (and Victoria Climbié) they are more likely to be presented as 'barbarians' and for the very reasons that Phillips suggests.

To make this point, we quote extensively from a later commentary on the Peter Connelly case. It typifies what this most recent child death scandal has come to represent. It rehearses the same failures of professionals but, like Phillips, it sees in the case a much greater, almost apocalyptic failure of far deeper structures and processes.

The piece is by Andrew Anthony, writing in the traditionally left-leaning and journalistically serious *Observer* in August 2009. In what might be regarded as a very well-written and challenging account, it establishes the context of Peter Connelly's death, both in a literal and a metaphorical sense. It describes the Tottenham in which Peter Connelly was living at the time of his death. In the narrative style of a gothic novel or a fairy story, it begins:

> The semi-detached house in which Peter Connelly spent the last hours of his brief life is bland and unremarkable. A slightly shabby prewar slice of suburbia, with bay windows and a side door, it does not stand out in a nondescript street a few minutes from the Tottenham Hotspur football ground. You would walk past without taking a second look. Which is exactly what the locals did.

It then sets out the nature of Peter Connelly's injuries in some detail, which do not require repetition, but the contrast between the inside and the outside of the house is powerfully evoked:

> The scene of the crime itself seemed to contain all the potent symbols and sordid realities of the feckless, desensitised version of contemporary life.
>
> Hardcore pornography, internet chat sites, vodka bottles, attack dogs, animal faeces, fleas, lice, Nazi paraphernalia, knives and replica guns formed the harsh backdrop to Peter's truncated life and brutal death.

The piece continues then to establish the frame of reference for Peter's death:

> As disturbing as the boy's death was, it was a long way from a unique crime. As many as 30 children have been killed in similar circumstances in this country since Peter, nearly all of them at the hands of a parent or carer. What made this case stand out was the failings of the local authority, Haringey,

which had also been judged to have been negligent in its protection of Victoria Climbié seven years earlier.

How the figure of '30 children' (more ghosts?) is arrived at, the reader is not told. What counts as 'similar circumstances' is not made clear – history lessons without dates, geography without places, numbers but few facts and already, the flow of the narrative has crossed over from the particular to the general. This is not now one case but many.

The article then constructs mini-biographies of each of the main protagonists starting – Mary O'Connor, Peter Connelly's grandmother:

> She lives in a small council flat in Islington, north London, with the alsatian that once belonged to her daughter. It is sparsely furnished and, when I visited, the dog was chained to a radiator to stop her attacking me. "She was raped by that lump of lard's [Barker's] rottweiler," O'Connor said, explaining the dog's nervousness with an image that conjured a climate of abuse that transcended species.

This is the metaphor of fable, as well as of myth.

There is evidence of a very hard life indeed but the depth of her own faults is left for her to express in her own words:

> She put her son in care, she says, because he made her life hell and "social services were on my back. I thought, sod the lot of you. So I took him down the social services. He didn't know. He thought we were going to get a new pair of trainers. I just turned round and said: 'See you.' I said to the woman: 'When you're fed up with him you can bring him back.'"
>
> "And almost to the day a year later, they brought him back to me. And they brought me a cooker. I said: 'If you want me to take him back, get me a cooker.'"

Anthony hints that another (unidentified) relative of Connelly's:

> ... was placed in care by Islington council. According to reports, this relative became involved in the alleged paedophile rings that operated in the authority's care system in the 1990s, as a victim, procurer and abuser. One of the reporters who exposed the rings attributed the problem to "5% corruption, 95% political correctness". The net result

was a damaging embarrassment for the Labour-run council in the short term but, argues the reporter, there was a more disturbing legacy: "Baby P is the evil fruit of that behaviour."

In a language that is both vague yet apparently precise, the article invokes the worst form of depravity to damn the wilful, politically motivated activities of the local authority children's services department.
Anthony reflects:

> Almost everywhere you look in this bleak tale, there is evidence or suggestion of child abuse that multiplies into an ever-expanding matrix of dysfunction. "Man hands misery to man," wrote Philip Larkin. "It deepens like a coastal shelf." And to examine the subterranean world of the people around Peter Connelly is to gain a vertiginous sense of unfathomable suffering.

There is then an anecdotal but not unsympathetic account of what happened in Haringey Social Services, post-Climbié, before an account of Barker's childhood, where the same pattern of hint, suggestion, implication and innuendo characterises an awful set of experiences:

> In 1995, [Barker and his older brother] moved into the Kent home of their grandmother, Hilda Barker. They waged a campaign of intimidation against the 82-year-old, terrorising her by wearing Halloween masks and stopping her from seeing her friends. She told police the brothers had locked her in a cupboard until she agreed to leave her money to them. They were charged with assault, but the charges were dropped after Hilda Barker died of pneumonia. Owen, who has five children from two different women, had convictions for arson and burglary. He was also accused of committing rape as a 13-year-old. As if to complete the portfolio of maladjustment, he was later investigated for victimising an Asian family.

No shades of grey – a thorough, unremitting and unredeemable cast of characters emerges:

> In court, it was possible to see Connelly's talent for manipulation. When the jury was out, she spent much of her time playing with her hair, looking bored and oblivious.

But as soon as the jurors returned, she would wear a face of anxious concern, and dab her eyes as she wept.

By contrast, Barker maintained an expression of gormless detachment throughout the proceedings, as though he wasn't able to grasp the moral gravity of child rape.

And so it continues to make its moral point. Anthony indirectly acknowledges that this is a form of storytelling in his final paragraph:

The Connellys and the Barkers were two families that were always unlikely to heal each other's brutalised psyches and self-inflicted wounds. When they came together, they instead turned a grim domestic drama into a social tragedy that reverberated far beyond the squalid confines of their semi-detached Tottenham home.

The specific lessons of this moral fable, he has already explained:

The ease with which people have children and the difficulty they have in looking after them is a recurring theme in stories of social breakdown. It is a symptom of a radically foreshortened perspective, in which future consequences seldom impinge on choices and actions in the present.

But it is also a function of a welfare system that allocates subsidies and material security to those with children. The noble intention is to arrest economic deprivation at birth, yet too often it helps foster the very conditions it seeks to combat. The more the state intervenes, the more it is required to intervene and therefore the more chance that its intervention will, as in the case of Baby P, not be enough.... There is no easy solution to the societal malaise this case highlights, but the fact remains, as many social workers will testify, there is a growing class of state dependants who have gained few if any life skills other than an ability to work the system.

Without making any judgement on the reasonableness or appropriateness of the opprobrium visited on the central characters in the death of Peter Connelly, Anthony is implying that it is the welfare state itself that has perpetuated if not actually spawned the very problems it was established to solve. Social work is directly implicated in this most perverse of unintended consequences. Far from simply failing to resolve the problems of families, the welfare state, not least through its social workers, has actually produced them. Just as misguided, arrogant and incompetent practice in the case of Maria Colwell ended so very badly, so too, in aggregate, has the sum total of 65 years of the postwar welfare state. This contrast with the expectations held for the fifth social service by Frederic Seebohm could not be more complete.

To understand how this transformation could have occurred, in the final part of this chapter we explore how the most obvious legacy of the Colwell Inquiry, the model of regulated practice that it produced, has played its part in creating the circumstances where such a view is even possible.

Governance in social work

In Chapter Six we described the framework of registers, area committees and other forms of organisational apparatus that flowed out of Whitehall in the aftermath of the Colwell Inquiry. If the history of the last 40 years has witnessed a meta-movement from govern*ment* to govern*ance* (Jessop, 1999, p 357), then the plethora of circulars and guidance with which central government sought to respond to concerns about child abuse represents a last high-water mark of 'government'. It stood firmly in the 'top-down', or Fordist, tradition of social policy making (see McDonald and Marston, 2002, and Powell, 2008, for an elaboration of this point), in which Whitehall and Westminster determined the objects of public policy, leaving its implementation to local agents in the NHS, or local authorities. Indeed, Ball (1998, p 166) suggests that, in retrospect, the Children Act 1975, and its attendant administrative machinery, can be seen to be the last of the legislative sequence under which the 'local authorities' responsibilities and discretionary powers multiplied with very little control of their interpretation'.

Nonetheless, a quarter of a century after the post-Colwell arrangements had been laid down, Farmer (1997, p 146) concluded that 'the procedures devised after the inquiry into her death have formed a blueprint for those still in use today. The emphasis present and past has been on setting up reliable procedures to identify children at risk and to maximise inter-professional coordination.' In Chapter Six we argued that the interprofessional forums established after Colwell were part of a new disciplinary framework in which social work was to be prevented from claiming a unique professional authority in relation to child welfare. That purpose remained intact throughout the twists and turns of policy change and the assaults of further high-profile child abuse scandals. Yet, below the surface, from 1979 onwards, the modes of operation characteristic of the Keynsian welfare state were eroding under a set of pressures, different in origin and nature, but uniform in effect.

For the neo-conservatives of the Thatcher era, the state was breaking down under its own weight, and that of general governmental 'overload' (see Moran, 2001, pp 414 ff, for an elaboration of this argument in the context of 'policy catastrophe'). For such theorists it was an article of faith that the welfare state was a problem, rather than a solution, generating the difficulties that it had, ostensibly, been set up to address. It was also self-expanding – always finding new problems to solve – and, in Jessop's (1999, p 352) terms, 'ultimately self-defeating as it becomes more complex, overloads itself with tasks and eventually produces a crisis of ungovernability'.

A leading article in *The Times* (4 December 1985), written in the aftermath of the Jasmine Beckford Inquiry, sums up the neoliberal reaction to social work. It identified the Maria Colwell case as a catalyst in the implementation of post-Seebohm reforms, in which a 'platform of collective thought ... and an atmosphere of optimistic utopianism and enforced egalitarianism' had produced 'a massive expansion of social work'. The patterns of thought characteristic of that mistaken era, the paper argued, meant that such expansion could only ever go on unchecked: 'If the customer is satisfied with his service the provider can ask for more money to keep up the good work. If the customer is dissatisfied he can ask for more money to put things right.'

Along with a never-satiated demand for public money went a boundary-less sense of what such a public service might achieve: 'the less the clarity about what social work was actually supposed to do, the more came the expectations that it could do almost anything'. The reality, the newspaper argued, was very different: 'the state's chief contribution to the Beckford tragedy was to move a four-year-old girl from foster parents who cared for her well to a natural parent in whose care she died.' Mrs Thatcher's next prime ministerial speech advocating 'the virtues of family life', the paper argued, would be most welcome 'if it were to include some reference to the value of caring foster parents'.

This sense that the virtues of family life had been eroded by the welfare state, in general, and by social work, in particular, reached a new pitch of rhetorical indignation around another, quite different, child welfare scandal. The Cleveland child abuse scandal occurred in 1987, where 121 cases of suspected child sexual abuse were diagnosed by Dr Marietta Higgs and Dr Geoffrey Wyatt, paediatricians at a

Middlesbrough hospital. A media storm had broken in which welfare services were accused of ripping children unjustly from the loving homes in which they had been carefully reared. In the process, Hill (1990, p 202) concludes, the media 'image of social workers was transformed from that of "wimp" to that of "bully"'. In *The Times* (19 December 1987), the accusation that social workers were 'riding roughshod over the rights of parents' was linked directly to the aftermath of the Maria Colwell Inquiry, an experience which 'hangs over the head of every social worker, affecting their attitude to their work and the decisions they take', and helping to explain 'the rise in the number of children taken into care and many of the 30,000 names on "at risk" registers'.

In governance terms, the general approach that successive Conservative governments of the 1980s and 1990s took to social work was infused with a belief that the primary responsibility for welfare services should lie, not with the state at all, but with families and charitable provision. Where the direct involvement of government was necessary, then this should be limited to supporting a vibrant pluralist economy of care, in which voluntary and charitable giving was to be combined with private enterprise and subject to the discipline and rigour of a free market, within the framework of the law. The specific tools through which the accompanying de-professionalisation and managerialism were pursued included ever more explicit manifestations of audit and inspection regimes that, as Parton (2009, p 70) suggests, produced 'a raft of tightly drawn legislation, guidance and procedures, particularly in the area of children's services so that social work had become an increasingly case-accountable and procedurally regulated activity'.

In this process, the early world of East Sussex Social Services Department had been left far behind. Then, the interests of welfare professionals, and those of the families they served, had been regarded as broadly the same. Parton and Martin (1989, p 33) describe the political consensus underpinning the postwar settlement as one 'imbued with an optimism which believed that measured and significant changes could be made to the lives of families, communities and society more generally, via the use of state interventions'. A direct line of common interest and shared concern ran between the state and its citizens, mediated through professional workers motivated by a sense of public service. The interests of patients and doctors, teachers and pupils, social workers and their clients were essentially identical and coterminous. 'Professional paternalism' was one of the hallmarks of the period. Within the family, too, a similar set of benign and paternalistic relationships were believed to operate in which 'individual family members did not have an identity or set of interests distinct from, or in opposition to, the family as a whole' (Parton and Martin, 1989, p 33).

Now, as Hill (1990, p 198) complained, the plethora of 'registers, case conferences, area child protection committees, procedure manuals' that followed from child abuse inquiries, had produced a 'disproportionate and distorting' impact on social work. The language of welfare had been replaced by one of child protection in which, as Parton and Otway (1995, p 608), writing at the end of the post-1979 Conservative period, concluded:

> ... we now have child protection strategy meetings, child protection case conferences, area child protection committees and child protection registers. Similarly most social services departments have child protection officers and teams, while many health authorities and trusts and police forces have staff specifically designated as specialising in child protection.

This was a process that was only to gather pace under the Blair administrations after 1997, with their mania for 'modernisation' and 'reform' – an obsession that Wallace (2009, p 249) concludes only became more insistent the longer New Labour remained in office. While different writers reach different conclusions as to the policy and practical impact of these commitments (see, for example, Clarke and Newman, 2004, p 53; 6 and Peck, 2005), there is a level of agreement among analysts that the decade after 1997 brought about an underlying, epochal re-articulation of the state, through a meta-movement from *government* to *governance* (Jessop, 1999, p 357) in which the modes of operation characteristic of the Keynsian welfare state have given way to those said to be required in a globalised era.

The suspicion with which Mrs Thatcher had regarded public services and public servants was replicated in the New Labour period. For the neo-conservatives such services were always best regarded as conspiracies against the public, monopolies in which workers held all the cards, and organised services to their own benefit, rather than those of users. In New Labour's hands, the argument became one that 'trust' could no longer be relied on as the basis for construction of welfare relationships. In the professional world of the Colwell era, trust relationships between users and providers, and between providers themselves, were at least believed to be the ambition of welfare services. Now, in its place, compliance replaced commitment and performance management replaced professional discretion. The familiar litany of 'policy guidelines, targets, standards, regulation, output-based commissioning, centrally determined access criteria, and assessment frameworks' (Newman et al, 2008, p 538) crowded out any sense of public service as an ethos. In the process, as Smith (2001) argues, the search for 'trust' in relationships between users and providers of services is replaced by an effort to generate 'confidence' in the services themselves. And 'confidence' in this sense has to be developed through the use of instrumental rationality – 'targets, objectives, performance indicators and (measurable) outcomes' (Smith, 2001, p 302).

The residualisation of the Keynsian welfare state, and the paradigm shift from trust to confidence, and from confidence to compliance, brought with it a recalibration in the relationship between users and services – and, in particular, with those users who were the object of New Labour's highly developed suspicion. At a general level, the combination is identified by McDonald and Marston (2002, p 387) as one in which governments 'seek to dismantle the social investment function of the state, while retaining and increasing its social control in the lives of the poor'. In the case of child welfare it produced a post-Laming Green Paper, *Every child matters* (Chief Secretary to the Treasury, 2003), which Munro (2004, p 83) suggests was characterised by a 'wholesale lack of trust' in both parents and the child welfare services available to help them.

Moran's (2001, p 418) analysis of policy catastrophes suggests that such events can be categorised in seven different ways, including what he calls the 'great leap forward' policy catastrophe, in which 'radical change demands rapid and irreversible institutional upheaval', in order to break with the culture of the past. The Children Act 2004, which followed from the Green Paper, has some of the hallmarks of this policy-making approach, in what Hudson (2005, p 519) calls its 'rapidly formulated top-down approach to policy-making'. In the process, it abandoned the 40-year pattern of local authority responsibility for children's services, embracing instead a set of untried procedures intended to create 'confidence' in 'modernised' patterns of delivery, closely overseen by a new, but entirely inexperienced, cadre of regulatory regimes.

In less than five years, and under the pressure of events surrounding the death of Peter Connelly, both these experiments in authoritarianism and centralism were exhibiting signs of acute failure. In terms of organisational reforms in October 2008, the Audit Commission (2008) had published a highly critical report on one of the major planks of the Act of 2004, the creation of children's trusts, concluding that their role was unclear and confusing, and reporting that one in ten councils had already either kept or reverted to a single organisational structure for children's services. In terms of regulation, the government, under intense media and political pressure, turned to the newly empowered Ofsted to carry out an investigation into the conduct of Haringey Council, with an instruction to report within two weeks. Invoking the case of Maria Colwell, 'more than three decades ago', the then leader of the opposition, David Cameron, criticised social workers involved in the case for their lack of 'common sense' – 'the common sense that says this child is being abused, and the responsibility to do something about it'. Where that responsibility had been shirked, he wrote, there had been 'professional negligence' and 'those who job it was to oversee the system must admit they have failed, and pay a price'.

Yet, almost immediately the first cracks in this regulatory wall were beginning to appear. A 'whistleblower' appeared to claim that regulators had already failed to respond to her complaints about the council's child protection services. Then newspapers discovered that Ofsted had only just published a report into the authority, which was almost uniformly congratulatory and which awarded Haringey's Social Work Services a maximum three star rating. Yet, when inspectors produced their new report, Ofsted now concluded that Haringey had the worst child protection systems of any borough scrutinised by a review in the last 12 months. In 2006, Ofsted had concluded that Sharon Shoesmith 'provides strong and dynamic leadership', a judgement endorsed in its 2007 report. Now, all this was reversed. 'Leadership and management' within the authority were 'inadequate'. Within a day Sharon Shoesmith had been relieved of her duties. Within a week, she had been sacked.

Unsurprisingly, such an emphatic *volte face* created a renewed interest in regulatory fallibility. In its restructuring of the state, New Labour had shifted responsibilities away from central government itself, outwards to new partnerships at local level, and upwards to newly strengthened regulatory regimes. In place of trust-based relationships between users and providers of services, it offered citizens the specialist, technical judgements of competent assessors and inspectors, through which confidence in the quality of otherwise-suspect local services could be measured and improved. In practice, the new arrangements turned out to be a means not of mitigating risk but of avoiding responsibility. Instead of protecting the public, the actions of agencies most closely involved – government ministers, Haringey bureaucrats and inspectorates alike – appeared more directed towards protecting themselves. The risks that were being managed, turned out to be risks to themselves, and their own reputations, even when, as in Ofsted's highly flexible judgements, attempts to do so appeared so deeply unconvincing and lacking in reassurance.

Writing in *The Guardian* (17 November 2008), Olive Stevenson reflected on the changes that had taken place in the years between the Maria Colwell case and that of Peter Connelly. In both, she concluded multi-agency working was at the heart of what went wrong. Yet in 1974, the section of the Colwell report that she had written on cross-agency cooperation had emphasised the importance of professional judgement and time for reflection in order better to understand risk and how to respond to it. In just one generation, the focus had shifted from dealing with risk to accounting for it, from a concern with promoting the complex decision making of professional staff to a preoccupation with procedures that ensured compliance, so that 'they can say they followed all the procedures to avoid the dreadful things happening'.

Conclusion: 'the arrogance of bureaucratic certainty'

Social work is far from unique in having adopted the credo of the new regulatory regimes of the last decade and managerialism, bureaucratisation and a performativity culture have penetrated deeply into other areas of welfare services such as hospitals and schools. It has, however, been uniquely damaging to social work, we would suggest, for a number of very particular reasons. First, it has apparently failed, even in its own terms, to produce the results that were intended. 'Lessons' are still not learned. Children still die and social workers are still found to be at fault. Second, it would seem that much of the regulatory apparatus is understood to be of social work's own making, a direct descendent of the Colwell Inquiry, and that it is imbued with the insensitive, nonsensical and incompetent arrogance that, for many, have always characterised the profession. It alienates those who might use the service and infuriates those who observe from a distance. Third, it has proven to be a Trojan horse, enabling what was always possible within the Seebohm vision for a family service, namely, a far from benign tutelage of those families identified as having or as simply being 'problems'. Taken together with 35 years of high profile, endlessly self-referencing and reinforcing scandals, what has emerged in the public consciousness is social work as a failed and scandalous profession. Whereas for Seebohm and his predecessors, social work was the answer, it is now simply another part of the problem.

The seeds of this were present in the social work practice that failed to prevent Maria Colwell's death and they were nurtured in the Inquiry that followed and the recommendations that it made. This was highlighted during the pre-publication discussion of the Report in Whitehall:

The story of Maria Colwell has something of the inevitability of the Greek tragedy; a group of adults preoccupied with their personal vendettas, emotional needs or psychological theories while the child herself, a predestined victim, seems at the end almost to have resigned herself to the inevitable. One cannot read the report without anger; a not particularly helpful reaction. The original mistake was, of course, the decision made at the case conference on 26th April 1971 to return the child to her mother. There appears to have been little to justify this decision and a great deal to suggest that it was wrong, not least the fact that Maria had been cared for by the Coopers since she was four months old. But the decision once made was relentlessly pursued with all the arrogance of bureaucratic certainty. The only person who seemed to know what was right for this child was Maria herself; and she was not consulted. Mrs [sic] Stevenson's minority report seems to me unfortunate. It is better not to try to excuse the inexcusable. [NA: BN 29/1412]

This is the judgement of senior Home Office official, Mrs Phyllis White, on the draft Colwell report submitted for her consideration in May 1974. Her reference to the 'arrogance of bureaucratic certainty' might be a description not just of the management of the specific case of Maria Colwell, but also a commentary on the last 10 years of modernised, 'Ofsteded', risk-averse, unprincipled, regressive social work practice with children and families of the New Labour period. Mrs White's judgement of the relative culpability of those involved in the Colwell case should perhaps be respected. Not only was she a principal in the criminal policy department of the Home Office, but when not undertaking her formal duties, she was also busy writing crime novels under her maiden name, P.D. James, under which title she was much better known. Her association of Maria Colwell and the narrative archetype of the Greek tragedy shows an instinctive appreciation of the scandalising process and the power of myth making.

At the time of writing, the struggle for the future shape and direction of social work is currently being carried on in the context of a new government, a new austerity and a whole new set of regulatory, representative and administrative structures. The trial continues but, as a serial offender – to extend the metaphor of this book one more time – while the jury is still out on this particular occasion, there can be little doubt as to the likely verdict on social work.

And yet, is there any mitigation to be offered? What we hope we have demonstrated in this book is the haphazard, contingent and uncertain circumstances in which a child's death might occur. What if Bill Kepple had been working away that weekend? What if Maria had already been in bed when he got home? We hope we have also demonstrated the complex, imprecise and deeply conflicted processes that constitute social work in such challenging circumstances and how mistakes are so much easier seen in hindsight. We have shown the integrity and unassuming commitment of Diana Lees and the pragmatic reliability of Daphne Kirby. We have shown just how difficult the work is and how important it is that it is done and done well. We may also have demonstrated that there is an urgent need, not for a residualist model of the welfare state where social work techniques are employed to defend managers and ministers and to deflect attention from failures operating more widely in our society, but for a larger, more ambitious and aligned form of social work that respects the complexity of human and social organisation and which is predicated on a commitment to achieve a similar form of social justice that motivated the original architects of the welfare state.

Maria Colwell – synopsis

Maria Colwell was born on 25 March 1965. She was the fifth child of Raymond and Pauline Colwell, née Tester, and Mrs Colwell's sixth child. Her parents had separated a few weeks before her birth and, within two months, in July 1965, Mr Colwell had died following a brief but catastrophic illness that, thereafter, gave rise to a substantial, sustained feud between his own family and that of his estranged wife.

Within a few weeks of Mr Colwell's death his wife, in the words of the Colwell Inquiry report, 'went completely to pieces'. The four elder Colwell children were received into local authority care, the younger two being placed with Mrs Colwell's mother, Mrs Tester. She already had care of Mrs Colwell's first child, who had been brought up to believe that she was Mrs Tester's daughter. No attempts were ever made, by Mrs Colwell, to resume the care of these children.

Maria, however, was placed by her mother, on a voluntary basis, in the care of her late husband's sister, Mrs Cooper. From the outset, that arrangement was a fraught one. Twice, within the first six months, Mrs Colwell removed Maria from her aunt and twice, on the intervention of the NSPCC, Maria was returned to Mrs Cooper. On the second occasion, the arrangement was formalised through a local authority Care Order. The basis on which Maria was then fostered by the Coopers was ambiguous and a matter of dispute before the Inquiry. It was clear that Mrs Colwell objected to the placement and that, in the first instance at least, it was clearly signalled to the Coopers that the arrangement was 'temporary', until a different, more permanent arrangement could be made. Nevertheless, no alternatives were ever put in place, and Maria remained in the care of Mr and Mrs Cooper for a further six years.

During this period, Mrs Colwell's contact with Maria was sporadic. By 1967 she had formed a new relationship with William ('Bill') Kepple, an Irishman in possession of a large number of aliases and a reputation for 'wildness'. Together they moved very rapidly through a large number of very substandard, privately rented addresses, with Mrs Colwell giving birth to children of the relationship in 1967, 1968 and 1970. Yet, throughout the period, and with growing insistence, Mrs Colwell expressed her intention of resuming care of Maria – an intention that much exacerbated the underlying family feud and, gradually, made Maria the main focus of it. On Mrs Colwell's side, she regarded the Coopers as obstructive and hostile. On the Coopers' side, they regarded her as irresponsible and interested only in her own needs and wishes, rather than in Maria's welfare.

In the years up to 1970, the strategy followed by social workers was to endorse Maria's placement with her aunt, while attempting to negotiate a level of contact with Mrs Colwell and the wider Tester family. On 1 April 1970, responsibility for Maria's supervision was transferred to Diana Lees, highly qualified with experience in medical social work, but taking her first post in local authority childcare. In August 1970, the Kepple family were allocated a council house by Brighton Corporation, moving to 119 Maresfield Road on the Whitehawk Estate. From this time onwards, with a fixed and permanent address, Mrs Kepple (as she was now known, and was soon to become in law) moved more directly and insistently to pursue Maria's return, making it clear that she would go to the courts if necessary.

By April 1971 East Sussex County Council Social Services Department had come to the conclusion that such court action could be delayed but not prevented, and that, given her settled address and relative success in bringing up those children of her relationship with Bill Kepple, Mrs Kepple's application would be likely to meet with success. They embarked on a programme of increasing contact between Maria and her mother, based essentially on the belief that reunion was inevitable, although not necessarily desirable. The part which a belief in the 'blood tie' played in this decision making was to become a matter of fundamental concern to the Inquiry.

Both the Coopers, and Maria herself, reacted badly to the new plan. Maria herself very actively resisted most, but not all, attempts to take her on visits to Maresfield Road. Frequency of contact, and Maria's opposition, increased together. Matters came to a head in the autumn of 1971 when Mrs Kepple made a formal court application for Maria's return to her care. After much debate, Maria was returned to her mother, on trial, in October and the application was not opposed at Hove Juvenile Court, in November. This was a decision that the Inquiry was to focus on in detail. Although Maresfield Road lay within the boundaries of Brighton's Social Services Department, it was agreed that supervision would be retained by East Sussex County Council's Social Services Department. From November 1971 to April 1972 matters were relatively quiet.

The first significant problem occurred over the Easter weekend of April 1972. Neighbours complained to the NSPCC of Maria's physical ill treatment and a considerable fracas occurred between the Kepples and other Maresfield Road residents, to which the police were called. A petition was got up among the neighbours calling for the Kepples to be re-housed elsewhere. Miss Lees and Mrs Kirby (of the NSPCC) visited and, after some considerable difficulty, Maria was seen. Despite visible bruising and a badly swollen eye, no action was taken, much to the disagreement of the Kepples' immediate neighbour, Mrs Rutson. The 'April incident', and the response of social workers to it, was to be a major focus of the Inquiry.

For six months after 1 June Miss Lees, heavily burdened with other cases, did not visit Maria. Mrs Kirby, more often in the area for other reasons, saw the Kepple children regularly but informally, while travelling through Maresfield Road. Her conclusion was that physical standards within the home were changing for the better and circumstances stabilising. Yet, as far as Maria was concerned, matters were to deteriorate from September onwards. At Whitehawk Junior School, to which she had moved after the summer, her class teacher was Mrs Turner, in her first teaching post. She became progressively more concerned about Maria. That concern was shared by the school's new education welfare officer, Mrs Dickenson, despite the fact that Mrs Turner and Mrs Dickenson never met. As newcomers, and outsiders, they made regular efforts to draw attention to Maria's ravenous hunger, the poor state of her clothing, her repeated lateness at school and rumours of complaints from neighbours and shopkeepers that she was being used as a 'drudge', for example in pushing home large sacks of coal in an old pram.

Over the autumn members of the public made a new series of complaints to the NSPCC about Maria's treatment. The number of these complaints was a matter of dispute, but the fact of their existence was not. With Mrs Kepple pregnant again, visits were now also paid by a health visitor, Miss Bodger, attached to the practice of the Kepples' family GP, Dr Barley.

From November 1972, further altercations took place with neighbours, involving the police. Maria now stopped attending school altogether. Mrs Dickenson's increasingly insistent visits now focused on obtaining a medical examination for Maria. This led to an angry confrontation with Mr Kepple at the start of December that, in turn, produced an emergency visit by Miss Lees. She found a steady domestic scene in which all family members were engaged together in apparent harmony. No action was taken. On the following day, 6 December, Maria was taken to Dr Barley who was, by now, alerted to the concerns of Mrs Dickenson, the education welfare officer. He examined Maria but, other than a scalp infection, found nothing to concern him. During the next three weeks, the family were visited and seen by a wide variety of social welfare workers, neighbours and relations. Their subsequent recollection of Maria's state of health also varied widely.

Once the Christmas holidays began, Maria's contact with the outside world was largely at an end. On the morning of Wednesday 3 January Mrs Kepple visited the WRVS. In her absence Mr Kepple hit Maria in the face because she had refused to answer him when he put a question to her. Her condition worsened over the following days, but neither parent took her for medical attention. On Saturday 6 January Mr Kepple was out of the house drinking for most of the afternoon, and all of the evening. He returned at about 11.30 pm. He found Mrs Kepple and all the children still up, watching television. He asked Maria about her eye which had been injured on the Wednesday. She again refused to answer him. A second major flare-up followed in which Maria was assaulted. On the morning of Sunday 7 January Maria was taken to Brighton's Children's Hospital where she was found to be dead on arrival. A post-mortem examination by forensic pathologist Professor Cameron was carried out five days later. It revealed a pattern of extensive, long-term physical damage, compounded by a final concentrated set of blows.

Maria Colwell – a chronology

1965, 25 March   Maria Colwell born in Hove, East Sussex, the fifth child of the marriage between Raymond and Pauline (née Tester) Colwell.

1965, 22 July   Death of Raymond Colwell, Maria's father. Maria is informally placed in the care of Raymond Colwell's sister and her husband, Doris and Ron Cooper.

1965, 15 Dec   The four older Colwell children are placed in the formal care of East Sussex County Council.

1966, June   Maria's mother removes her from the care of the Coopers and places her with 'a friend'.

1966, 17 Aug   Maria is placed under the formal care of East Sussex County Council and returns to live with the Coopers.

1971, 26 April   Case conference held to review Maria's position.

1971, 22 Oct   Maria is returned, 'on trial', to the care of her mother.

1971, 17 Nov   Hove Juvenile Court revokes the Care Order in respect of Maria and replaces it with a Supervision Order in favour of the County Borough of Brighton.

1972, 20 May   Pauline Colwell marries William Kepple.

1973, 6 Jan   Maria is killed at her home in Maresfield Road, Brighton.

1973, 17 April   William Kepple is convicted of Maria's murder although, on appeal, he is subsequently convicted of her manslaughter and sentenced to eight years imprisonment.

1973, 24 May   Public inquiry into Maria Colwell's death is announced.

1974, 5 Sept   Report of the public inquiry is published.

References

Books and articles

6, P. and Peck, E. (2005) 'Modernisation: the 10 commitments to New Labour's approach to public management', *International Public Management Journal*, vol, 7, no 1, pp 1-18.

Abse, L. (1973) *Private member*, London: Macdonald and Co.

Alcock, P. (2002) 'Editorial', *Benefits*, vol 10, no 3, pp 177-8.

Andrews, C. (1975) 'The Children Bill – BASW must intensify its campaigning', *Social Work Today*, vol 5, no 25, pp 777-9.

Anthony, A. (2008) 'The killers of Baby P came from decades of abuse and dysfunction', *The Observer*, 16 August.

Audit Commission (2008) *Are we there yet? Improving governance and resource management in children's trusts*, London: Audit Commission.

Ayre, P. (2001) 'Child protection and the media', *British Journal of Social Work*, vol 31, no 6, pp 887-901.

Bailey, R. and Brake, M. (1975) *Radical social work*, London: Hodder and Stoughton.

Bailey, R. and Brake, M. (1980) *Radical social work and practice*, London: Edward Arnold.

Ball, C. (1998) 'Regulating child care: from the Children Act 1948 to the present day', *Child and Family Social Work*, vol 3, no 3, pp 163-71.

Bilton, K. (1979) 'Origins, progress and future', in J. Cypher (ed) *Seebohm across three decades*, Birmingham: BASW Publications, pp 5-26.

Blacker, C. (1952) 'Introduction', *Problem families: Five enquiries*, London: Eugenics Society.

Bogdanor, V. (1996) 'The fall of Heath and the end of the postwar settlement', in S. Ball and A. Seldon (eds) *The Heath government 1970-1974: A reappraisal*, London: Longman, pp 371-89.

Bradley, D. (1976) 'Children Act 1975', *Modern Law Review*, vol 33, no 4, pp 452-61.

Brown, A.D. (2003) 'Authoritative sense-making in a public inquiry report', *Organisational Studies*, vol 21, no 1, pp 95-112.

Brown, M. and Madge, N. (1982) *Despite the welfare state: A report on the SSRC/DHSS programme of research into transmitted deprivation*, London: Heinemann Educational.

Butler, D. and Pinto-Duschinsky, M. (1971) *The British General Election of 1970*, London: Macmillan.

Butler, I. and Drakeford, M. (2005) *Scandal, social policy and social welfare* (2nd revised edn), Bristol/London: The Policy Press/BASW.

Castle, B. (1980) *The Castle diaries*, London: Weidenfeld and Nicolson.

Chief Secretary to the Treasury (2003) *Every child matters*, Cm 5860, London: The Stationery Office.

Clarke, J. (1980) 'Social democratic delinquents and Fabian families', in National Deviancy Conference *Permissiveness and control: The fate of the sixties legislation*, London and Basingstoke: Macmillan, pp 72-95.

Clarke, J. and Newman, J. (2004) 'Governing in the modern world', in D.L. Steinberg and R. Johnson (eds) *Blairism and the war of persuasion: Labour's passive revolution*, London: Lawrence and Wishart, pp 53-65.

Collison, M. (1980) 'Questions of juvenile justice', in P. Carlen and M. Collison (eds) *Radical issues in criminology*, Oxford: Martin Robertson, p 63.

Community Care (1974) 'National coverage was fair', 11 September, p 5.

Cooper, J. (1983) *The creation of the British personal social services 1962-1974*, London: Heinemann.

Corrigan, P. and Leonard, P. (1978) *Social work practice under capitalism: A Marxist approach*, London: Macmillan.

Crossman, R. (1977) *The diaries of a cabinet minister. Volume One: Minister of Housing 1964-66*, London: Hamish Hamilton and Jonathan Cape.

Crossman, R. (1978) *The diaries of a cabinet minister. Volume Three: Secretary of State for Health and Social Services 1968-70*, London: Hamish Hamilton and Jonathan Cape.

Curtis, M. (1946) *Care of Children Committee Report*, Cmd 6760, London: HMSO.

Dean, M. (1985) 'Jasmine death may thwart child care changes', *The Guardian*, 15 April.

Denham, A. and Garnett, M. (2001) 'From "guru" to "godfather": Keith Joseph, New Labour and the British Conservative tradition', *Political Quarterly*, vol 72, no 1, pp 97-106.

Denham, A. and Garnett, M. (2002) 'From "cycle of enrichment" to the "cycle of deprivation", Sir Keith Joseph, "problem families" and the transmission of disadvantage', *Benefits*, vol 10, no 3, pp 193-8.

DHSS (Department of Health and Social Security) (1974a) *Report of the Committee of Inquiry into the Care and Supervision Provided in Relation to Maria Colwell*, London: HMSO.

DHSS (1974b) *Non-accidental injury to children*, LASSL(74)13, London: DHSS.

Dingwall, R., Eekelaar, J. and Murray, T. (1983) *The protection of children: State intervention and family life*, Oxford: Blackwell.

Donnison, D. and Stewart, M. (1958) *The child and the social services*, Fabian Pamphlet, London: Fabian Society.

Donnison, D., Jay, P. and Stewart, M. (1962) *The Ingleby Report: Three critical essays*, Fabian Pamphlet, London: Fabian Society.

Donoughue, B. (2005) *Downing Street diary*, London: Jonathan Cape.

Drakeford, M. and Butler, I. (2008) 'Booing or cheering? Ambiguity in the construction of victimhood in the case of Maria Colwell', *Crime Media Culture*, vol 4, no 3, pp 367-85.

Farmer, E. (1997) 'Protection and child welfare: striking the balance', in N. Parton (ed) *Child protection and family support: Tensions, contradictions and possibilities*, London: Routledge, pp 146-64.

Fox-Harding, L. (1997) *Perspectives in child care policy* (2nd edn), London: Longman.

Franklin, B. and Parton, N. (eds) (1991) *Social work, the media and public relations*, London: Routledge.

Freedman, M.D.A. (1976) *The Children Act 1975: Text with concise commentary*, London: Sweet and Maxwell.

Gans, H. (1995) *The war against the poor: The underclass and antipoverty policy*, New York, NY: Basic Books.

Gladstone, D. (1999) 'Renegotiating the boundaries: risk and responsibility in personal welfare since 1945', in H. Fawcett and R. Lowe (eds) *Welfare policy in Britain: The road from 1945*, London: Macmillan, pp 34-51.

Golding, P. and Middleton, S. (1982) *Images of welfare: Press and public attitudes to poverty*, Oxford: Robinson.

Greenland, C. (1986) 'Inquiries into child abuse and neglect (CAN) deaths in the United Kingdom', *British Journal of Criminology*, vol 26, no 2, pp 164-72.

Hall, P. (1976) *Reforming the welfare: The politics of change in the personal social services*, London: Heinemann.

Hammond, P. (1973) 'Personal services to the family', in J. Stroud (ed) *Services for children and their families: Aspects of child care for social workers*, Oxford: Pergamon Press, pp 31-43.

Harris, J. (2008) 'State social work: constructing the present from moments in the past', *British Journal of Social Work*, vol 38, no 4, pp 662-79.

Hebbert, M. (2008) 'William Robson, the Herbert Commission and "Greater London"', in B. Kochan (ed) *London Government 50 Years of Debate*, London: LSE, pp 23-32.

Hendrick, H. (1994) *Child welfare: England 1872-1989*, London: Routledge.

Hendrick, H. (2003) *Child welfare: Historical dimensions, contemporary debate*, Bristol: The Policy Press.

Herbert, E. (1960) *The Royal Commission on local government in Greater London*, London: HMSO.

Heywood, J.S. (1973) 'Services for children and their families', in J. Stroud (ed) *Services for children and their families: Aspects of child care for social workers*, Oxford: Pergamon Press, pp 1-13.

Hill, M. (1990) 'The manifest and latent lessons of child abuse inquiries', *British Journal of Social Work*, vol 20, no 3, pp 197-213.

Hitchins, P. (2009) 'Marriage is dead on its feet, but it's still the best safeguard for a future', *Mail on Sunday*, 10 May.

Holden, A. (ed) (1986) *A review of the Children Act 10 years on: The effect on foster care policy and practice*, London: National Foster Care Association.

Holman, R. (1973) 'Supportive services to the family', in J. Stroud (ed) *Services for children and their families: Aspects of child care for social workers*, Oxford: Pergamon Press, pp 14-30.

Holman, B. (2005) 'Knock it down and start again', *Community Care*, 20 October, p 23.

Holman, R. (1988) *Putting families first*, Basingstoke: Macmillan.

Horner, N. (2003) *What is social work?*, Exeter: Learning Matters.

Houghton, W. (1972) *Report of the Departmental Committee on the Adoption of Children*, Cmnd 5107, London: HMSO.

Howells, J.G. (1974) *Remember Maria*, London: Butterworths.

Hudson, B. (2005) '"Not a cigarette paper between us": integrated inspection of children's services in England', *Social Policy and Administration*, vol 39, no 5, pp 513-27.

Ingleby Committee (1960) *Report of the Committee on Children and Young Persons*, Cmnd 1191, London: HMSO.

Jackson, S. (1977) 'The Children Act 1975: parents' rights and children's welfare', *British Journal of Law and Policy*, vol 3, no 1, pp 85-90.

James, A. (1998) 'Supporting families of origin: an exploration of the influence of the Children Act 1948', *Child and Family Social Work*, vol 3, no 3, pp 173-81.

Jessop, B. (1999) 'The changing governance of welfare: recent trends in its primary functions, scale, and modes of coordination', *Social Policy and Administration*, vol 33, no 4, pp 348-59.

Johnson, P. (2004) 'The welfare state, income and living standards', in R. Floud and P. Johnson (eds) *The Cambridge economic history of Britain, vol 3: Structural change and growth, 1939-2000*, Cambridge: Cambridge University Press, pp 213-37.

Jordan, B. (1974) *Poor parents: Social policy and the 'cycle of deprivation'*, London: Routledge and Kegan Paul.

Joseph, Sir Keith (1972) 'The cycle of deprivation', Speech to Conference of Pre-School Playgroups Association, 29 February, reprinted in K. Joseph, *Caring for people*, London: Conservative Political Centre.

Kavanagh, D. (1996) 'The fatal choice: the calling of the February 1974 election', in S. Ball and A. Seldon (eds) *The Heath government 1970-1974: A reappraisal*, London: Longman, pp 351-70.

London Borough of Brent (1985) *A child in trust: The report of the Panel of Inquiry into the Circumstances Surrounding the Death of Jasmine Beckford*, London: London Borough of Brent.

London Borough of Greenwich and Greenwich Health Authority (1987) *A child in mind: Protection of children in a responsible society. The report of a Commission of Inquiry into the Circumstances Surrounding the Death of Kimberley Carlile*, London: London Borough of Greenwich.

London Borough of Haringey (2009) *Serious case review: Baby Peter*, Local Safeguarding Children Board, London: London Borough of Haringey.

London Borough of Hillingdon Area Review Committee (1986) *Report of the Review Panel of the London Borough of Hillingdon Area Review Committee on Child Abuse into the Death of Heidi Koseda*, London: London Borough of Hillingdon.

London Borough of Lambeth (1987) *Whose child? The report of the Public Inquiry into the Death of Tyra Henry*, London: London Borough of Lambeth.

Longford Study Group (1964) *Crime: A challenge to us all*, London: Labour Party.

Lowe, R. (1996) 'The social policy of the Heath government', in S. Ball and A. Seldon (eds) *The Heath government 1970-1974: A reappraisal*, London: Longman, pp 191-214.

McDonald, C. and Marston, G. (2002) 'Patterns of governance: the curious case of non-profit community services in Australia', *Social Policy and Administration*, vol 36, no 4, pp 376-91.

Macnicol, J. (1999) 'From "problem family" to "underclass", 1945-95', in H. Fawcett and R. Lowe (eds) *Welfare policy in Britain: The road from 1945*, London: Macmillan, pp 69-93.

Martin, B. (1988) 'Moral messages and the press: newspapers responses to "A child in trust"', in G. Drewry, B. Martin and B. Sheldon (eds) *After Beckford: Essays on themes related to child abuse*, London: Department of Social Policy, Royal Holloway and Bedford New College.

Mayer, J.E. and Timms, N. (1970) *The client speaks: Working class impressions of casework*, London: Routledge and Kegan Paul.

Moran, M. (2001) 'Not steering but drowning: policy catastrophes and the regulatory state', *Political Quarterly*, vol 72, no 4, pp 414-27.

Mumford, G.H.F. and Selwood, T.J. (1976) *A guide to the Children Act 1975*, London: Shaw and Sons Limited.

Munro, E. (2004) 'Child abuse inquiries since 1990', in N. Stanley and J. Manthorpe (eds) *The age of the inquiry: Learning and blaming in health and social care*, London: Routledge, pp 75-91.

Newman, J., Glendinning, C. and Hughes, M. (2008) 'Beyond modernisation? Social care and the transformation of welfare governance', *Journal of Social Policy*, vol 37, no 4, pp 531-57.

Owen, D. (1986) 'The objectives of the Children Act', in A. Holden (ed) *A review of the Children Act 10 years on: The effect on foster care policy and practice*, London: National Foster Care Association, pp 1-7.

Parton, N. (1985) *The politics of child abuse*, London: Macmillan.

Parton, N. (2009) 'From Seebohm to *Think family*: reflections on 40 years of policy change of statutory children's social work in England', *Child and Family Social Work*, vol 14, no 1, pp 68-78.

Parton, N. and Martin, N. (1989) 'Public inquiries, legalism and child care in England and Wales', *International Journal of Law and the Family*, vol 5, no 1, pp 21-39.

Parton, N. and Otway, O. (1995) 'The contemporary state of child protection policy and practice in England and Wales', *Children and Youth Services Review*, vol 17, nos 5/6, pp 599-617.

Phillips, M. (2008) 'The liberals who did so much to destroy the family must share the blame for Baby P', *Daily Mail*, 17 November.

Philp, F. and Timms, N. (1962) *The problem of the problem family*, London: Family Service Units.

Pinchbeck, I. and Hewitt, M. (1973) *Children in English society*, London: Routledge and Kegan Paul.

Powell, M. (ed) (2008) *Modernising the welfare state: The Blair legacy*, Bristol: The Policy Press.

Ramsden, R. (1996) 'The Prime Minister and the making of policy', in S. Ball and A. Seldon (eds) *The Heath government 1970-1974: A reappraisal*, London: Longman, pp 21-46.

Reder, P., Duncan, S. and Gray, M. (1993) *Beyond blame: Child abuse tragedies revisited*, London: Routledge.

Rose, N. (1985) *The psychological complex: Psychology, politics and society in England 1869-1939*, London: RKP.

Rowe, J. (1986) 'Piecemeal distortion', in A. Holden (ed) *A review of the Children Act 10 years on: The effect on foster care policy and practice*, London: National Foster Care Association, pp 39-47.

Rowe, J. and Lambert, L. (1973) *Children who wait*, London: Association of British Fostering and Adoption Agencies.

Seebohm, F. (1968) *The report of the Committee on Local Authority and Allied Personal Social Services (Seebohm Report)*, Cmnd 3703, London: HMSO.

Seebohm, F. (1977) 'Address at BASW London Branch', in F. Seebohm (1989) *Seebohm: Twenty years on – Three stages in the development of the personal social services*, London: Policy Studies Institute.

Seebohm, F. (1989) *Seebohm: Twenty years on – Three stages in the development of the personal social services*, London: Policy Studies Institute.

Seldon, A. (1996) 'The Heath government in history', in S. Ball and A. Seldon (eds) *The Heath government 1970-1974: A reappraisal*, London: Longman, pp 1-19.

Short, R. (1984) *Second report from the Social Services Committee, Session 1983-4, Children in Care (Short Report)*, London: HMSO.

Sinfield, A. (1970) 'Which way for social work?', in *The fifth social service: A critical analysis of the Seebohm proposals*, London: Fabian Society, p 64.

Smith, C. (2001) 'Trust and confidence: possibilities for social work in "high modernity"', *British Journal of Social Work*, vol 31, no 2, pp 287-305.

Social Work Today (1973) 'Editorial', 11 January.

Starkey, P. (2001) *Families and social workers: The work of Family Service Units, 1944-1985*, Liverpool: Liverpool University Press.

Such, E. and Walker, R. (2002) 'Falling behind? Research on transmitted deprivation', *Benefits*, vol 10, no 3, pp 185-92.

Terry, J. (1979) *A guide to the Children Act 1975* (2nd edn), London: Sweet and Maxwell.

Timmins, N. (2001) *The five giants: A biography of the welfare state* (2nd edn), London: Harper Collins.

Timms, N. (1964) *Psychiatric social work in Great Britain*, London: Routledge.

Tomlinson, J. (2008) 'The 1964 Labour government, poverty and social justice', *Benefits*, vol 16, no 2, pp 135-45.

Triseliotis, J. (1986) 'Substitute care and permanence', in A. Holden (ed) *A review of the Children Act 10 years on: The effect on foster care policy and practice*, London: National Foster Care Association, pp 28-38.

Trimingham, A. (unpublished) 'Maria Colwell'.

Trimingham, A. (1978) 'Maria Colwell inquiry – a trial without a crime', Argus 20 March

Tunstill, J. (1986) 'An overview of how the Children Act has affected child care policy', in A. Holden (ed) *A review of the Children Act 10 years on: The effect on foster care policy and practice*, London: National Foster Care Association, pp 8-18.

Wallace, A. (2009) 'Governance at a distance? The turn to the local in UK social policy', in K. Rummery, I. Greener and C. Holden (eds) *Social Policy Review 21*, Bristol: The Policy Press for the Social Policy Association, pp 245-66.

Watson, S. (1973) 'The Children's Department and the 1963 Act', in J. Stroud (ed) *Services for children and their families: Aspects of care for social workers*, Oxford: Pergamon Press, pp 44-59.

Welshman, J. (2002) 'The cycle of deprivation and the concept of the underclass', *Benefits*, vol 35, no 10, pp 199-204.

Welshman, J. (2005) 'Ideology, social science, and public policy: the debate over transmitted deprivation', *Twentieth Century British History*, vol 16, no 3, pp 306-41.

White, T. (1986) 'Changing perceptions', in A. Holden (ed) *A review of the Children Act 10 years on: The effect on foster care policy and practice*, London: National Foster Care Association, pp 19-27.

Women's Group on Public Welfare (1943) *Our towns: A close-up*, London: Oxford University Press.

Wroe, A. (1988) *Social work, child abuse and the press*, Social Work Monographs, Norwich: University of East Anglia.

Younghusband, E.L. (1959) *Social workers in the local authority health and welfare services: Report of the Working Party on Social Workers*, London: HMSO.

Newspapers

Argus (1973) 'Husband denies murdering girl', 7 and 8 January.

Argus (1973) 'New vicar is East Sussex man', 22 January.

Argus (1973) 'Neighbours remember little Maria', 25 January.

Argus (1973) 'Shouts at the cemetery as little Maria is buried', 26 January.

Argus (1973) 'Maria's mother tells of "my lies"', 17 April.

Argus (1973) 'Murdered Maria: probe is ordered', 17 April (a).

Argus (1973) 'Little Maria: how did it happen?', 24 April.

Argus (1973) 'Maria probe in secret', 26 April.

Argus (1973) 'Maria: let us hear all the facts', 27 April.

Argus (1973) 'Maria: call for wider inquiry', 28 April.

Argus (1973) 'Sir Arthur Bliss joins Maria inquiry call', 30 April.

Argus (1973) 'Maria inquiry "must be in public"', 5 May.

Argus (1973) 'Let Home Office take over', 8 May.

Argus (1973) 'Justice must be seen in Maria case', 11 May.

Argus (1973) 'Maria: petition in', 11 May (a).

Argus (1973) 'Maria: MP calls for public inquiry', 12 May.

Argus (1973) 'County under attack as Maria probe team meets – in private. Procedures "cold, aloof" – Sheldon', 15 May.

Argus (1973) 'Maria's teacher tells of "my fears"', 16 May.

Argus (1973) 'The real memorial to Maria', 17 May.

Argus (1973) 'Appeal move by Maria's stepfather', 17 May (a).

Argus (1973) 'Shock move halts Maria inquiry', 18 May.

Argus (1973) 'Sterilisation – that's the only answer', 19 May.

Argus (1973) 'Minister in more talks on Maria', 22 May.

Argus (1973) 'The real memorial to Maria', 24 May.

Argus (1973) 'Now for the facts', 25 May.

Argus (1973) 'Memorial fund announced', 31 May.

Argus (1973) 'Maria: QC will head probe team', 23 July.

Argus (1973) 'Maria: a top level probe: social experts on inquiry team', 24 July.

Argus (1973) 'Maria: death probe will start in public', 4 August.

Argus (1973) 'Maria probe should be held in Brighton', 20 August.

Argus (1973) 'Victory! Maria probe will be in public and in Brighton', 24 August.

Argus (1973) 'Mrs Kepple calls at offices', 24 October.

Argus (1973) 'Another setback as five quit Maria fund', 15 November.

Argus (1974) 'A report fit for the dustbin', 29 March.

Argus (1974) 'Maria report out in July', 23 May.

Argus (1974) 'Maria inquiry report delayed', 9 July.

Argus (1974) 'Maria demo aims to "shame" Harold', 28 August.

Argus (1974) 'Maria: Castle speaks out', 29 August.

Argus (1974) 'The system failed Brighton's child of tragedy', 4 September.

Argus (1974) 'Maria: no scapegoats but a lesson to be learned', 5 September.

Argus (1974) 'Fourth reprint of Maria report', 18 October.

Argus (1975) 'This is a triumph for the people says Mayor', 24 January.

Argus (1975) 'At last, a charter for childhood', 27 January.

Argus (1975) 'We must not react too strongly – JP', 29 January.

Argus (1975) 'The Children Bill – a memorial to Maria', 1 February.

Argus (1975) 'No one could stop another Maria tragedy', 29 April.

Argus (1975) 'Maria and the blood-tie', 2 May.

Argus (2000) 'Demanding a debate on child cruelty', 24 March.

Argus (2000) 'The Sage of Sussex', 8 April.

Daily Express (1973) 'Tug-of-love "error" led to murder', 17 April.

Daily Express (1973) 'Council let her stay with killer', 10 October.

Daily Express (1973) 'I saw no risk to Maria', 6 November.

Daily Express (1973) 'Maria social worker gets bodyguard', 14 November.

Daily Express (2008) 'Baby died after being used as "a punchbag"', 12 November.

Daily Mail (1973) 'How Maria was torn between two families', 6 November.
Daily Mail (1973) 'Maria's "happy family" life', 8 November.
Daily Mail (2008) 'Spiv. Gangster. Playboy. There wasn't much to love about Harvey Holford. So why, when he executed his wife and butchered her body, was he treated like a national hero?', 8 July.
Daily Mail (2008) 'The woman who puts performance graphs before a baby's life', 13 November.

Daily Mirror (1973) 'Woman witness thrown to the ground in "witch" taunt at Maria's mother', 1 November.
Daily Mirror (1973) 'I have nothing to hide', 2 November.
Daily Mirror (1973) 'The case which shocked Britain', 3 November.
Daily Mirror (1973) 'Mob jeer social worker after fury at inquiry', 6 November.
Daily Mirror (1973) 'Wanted: a Britain that really cares...', 29 November.
Daily Mirror (1973) 'The agony of Maria's Mother – by a woman barrister', 7 December.
Daily Mirror (1974) 'The lifesaver: Barbara speeds up report to help the battered babies', 2 September.
Daily Mirror (2008) 'Cops fought with social workers over boy's fate', 17 November.

Daily Star (2008) 'Boss off to races', 14 November.

Daily Telegraph (1973) '"Maria not exploited" says social worker', 8 November.
Daily Telegraph (1973) 'Maria was "sad and afraid"', 7 December.
Daily Telegraph (2008) 'Another child's death that should have been avoided', 12 November.

Guardian, The (1973) 'Case "code" led to tragedy of Maria', 8 November.
Guardian, The (1985) 'Inquiry starts into battered girl', 29 March.
Guardian, The (1985) 'Child abuse deaths and the Jasmine Beckford inquiry', 29 June.
Guardian, The (2008) 'Social work experts discuss child protection', 17 November.

London Evening Standard (1973) 'Foster girl's death: change law plea', 24 August.

News of the World (2008) 'Now teach the sinks to swim', 7 December.

Observer, The (1970) 'Wilson to win', 7 June.
Observer, The (2008) 'Why children are left to die beyond help's reach', 16 November.

Sun, The (1973) 'Anger flares the Maria Inquiry', 1 November.
Sun, The (1973) 'I'm so scared, says Maria's mum', 2 November.
Sun, The (1973) 'Maria case woman is chased by angry mob', 6 November.
Sun, The (1973) 'The torment of Maria's mother – tears as inquiry hears of poison pen campaign', 7 December.
Sun, The (2008) 'Blood on their hands', 12 November.
Sun, The (2008) 'Incompetent, politically correct and anti white', 14 November.
Sun, The (2008) 'Fixing broken Britain', 27 November.

Sunday Mirror (1999) 'Why we can't let them break up runaway family', 17 January.

Sunday Times (1973) 'Battered Maria: neighbours "tried to warn officials"', 22 April.
Sunday Times (1973) 'Let us end the killings', 11 November.
Sunday Times (1973) 'Problem parents should lose adult rights', 18 November.
Sunday Times (1973) 'The battered babies scandal', 25 November.

Times, The (1973) 'Wider power aim in adoption Bill changes', 23 November.
Times, The (1985) 'Catalogue of failure in infant abuse deaths', 27 July.
Times, The (1985) 'Profession of care: the implications of the Jasmine Beckford Inquiry', 4 December.
Times, The (1987) 'Danger – child abuse inquiry at work', 19 December.
Times, The (2008) 'Baby P: the lessons, the rights and the wrongs', 17 November.

Index

A

Abse, Leo 140, 175
Adey, Dr 3
adoption 140, 179, 181–2
Al-Zayyat, Dr Sabah 200
Allen, Denis 94, 130–1, 143, 169–70
American Humane Association 141
amicus curiae 164–5, 177–8, 180
Andrews, Chris 188
Anthony, Andrew 202–6
April incident 19–20, 120–4, 216–17
area review committees 171, 174
Argus viii
  blood tie 140
  Castle interview 167
  Children Act 1975 182
  Christmas parcels 51
  Inquiry report 163, 169
  Pauline Kepple 19, 111
  Bill Kepple's trial 92
  later child abuse cases vii, viii, 194–6
  Maria Colwell Memorial Fund 99
  public inquiry campaign 94–7, 98
  sterilisation 87
  Whitehawk Estate 2
Atkinson, Tony 86
Attlee, Clement 74
Auckland, John 185
Auckland, Susan 185
Audit Commission 210–11

B

Baby P *see* Connelly, Peter
Bacon, Alice 69
Baker, Mr 30–1, 50
Ball, C. 191, 206
Bampflyte, Mr 146, 147
Barker, Hilda 204
Barker, Steven 196, 203, 204, 205
Barley, Dr
  and Miss Bodger 46
  and Mrs Dickenson 45, 46
  at Inquiry 48, 111, 148
  Inquiry majority report 157
  Bill Kepple's call 40
  Bill Kepple's trial 93
  contact with Maria 43, 56, 217
  and NSPCC 154
  prescription 46, 48
Barnett, Joel 68
Barnsley Metropolitan Borough
  Council 186

Barrow, Ruby 50
BASW (British Association of Social
  Workers) 10, 177, 187–8
'Battered Babies' campaign 87–8
battered baby syndrome 141
Beaumont, Robert 99–100, 112, 166,
  170
Beckford, Jasmine 194, 198
Beckford Inquiry 198, 207
Beloff, Nora 81–2
Bennett, Mr 141
Bennion, Francis 179
Bliss, Sir Arthur 95
blood tie 139–45, 169, 179, 188–9, 190,
  216
Bloom, John 99
Bodger, Miss 56, 217
  and Dr Barley 42
  December 1972 34, 43, 46–7, 49, 57
  and Mrs Dickenson 35, 42, 43, 109
  at Inquiry 111
  and Mrs Kirby 48–9, 50–1
  November 1972 23
  and NSPCC 154
Bogdanor, V. 83–4
Bowden, Andrew 91, 94, 95, 96, 170
Bradley, David 189
Brashill (Brasil, Brazil), Mr 22, 23, 30
Brashill (Brasil, Brazil), Betty 30, 32, 44,
  54, 111–12
Brighton 194–6
  Whitehawk Estate 2, 19–20, 196–7
Brighton Evening Argus see Argus
Brighton Social Services Department
  5, 21, 29, 37–8, 55, 104
  see also McBurney, Mr
Brown, A.D. 94
Brown, Muriel 10–11
Butler, D. 81
Butler, I. 7, 58
Butt, Ronald 82

C

Caffyn, Brigadier Sir Edward 95
Callaghan, Audrey 71
Callaghan, James 71, 78, 79–80, 140
Cambridgeshire Social Services 199
Cameron, David 211
Cameron, Professor James 3, 7, 151
  at Inquiry 93, 110
  NSPCC 154
  post-mortem examination 3–4, 218
Carlile, Kimberley 198

casework model 74
Castle, Barbara 171–2, 192
  BASW speech 177
  Children Act 1975 177, 178
  Inquiry Report 163, 166, 167–9, 170
Certificate in Social Work 65
Chapman, Mrs 31, 45
child protection 209
child protection registers 171, 174–5
Children Act 1948 12, 60
Children Act 1975 8, 166, 169, 192,
    206
  and Auckland case 187
  Conservative Party 175–7
  impact 190–1
  implementation 189
  Labour Party 177–85
  reaction to 187–9
  Short Report 189–90
Children Act 2004 210
Children and Young Persons Act 1963
    62, 64
Children who wait (Rowe and Lambert)
    181–2, 191
children's trusts 210–11
Clarke, J. 66, 67
Cleveland child abuse scandal 207–8
Climbié, Victoria 193–4, 196, 203
Clough, Gill 196–7
Coe, Dr 156
Collison, M. 74
Colwell, Maria vii–viii, 19–22
  chronology 5, 20–1, 219
  death 3, 13–18
  December 1972 33–56
  funeral 19
  Keith Joseph's comments 88
  and later child abuse reporting 193–8,
    201
  local authority and agency
    involvement 5, 21, 23, 24, 26–58
  neighbours' concerns 19–20
  November 1972 22–33
  post-mortem examination 3–4
  scandal 6–8
  synopsis 215–18
  weight 4, 30, 33–4, 102, 108, 110
Colwell, Pauline *see* Kepple, Pauline
Colwell, Raymond 4, 5, 215
Colwell Inquiry 91–4, 126–7
  administrative and procedural reforms
    171–5, 206–7
  and Auckland case 185–7
  blood tie 139–45
  and Children Act 1975 175–85,
    190–1
  common sense 115–19
  community social work 133

East Sussex Social Services
    Department 130–1
  government response 163–71, 192,
    212–13
  hearing the evidence 105–15
  moral relativism 150–1
  neighbours 19, 119–26
  origins 94–9
  principal players 103–5
  problem families 145–9
  purpose 20
  report 161–3
  rule of optimism 151–2
  scope 13
  setting the tone 99–103
  social work 74, 129–30, 157–9, 191,
    199
  social work boundaries 152–7
  social work incompetence 136–9
  social workers 131, 132–6
  Trimingham 195
common sense 91–2, 115–16, 127, 129,
    211
  Cooper family 116–19
  neighbours 119–26
Community Care 169
community social work 75, 133
confidence 210, 211
Connelly, Peter 193, 196, 210
  media reporting 199–201, 202–6
Connelly, Tracey 196, 204–5
Conservative Party 80–1, 82–9, 163
  Children Act 1975 175–7
  social work governance 207, 208
Cooper, Bob vii, 21
Cooper, Doris vii, 5, 21, 215
  at Inquiry 106, 119
  Bill Kepple's trial 93
  and Miss Lees 54
Cooper, Joan 80, 97–8, 131
  Auckland case 185–6, 187
  Colwell Inquiry 97–8
  Houghton Committee 175
  Seebohm Committee 71, 72, 76, 89
Cooper family
  at Inquiry 116–19
  Inquiry majority report 137–8, 140
  Inquiry minority report 137
  and Kepples 24–5, 215–16
  see also Shirley, Mrs Pearl
Cornwall, Mr 31
Coulthard, Miss 37
Council for Training in Social Work 65
Court, Joan 134, 185
courts 169
  children's representation 164–5,
    177–8, 180, 183
  see also Hove Juvenile Court

Crichton, Charlotte 104–5, 111,
  114–15
Crosland, Tony 80
Crossman, Richard 70–1, 77–80, 81
Curran, Inspector 109, 121, 150, 153
Curtis, Myra 12
cycle of deprivation theory 85–9, 170

D

Daily Express 103, 113–14, 140, 151,
  199
Daily Mail 145, 151, 199, 200, 201
Daily Mirror
  Inquiry 101, 111–12, 113, 114–15
  Inquiry report 167–8, 169
  Sir Keith Joseph interview 88–9
Daily Star 200
Daily Telegraph 115, 151, 169
Davey, Alderman Margaret 97, 103, 104
  hearing the evidence 107
  moral relativism 151
  social work boundaries 156, 173
Dean, Miss 107, 109
delinquency 62, 66, 67
Denham, A. 85
Department of Education and Science
  173
Department of Health and Social
    Security (DHSS)
  administrative and procedural reforms
    171–3
  Auckland case 185, 186
  Castle 163
  Children Act 1975 177
  Inquiry report 163
  Joseph 84
  Working Group 86–7
  see also Colwell Inquiry
deprivation 85–9, 141, 142–3, 170
Desborough, Christine 98
Dickenson, Mrs
  and Dr Barley 40, 43, 45, 217
  and Miss Bodger 35, 42, 46
  and Brighton Social Services
    Department 34–5, 43–4
  and Mrs Chapman 45
  December 1972 35–7, 44–5, 47, 54,
    57
  at Inquiry 108–9
  January 1973 56
  Mr Kepple's hostility towards 41,
    42–3, 45, 47
  and Mrs Kirby 32, 33, 35, 39
  and Miss Lees 37, 42
  and Mr Masters 31, 34
  November 1972 24, 27, 29, 32–3, 57,
    217
  and Mrs Tattam 37

Dingwall, R. 151
doctor *see* Barley, Dr
Donnison, David 66, 67, 76
Drakeford, M. 7, 58
Driscoll, DI 14–15

E

East Sussex County Council
  review panel 58, 95, 96
  Social Services Committee 94
East Sussex Social Services Department
  5, 20, 21, 130–1, 216
  at Inquiry 104, 114
  Inquiry minority report 158
  see also Lees, Diana
educational welfare officer *see*
    Dickenson, Mrs
Edwards, Pauline 52–3, 149
Egan, Margaret 37
Elton, Lord 182–3
Eugenic Society 146, 149
Evening Argus see Argus
Every child matters 210

F

Fabian Society 66, 67
family planning 87, 89, 162, 172
family service 62, 65–71, 72, 74
Farmer, E. 191, 206
Field-Fisher, Thomas 97, 98, 100,
    101–2, 103, 104
  hearing the evidence 106, 107, 109,
    112, 113, 119
  problem families 149
  report 161–3
  social work boundaries 155, 156, 173
Fox-Harding, L. 191
Franklin, Dr Alfred White 101, 102,
    114, 140–1, 174
Freedman, Maurice 86
Fry, WPS Gillian 3, 6

G

Gans, Herbert 86
Garnett, M. 85
Goodman, Mrs 30, 50
governance 206–12
GP *see* Barley, Dr
Greenland, C. 198
guardian at litem 180, 183
Guardian, The 113, 145, 169, 212

H

Hall, Phoebe 60, 72, 76, 78–9, 83
Hammond, P. 75
Hargrove, Bernard 104, 124, 125
Haringey Council 196, 200–1, 202–3,
    211

Harris, J. 76
Hart, Graham 178, 192
Hawkins, DCI 14
health visitor *see* Bodger, Miss
Heath, Edward 82, 83, 163, 167
Hendrick, H. 140, 191
Henry, Tyra 194, 198
Herbert Commission 61–2
Hidden, Anthony 104, 110
Higgs, Dr Marietta 207–8
Hill, M. 208, 209
HMSO 164, 165
Hodgson, Miss 34–5, 154
Holden, A. 189
Holford, Christine 99
Holford, Harvey *see* Beaumont, Robert
Holman, Bob 75, 133
Home Office 61, 69
  administrative and procedural reforms
    173
  amicus curiae 165, 177–8
  Auckland case 187
  Callaghan 78, 80
  custodians 179–80
  guardian at litem 180
  Houghton Committee 175
  Inquiry 94, 96
  Inquiry report 163, 164, 166, 171
  Seebohm Committee 71, 72
Horner, N. 191
Houghton, Douglas 69, 70, 71
Houghton, Sir William 175
Houghton Committee 140, 175–6,
  179, 192
House of Commons Social Services
  Committee 189–90
housing department 23, 24, 25–6, 56,
  125
  see also Smith, George
Hove Children's Department 5
Hove Juvenile Court 5, 26, 137, 164,
  165, 170, 216
Hudson, B. 210
Huws Jones, Robin 70

I

Ingleby Committee 62, 65–6
interdisciplinary working 152–7, 172–3

J

Jackson, Sonia 188–9
James, Ann 191
James, P.D. 213
Jay, Peggy 66
Jessop, B. 207
Johnson, P. 68
Jordan, Bill 85, 86
Joseph, Sir Keith 84–5, 140, 171

child abuse 141
Children Act 1975 175, 176, 177
Colwell Inquiry 91, 96–7
cycle of deprivation 85, 86–9, 170
monetarism 167
problem families 85, 134, 145

K

Kavanagh, D. 82
Kempe, Dr Henry 141
Kepple, Bill 4–5, 215, 216
  appeal vii, 93, 96, 97
  April incident 121–2, 216–17
  and Dr Barley 40, 43
  and Miss Bodger 46–7
  and Mr Brashill 22, 23
  and Mrs Dickenson 24–5, 32–3,
    36–7, 38, 41, 42–3, 45, 217
  and housing department 25–6
  and Mrs Kirby 40–1, 50
  and Miss Lees 42–3, 47
  Maria's death vii, 13, 14–15, 18, 218
  moral relativism 151
  November 1972 23, 24, 27, 28
  problem family 147
  and Rutsons 55, 122, 124, 125
  state benefits 85, 134
  and Sandra Tester 28, 56
  trial vii, 92–4
Kepple, Pauline 4–5, 215
  anger towards 19
  April incident 19, 121, 122–3,
    216–17
  blood tie 139, 141–2, 144
  and Miss Bodger 46, 49
  and Coopers vii, 5, 215–16
  and Mrs Dickenson 27, 29, 34, 35–6
  and Miss Edwards 52, 53
  at Inquiry 104–5, 111–12, 114–15,
    116
  in Inquiry report 162
  Bill Kepple's trial 92, 93
  and Mrs Kirby 32, 40, 42, 50, 51–2,
    133
  and Miss Lees 28, 29–30, 33, 38–9,
    47–8
  Maria returned to vii, 5, 216
  Maria's death 13–14, 15–18, 218
  Maria's funeral 19
  media reporting 114–15, 201
  moral relativism 150, 151
  November 1972 23, 25
  problem family 146–7, 148–9
  and Rutsons 120, 122
  and Mrs Shirley 117
  state support 55, 133–4
  and Mrs Tester 49
  and Sandra Tester 52, 53–4

Kilbrandon Commission 78
Kirby, Mrs Daphne 21, 56, 131, 132,
    154, 214, 217
  April incident 121, 122–3, 217
  blood tie 143
  and Miss Bodger 48–9, 50–1
  Christmas Party 49–50
  December 1972 40–2, 50, 51–2, 57
  and Mrs Dickenson 33, 34–5
  at Inquiry 110–11, 121, 132–4
  Bill Kepple's trial 93
  and Miss Lees 31–2, 33, 47, 50, 51,
    57, 122–3, 153–4
  and Mr Masters 39–40
  November 1972 29, 31, 32, 33, 57
  problem families 148–9
  and Mrs Tattam 39
Koseda, Heidi 198

L

Labour Party 70, 76–80, 81–2, 163
  Children Act 1975 177–85
  family service 66–7
  response to Inquiry report 163–71
  social spending 68–9
  see also New Labour
Lambert, Lydia 181–2, 191
Lawson, Mr Justice Neal 186
Lees, Miss Diana 21, 56, 131, 134, 214,
    216, 217
  April incident 121, 122–4, 126, 217
  blood tie 139, 141–2, 144, 145
  and Coopers 54
  December 1972 33–4, 37–9, 43,
    47–8, 49, 57, 217
  and Mrs Dickenson 37, 42, 57
  at Inquiry 103, 113–14, 123–4, 126,
    134–6
  Inquiry majority report 136–9, 163,
    170
  Inquiry minority report 137, 158
  Bill Kepple's trial 93
  and Mrs Kirby 31–2, 42, 50, 51, 57,
    110
  and Mr McBurney 44
  moral relativism 151
  November 1972 28, 29–30
  and NSPCC 153–4
  and other professionals 155–7, 174
  police statement 56, 135
  rule of optimism 152
  and Mrs Rutson 46
  and Mrs Shirley 116–18
  and Mrs Tattam 42, 43
  and Testers 26–7, 28, 56, 57
  and Whitehawk Junior School 31, 42
Linge, Mr 166
local authorities

children's services 60–3
  family service 62, 65–71, 72
  see also social services departments
Local Authority Social Services Act
    1970 59, 80, 81, 129, 130
Locke, Miss 144
Longford Study Group 67–8, 69, 76
Lowe, R. 82–3
Luck, WPC 23, 27
Lyon, Alex 165

M

McBurney, Mr 29, 34, 35, 38, 39, 43–4
  April incident 123, 124, 126
  and NSPCC 153
McDonald, C. 219
Macnicol, J. 86, 146
Malone, Carole 199
Maria Colwell Memorial Fund 99,
    100, 166
Marston, G. C. 219
Martin, Miss 111
Martin, B. 198–9
Martin, N. 208–9
Masters, Mr 31, 34, 39–40
Matthews, Robin 86
Mayer, J.E. 74
media
  later child abuse cases 193–8
  social work 198–201
Mees, Paddy 53
Mildon, Arthur 104
  and Mrs Kirby 142–3, 148–9
  and Miss Lees 103, 123, 137, 142,
    145, 155–6
  opening statement 103, 105–6, 137
  problem families 145–6
  and Mrs Rutson 120
Miles, Mrs 23
Ministry of Education 61
Ministry of Health 61, 77–8
Ministry of Housing 61
moral relativism 150–1
Moran, M. 210
Mumford, G.H.F. 184
Munro, E. 210

N

National Institute for Social Work
    Training 65, 70, 72
Neave, Rikki 199
neighbours 20
  April incident 216–17
  and housing department 23, 24, 125
  at Inquiry 91, 106–7, 119–26
  see also Brashill, Betty; Brashill, Mr;
    Rutson, Mrs Shirley Jean
neoliberalism 207

New Labour 209–11, 213
see also Labour Party
Newman, J. 210
NSPCC 5, 20, 21
　anonymous calls 28, 50, 56, 57
　Battered Child Research Unit 141
　Mrs Brashill's call 30–1, 44
　Christmas Party 49–50
　Coopers 215
　at Inquiry 104, 109, 111
　Mrs Rutson's call 19, 120, 121, 122,
　　125
　and social services departments 152–5
　see also Inspector Curran; Kirby, Mrs
　　Daphne

O

Observer, The 196, 202–6
O'Connor, Mary 203
Ofsted 211
Oliver, Leonard 114
optimism 151–2, 174
Otway, O. 209
Our Towns (Women's Group on Public
　Welfare) 86
Owen, Dr David
　amicus curiae 164–5, 177–8
　Auckland case 185–6
　Children Act 1975 177, 179, 190
　Private Member's Bill 176–7
Owen, Jason 196, 204

P

paramountcy principle 183–4, 188–9
Parker, Roy 86
Parker, Dr William 87–8
Parton, N. 208–9
Phillips, Melanie 201
Pinto-Duschinsky, M. 81
police
　and Kepples 22–3, 27, 56
　Maria's death 2–3, 6
Pomfret, Mrs 87
Poor Law 63, 66, 73, 89
Pratt, PC Roger 22–3
Prentice, Reg 168
problem families 7, 74, 85–6, 87–8, 212
　administrative and procedural reforms
　　174–5
　Kepples 26, 53, 96–7, 134, 145–9
　Whitehawk Estate 2, 107, 196–7
Probyn, Alan 114
Proops, Marjorie 88–9
public inquiries 7, 185–7
　see also Colwell Inquiry

R

Reader, Richard 99
Rees, Sir Stanley 92, 93
Rickworth, Mrs 55
Robinson, Dr 156
Robinson, Kenneth 70
Rowe, Jane 175, 181–2, 190–1
*Royal Commission on local government in
　Greater London* 61–2
rule of optimism 151–2, 174
Rutherford, Mr 37–8
Rutson, Mr Graham 16, 119
Rutson, Mrs Shirley Jean 19, 106,
　119–20, 124–6
　April incident 19–20, 120–2
　call to school secretary 31
　December 1972 44, 45–6, 55
　at Inquiry 19, 106, 119–26
　and Miss Lees 46, 47, 57, 122–3, 124,
　　126
Rutter, Michael 86

S

Sansom, PC Bill 101, 111–12, 195
scandals 6–8, 91–2
schools 168
　see also Whitehawk Junior School
Seebohm, Frederic 63, 71–2, 89, 129
　and Crossman 77
　passion to know 59, 91
Seebohm Committee 68, 71, 72–7,
　133, 212
Seebohm Implementation Action
　Group 79
Seebohm Report 59–60, 64, 77, 78–80,
　127, 130, 206
Seldon, A. 82
selectivity 84–6
Selwood, T.J. 184
Sheldon, Danny 94, 95, 170, 194
Sheldon, John 194
Shirley, Mrs Pearl 23, 24, 112, 116–19
Shoesmith, Sharon 200, 211
Short, Renee 189
Short, Ted 178
Short Report 189–90
Simey, Thomas 74
Simpson, Miss 134–5, 141–2, 143
Sinfield, Adrian 74–6
Smith, C. 210
Smith, George 24, 26, 29, 147–8
Smith, Mrs Muriel 45, 48, 49
Social Science Research Council
　(SSRC) 86
social services departments 9–12, 61–2,
　78, 80, 82–3

government response to Colwell
Inquiry 168–9
and NSPCC 152–5
Seebohm Committee 59–60, 71, 72, 76
see also Brighton Social Services Department; East Sussex Social Services Department
social work 21, 129, 213–14
administrative and procedural reforms 171–5
arrogance of bureaucratic certainty 212–13
before Seebohm 59–65
boundaries 152–7, 173–4
Colwell Inquiry 129–30, 157–9
and common sense 115–26, 127
East Sussex Social Services Department 130–1
exercise of judgement 150–2
family service 65–71
from Seebohm to Local Authority Social Services Act 77–81
fundamental assumptions 139–49
ghosts 193–8
governance 206–12
government response to Colwell Inquiry 163, 168–9
incompetence 136–9
Sir Keith Joseph and the 'cycle of deprivation' 81–90
media reporting 198–201
organisation and leadership 8–13
and other professions 155–7
Seebohm 59, 71–7
training 64–5, 72
see also Kirby, Mrs Daphne; Lees, Miss Diana
Social Work Today 8–13, 60, 153
Children Act 1975 188
sterilisation 87, 89, 162
Stevenson, Olive 97–8, 100, 102, 103, 104, 114
Mr Beaumont 112
blood tie 144
Cooper family 117, 118
Inspector Curran 109
Mrs Dickenson 108
majority report 161–3
minority report 116, 126, 162, 213
multi-agency working 212
neighbours 106–7
NSPCC 111
rule of optimism 152
social work 158–9
social work boundaries 156–7
social work incompetence 137, 138–9
Mrs Turner 107

Stewart, Mary 66
Stockton, Judge 175
Streatfield, Justice 99
Sun, The
Baby P case 200–1
Colwell Inquiry 111, 112, 113, 115, 169
Sunday Mirror, The 199
Sunday Times 186
'Battered Babies' campaign 87–8
Supervision Orders 5, 29, 35, 39, 149, 154, 164

T

Tattam, Mrs 37, 39, 42–3, 44, 144
Telegraph 113
Terry, Jennifer 189
Tester, Mrs Lilian 5, 49, 56, 215
and Miss Lees 26–7, 28, 33, 54, 57
Tester, Pauline *see* Kepple, Pauline
Tester, Miss Sandra 27, 52, 55, 57, 215
at Inquiry 111, 112
Maria locked in room 53–4
Maria slapped by Kepple 28, 56
Times, The 113, 169, 186–7, 207, 208
Timmins, N. 76, 84
Timms, N. 74
Titmuss, Richard 69–71, 72–3, 74
Topley, Mr 24, 25–6
Townsend, Peter 66
Trimingham, Adam 2
Inquiry 102, 195
Inquiry members and legal representatives 103, 104, 105
Inquiry room 100
Mrs Kirby 110
Miss Lees 113
neighbours 106
Mrs Turner 107
Whitehawk Estate 2
trust 209, 210, 211
Tunbridge Wells Study Group 140–1
Tunstill, Jane 190
Turner, Mrs Ann 217
in *Argus* 95, 195–6
December 1972 50
and Mrs Dickenson 24, 27, 57, 109
at Inquiry 107–8
November 1972 27, 31

U

underclass 86, 197

V

Vickers, Dame Joan 175

W

Wall, Miss 37

Wallace, A. 209
Watson, Sylvia 61, 63
Webster, Peter 104
welfare state 205–6, 207
Weller, Patricia 3
Welshman, J. 85, 86, 87
White, Margaret 16
White, Mrs Phyllis 163, 212–13
Whitehawk Estate 2, 19–20, 119,
    196–7
  see also neighbours
Whitehawk Infant School 138
Whitehawk Junior School 28, 31, 45,
    57, 107, 108, 138, 217
  see also Masters, Mr; Turner, Mrs Ann
Wigoder, Lord 183–4
Willmott, Peter 86
Wilson, Harold 68–9, 78, 81–2, 163,
    166–7, 170
Winterbottom, Lord 183
Women's Group on Public Welfare 86
Wootton, Barbara 74
Wright, Inspector Jack 2–3
WRVS 55, 56, 218
Wyatt, Dr Geoffrey 207–8

Y

Younghusband, Dame Eileen 70, 129
Younghusband Committee 60, 62,
    64–5, 70